Siebel CRM 8.1

Navigation and Configuration

Siebel CRM 8.1
Navigation and Configuration

Rishi Kumar Shrivastava
Tata Consultancy Services
Gurgaon

Tata McGraw Hill Education Private Limited
NEW DELHI

McGraw-Hill Offices

New Delhi New York St Louis San Francisco Auckland Bogotá Caracas
Kuala Lumpur Lisbon London Madrid Mexico City Milan Montreal
San Juan Santiago Singapore Sydney Tokyo Toronto

Tata McGraw-Hill

Published by Tata McGraw Hill Education Private Limited,
7 West Patel Nagar, New Delhi 110 008

ISBN-13: 978-1-25-906132-5
ISBN-10: 1-25-906132-9

Vice President and Managing Director—Asia Pacific Region: *Ajay Shukla*
Publishing Manager—Professional: *Praveen Tiwari*
Asst. Sponsoring Editor—Science, Technology and Computing: *Simanta Borah*
Editorial Researcher—Science, Technology and Computing: *Sushil Gupta*
Sr. Copy Editor: *Neha Sharma*
Manager—Production: *Sohan Gaur*
Asst. General Manager—Sales and Business Development—Professional: *S Girish*
Deputy Marketing Manager—Science, Technology and Computing: *Rekha Dhyani*
General Manager—Production: *Rajender P Ghansela*
Manager—Production: *Reji Kumar*

Typeset at SP Graphics, 130 DDA Flats, 1st Floor, Todapur (Opp. Pusa Institute), New Delhi-110 012 and
printed at

Cover Printer:

Cover Designer: Mukul Khattar

To
my father Dr. M.K. Shrivastava,
my mother Mrs. Sudha Shrivastava
and
my sister Mrs. Richa Gaur
for their support and well wishes at every stage in my life

PREFACE

The idea of writing "Siebel CRM 8.1: Navigation and the Configuration" came to my mind during a knowledge transition session with my juniors in office. While explaining them the concepts, I was reminded of the days when I started my journey in this industry. I used to have several million questions running through my mind starting from "Where should I start", "What is CRM", "What is Siebel" till "When I will start working in Siebel" and "When I will become perfect in it". I used to attack my seniors with a lot of doubts that I used to have during my initial days. Obviously, the most common suggestions included digging through thousands of pages of study material available across documentations, online tutorials, blogs etc but I was too lazy (and still I am) to go through that much information for deriving knowledge out of it. I desperately needed a book that could provide me a guided path to get used to with Siebel in minimum possible words.

This book is especially designed for those lazy beginners like me who want to get the basic idea of Siebel CRM Navigation and Configuration in minimum possible words. It follows the same path that I followed while learning. While writing this book, I have shared experiences of lot of Siebel professionals around me to get their suggestions and feedbacks on my approach. As an author, I have tried my best to keep the language as simple and interesting as possible so that you don't fall asleep while reading.

The book starts with "Introduction to CRM". As Siebel is a CRM tool, readers should have a clear picture of CRM, its significance and use. This part is followed by Siebel Navigation, where readers will get the first look and feel of Siebel Enterprise Applications and Siebel tools. The next part covers details about Configuring Siebel Applications, where readers will get to know about various Siebel object types and their properties. Finally, the book discusses about Implementing Siebel Enterprise Applications. This part will provide a big picture to readers on how Siebel applications are implemented and used. As an add-on, I have added Sample Project and Practice questions towards the end of book which will work as a refresher for the readers. In short, I have tried to answer all the questions that a typical beginner gets in his mind while starting his journey as a Siebel professional. This book can also be used as a reference by experienced professionals, as it contains some best practices to be followed while configuring Siebel applications.

Rishi Kumar Shrivastava

ACKNOWLEDGEMENTS

Writing a book is near to impossible without support from others, and I am not an exception. I have got a long list of people whom I want to acknowledge. I would like to start with Mr. Saravanan P., working as IT Analyst with Tata Consultancy Services Ltd., Chennai for playing the role of a teacher during my learning phase and a reviewer during the writing phase. Also, special thanks to Mr. C. Raghunath, Technical Architect, Tata Consultancy Services Ltd., Chennai, Mr. Govindaraj R., IT Analyst, Tata Consultancy Services Ltd., Chennai and Mrs. Deepa Aiyer for their encouragement and guidance during my writing phase. Also, I have got lot of support, encouragement and co-operation from my colleagues in "C2 - 16" group in completing this book. Thanks to all of you guys. Towards the end, I would like to thank all those associates in TCS - American Airlines relationship who helped me during my learning phase, as without their support, I would not have succeeded in bringing this book to its current state.

Thank you all!!!!

Rishi Kumar Shrivastava

CONTENTS

PART I

CUSTOMER RELATIONSHIP MANAGEMENT

Let us begin our mission of learning Oracle's Siebel CRM 8.x Navigation and Configuration. From here onwards, wherever I say the word "Siebel," I'll be referring to Oracle's Siebel CRM 8.1 solution. In this part of book, I'll try to make you familiar with the concept Customer Relationship Management (CRM). As Siebel is a CRM tool, it is mandatory to know the meaning and significance of Customer Relationship Management in the growth of an organization. The major topics covered in this part are:

- Introduction to CRM
- Basic definitions of CRM
- Customer Centricity
- Customer Responsiveness
- Customer Loyalty
- Customer Lifecycle Management
- Customer Value Management
- Gartner's 8 Building Blocks of CRM
- Customer Relationship Management Systems
  - Operational CRM Systems
  - Collaborative CRM Systems
  - Analytical CRM Systems.
- Electronic CRM Systems (eCRM)
- Difference between CRM and eCRM
- eCRM Systems over CRM Systems.
- Myths related to CRM

Chapter 1

INTRODUCTION TO CUSTOMER RELATIONSHIP MANAGEMENT

1.1 CUSTOMER RELATIONSHIP MANAGEMENT

So guys, let us tighten our shoes to start our mission Oracle's Siebel CRM 8.x Navigation and Configuration. Siebel is basically a CRM solution. Therefore, before starting our mission of learning Siebel, we should understand meaning and importance of customer relationship management (CRM). Throughout the book, we will use the term CRM to refer to customer relationship management, obviously to save some papers (save paper, save trees, and go green☺).

If we look at the name "customer relationship management," we can get some idea of it. At this point of time, let us just say that a CRM is "management of relationships with customers." Throughout the chapter, we will elaborate this definition. CRM starts with a customer, the most crucial factor for any business. For explaining the definition, I will take "you" as my example. All of you are customers to some business in your day-to-day life, either directly or indirectly. Let us just take the example of a small retail shop in your locality. You might have experienced a lot of things, when you go to the shop. The shopkeeper always welcomes you with smile, tries to take care of all your demands, gives offers on products, keeps track of your choices, asks for the feedbacks, provides the service of home delivery for your comfort, and so on. If we try to find out the reason behind this behavior, we will get that he tries to make sure that we go to his shop again, and again. He tries to manage the relationship with you, and all other customers. In turn, you make repeated purchases to his shop and recommend others too. In short, you remain *loyal* to him. The various strategies used by the shopkeeper groups together to form the CRM.

With an increase of super markets and big departmental stores, customers were provided most of the things of their needs at the same place, with a better quality assurance and lower prices. But, it made difficult for the businesses to maintain personal relationships with customer. Due to large size of business and its market, the face-to-face interaction between a supplier and a customer became near to impossible, making it difficult for business to know its customers and their preferences. Although customers used to get a wide range of products and good offers, the customer mobility increased. Customers always tried to find out the supplier who can provide the goods at cheapest rate, or with more features. This resulted in reduction of customer loyalty.

Other businesses across the globe, small, mid, or large sized, are not the exceptions. The same problem is faced by almost every business. With the increase in size and market share, it becomes difficult for them to retain their existing customers. This gave rise to the need of a CRM solution that can equip businesses to manage their relationships with their customers. It is always cheaper and profitable to retain an existing customer, then to acquire a new one. Certain points justifying this statement are [1] as follows:

- By Pareto's principle, it is assumed that 20% of a company's customers generate 80% of its profits.
- In industrial sales, it takes an average of 8–10 physical calls in person to sell a new customer, and 2–3 calls to sell an existing customer.
- It is 5–10 times more expensive to acquire a new customer than obtain repeat business from an existing customer. For example, according to the Boston Consulting Group [Hildebrand, 2000], the cost to market to existing Web customers is $6.80 compared to $34 to acquire a new Web customers.
- A typical dissatisfied customer tells 8–10 people about his or her experience.
- A 5% increase in retaining existing customers translates into 25% or more increase in profitability.

All the businesses, small, mid-sized, or large, depend heavily on CRM, in order to optimize their revenue and profits. The next section will focus on formally defining a CRM, along with some of the definitions given by CRM experts.

1.2 DEFINITIONS OF CRM

CRM, or Customer Relationship Management, is basically a business strategy that enables organizations to find their potential customers and manage relationships with their most profitable customers, using efficient marketing, sales and service, ultimately resulting in an overall growth in organization's revenue and customer satisfaction. Despite of traditional offerings – centric business strategies – CRM is a customer-centric business strategy (Customer Centricity is covered in next section). It focuses on getting profits from existing customers, by encouraging them for repeated purchases, cross-sell and up-sell, using effective CRM strategies.

Following are various definitions of CRM, provided by some CRM experts:

1. Ref. [2] states that "*Customer relationship management (CRM) is a business strategy to acquire and manage the most valuable customer relationships. CRM requires a customer-centric business philosophy and culture to support effective marketing, sales, and service processes. CRM applications can enable effective customer relationship management, provided that an enterprise has the right leadership, strategy, and culture.*"
2. According to **Siebel.com [3]** "*CRM is an integrated approach for identifying, acquiring, and retaining customers. By enabling organizations to manage and coordinate customer interactions across multiple channels, departments, lines of business, and geographies, CRM helps organizations maximize the value of every customer interaction and drive superior corporate performance.*"

3. **destinationcrm.com [4]** defines CRM as "*CRM, or Customer Relationship Management, is a company-wide business strategy designed to reduce costs and increase profitability by solidifying customer satisfaction, loyalty, and advocacy. True CRM brings together information from all data sources within an organization (and where appropriate, from outside the organization) to give one, holistic view of each customer in real time. This allows customer facing employees in such areas as sales, customer support, and marketing to make quick yet informed decisions on everything from cross-selling and up-selling opportunities to target marketing strategies to competitive positioning tactics.*"

1.3 CONCEPTS USED IN CRM

This section covers the discussion on some of the concepts that are commonly used while talking about CRM. Understanding these terms is quite necessary to have a clear picture about CRM. The section covers following:

- Customer Centricity
- Customer Responsiveness
- Customer Loyalty
- Customer Lifecycle Management
- Customer Value Management

1.3.1 Customer Centricity

Customer centricity is a business logic, in which organizations focus more on the needs and demands of customers, rather than internal factors, such as quick wins and short-term profits. A true customer-centric business always maintains the primacy of its customers, and develops the products based on customer responses and behavior.

Apart from customer centricity, three other business logics are identified. They are Product Centricity, Production Centricity and Sales Centricity. Following table shows the comparison of all:

Table 1.1 Comparison of Customer Centricity, Product Centricity, Production Centricity, and Sales Centricity

Serial number	*Customer centricity*	*Product centricity*	*Production centricity*	*Sales centricity*
1.	The main focus is on customers, their responses, and behavior	Main focus is on the quality of product. This logic states that customers always buy the product with the best quality and features	Main focus is on the cost of product. This logic assumes that customer buys the product with lower cost	Main focus is on increasing sales, by advertising, public relations, and sales promotion

Serial number	*Customer centricity*	*Product centricity*	*Production centricity*	*Sales centricity*
2.	As products are based on customer feedbacks and their specific wants, they are quite attractive to customers	As the quality of product is kept at primacy, typically the products are quite costly for majority of customers	As the ultimate goal is to keep the product cost low, the organizations working on this logic strive to keep operating costs low	Advertising and public relations are given more importance over the quality and price of product

According to Michael T. Bosworth and John R. Holland [5], there are seven basic tenets of Customer Centric behavior that sets it apart from other traditional selling behaviors. They are as follows:

1. Having situational conversations *versus* making presentations

Traditional salespeople rely on making presentations because they believe this approach gives them the opportunity to add excitement to an offering with snazzy visuals and the supposed innovative use of presentation tools, such as PowerPoint. Such dramatics, however, are unnecessary. In order to be effective, a salesperson must be able to relate his or her offering to the buyer in a way that will enable the buyer to visualize using the offering to satisfy his or her needs. The most effective way to determine those needs is through honest conversations with the buyer.

2. Asking relevant questions *versus* offering opinions

People love to buy, but hate feeling sold to. Most salespeople come to a vision of the buyer's problem before the buyer does, usually to the buyer's chagrin. Customer-centric salespeople use their expertise to frame interesting and helpful questions, rather than to deliver opinions, drawing out of the buyer a realization of his or her needs, and building toward a more useful solution.

Earn the Buyer's Respect

3. Solution-focused *versus* relationship-focused

Salespeople who are not trained to converse with decision makers about product usage gravitate toward focusing on their relationship with their buyers, which can be fleeting, depending on the product and market. In situations where the buyer is attempting to satisfy a need, the successful seller must first earn the buyer's respect by knowing how his or her wares can provide a solution to that need.

4. Targeting businesspeople *versus* gravitating toward users

Traditional salespeople gravitate toward the users of their products, while customer-centric salespeople target business decision makers. Most traditional salespeople can talk a great deal about a product's features, but a very little about how it is used in day-to-day applications. Customer-centric sellers, conversely, focus on how to use a product and what results can be expected, and how much it costs *versus* the benefits it presents.

5. Relating product usage *versus* relying on a product

Traditional salespeople educate buyers about a product, and assume buyers will know how to apply the product's features to meet their needs. Customer-centric sellers are able to relate conversationally with buyers about product usage.

Monitor Progress When Necessary

6. Managing their managers *versus* needing to be managed

Traditional sales managers monitor activity, rather than progress; they are promoted to management positions, in part, because they were good salespeople – management skills are rarely used as criteria for promotion. Managers of customer-centric salespeople, on the other hand, must only monitor their charges' progress and, when necessary, provide company resources to help them make a sale.

7. Empowering buyers *versus* attempting to sell them

Selling is not about persuasion, pressure, or coercion; it is about empowerment. A seller's objective, going into a new customer relationship, should be to help the buyer solve a problem, satisfy a need, or achieve a goal. The difference between the two sales approaches is fundamental.

1.3.2 Customer Responsiveness

Customer responsiveness, as the name suggests, is the organization's readiness to accept new suggestions, ideas, or opinions of customers, by taking their feedbacks on the products and services provided. With an increasing cost of acquiring new customers, organizations these days are focusing more on retaining their existing customers. Customer responsiveness plays a significant role in helping organizations to retain their existing customers.

Traditionally, organizations were focused mainly on mass marketing, targeted to increase the sales transactions, by providing different offerings. The major goal of mass marketing was to sell the product to as many customers as possible, with minimal attention on customer feedbacks. This approach was quite inflexible, as products and solutions were made based on the forecast of customer needs, before interacting with them. The major drawbacks of this approach are reduction in customer loyalty and increase in the cost, incurred on acquiring new customers.

In the modern approach of customized marketing, organizations focus more on customer responsiveness. This approach is comparatively more flexible, and the main focus in on the efficacy of delivered solution, that is, how the solution tackles individual's problems. Unlike the mass marketing approach that tries to sell a solution to as many customers as possible, customized marketing approach aims at selling as much products as possible to a single existing customer, via different product lines. Also, this approach allows the organizations to have a one-to-one discussion with individual customers to understand their needs, based on which the solution is designed and customized. As the solutions are designed based on the individual's needs that are not known to competitors, the organization gets a competitive advantage.

Customized marketing approach stands on the concept of customer responsiveness. Therefore, the organizations practicing this approach should focus on making their customer responsiveness efficient. For achieving an efficient customer responsiveness, the organizations should:

- deeply understand the customer behavior, and do its necessary profiling.
- concentrate on real time customer profiling and loyalty management.
- practice highly customer-targeted promotion activities.
- be agile to respond to the changing market scenarios.

Certain advantages of efficient customer responsiveness are as follows:

- Minimization of the gap between the customers' needs and delivered solution.
- Reduction in the cost.
- Enterprises become more agile to frequent changes.
- All the above-mentioned advantages ultimately result in increased customer loyalty and competitive advantage.

1.3.3 Customer Loyalty

Customer loyalty plays a significant role in increasing the revenues and profits of organization. A customer can be said loyal if he does repeated and regular purchases, along several product and service lines. A loyal customer remains immune to the competitor's pull and refers the organization to others as well.

In traditional marketing approaches, the main aim was to acquire more and more customers, by mass marketing and advertising, with a minimal attention on retaining existing customers. Organizations following this principle faced following losses:

- Huge marketing and customer acquisition costs
- More transaction costs
- Low cross-selling and up-selling
- Lack of support from customer's "word of mouth"

But, as the Internet grew and became popular among customers, the way customers used to connect to organizations changed drastically. Their expectations with organizations also changed with time. Unlike traditional marketing approaches that were focused on one-way flow of marketing and sales information from organization to customers, customized marketing focuses on two-way flow of information, both from organizations to customers, and vice versa. Organizations provide marketing and sales information to customers, and collect their feedbacks and future demands. In addition, organizations started allowing customers to pull the product details as and when they require, and purchase the product on the terms that best suit them. Also, as organizations realized that the cost of acquiring a new customer is much more then retaining an existing customer, their focus and efforts also shifted from customer acquisition to customer retention, that is, turning a "first-time buyer" to "lifetime customer." Some benefits of turning a "first-time buyer" to "Lifetime customer" are as follows:

- As the customer is loyal to the organization, he will purchase more from it. This will increase organization's sales, with a minimal advertising and marketing costs.
- A loyal customer is resistant to the discounts and luring offers from competitors. This insulates the organization from price competition.
- A satisfied and loyal customer always refers the organization to others, thereby helping the organization to achieve more market share, with minimum marketing costs.
- Finally, an organization saving huge marketing costs via customer retention can provide a better pay to its employees, resulting in employee loyalty.

1.3.4 Customer Life Cycle Management (CLM)

An efficient customer-centric organization requires three core customer management processes: **Get a customer (Customer Acquisition), retain the customer (Customer Retention), and develop the customer from first-time buyer to lifetime customer (Customer Development)**. These three core processes together form a Customer Life Cycle (CLC).

Customer's expectations from organizations vary with the Customer - Organization relationship stage. CLC encompasses these stages, allowing organizations to analyze the needs and expectations of customers at each stage of relationship. Based on the relationship, customers are of four types:

1. **Potential customers:** Customers falling under this category are not exactly the customers, but they form the future market for the company. They are the potential buyers for the organization, who are most likely to become the customers in future. While making marketing and advertising strategies, organizations should take a great care of customers in this group.
2. **First-time buyers:** As the category's name suggests, these customers are the first-time buyers of organization's products and services. These customers have a huge potential for organization's future revenues and profits. An utmost care is taken by organizations to satisfy their first-time buyers and convert them to loyal customers. At this stage, a customer is highly susceptible to "churn" due to better competitor's offerings, or even minor disappointment.
3. **Loyal customers:** Customers falling in this category form the core of organization's customer base. These are the customers that do repeated purchases from organization, and have a stable relationship with it. The organization's relationship with these customers is insulated from small and occasional defects in products and services. Also, the needs and expectations of these customers with organization are stable, and do not change frequently with time. As this group of customers is loyal to organization, they account for the highest sales per customer and have highest retention rates.
4. **Turncoats:** Repeated failures in products or services from organization, recursive offerings from competitors that are too attractive, or continuous ignorance by the

organization results in customers of this category. These customers join hands with competitors, breaking their relationships with the organization.

Organization's strategies vary with the customer–organization relationship stage. Apart from these stages, organizations should also take care of various stages of customer in CLC. Figure 1.1 illustrates various stages of CLC.

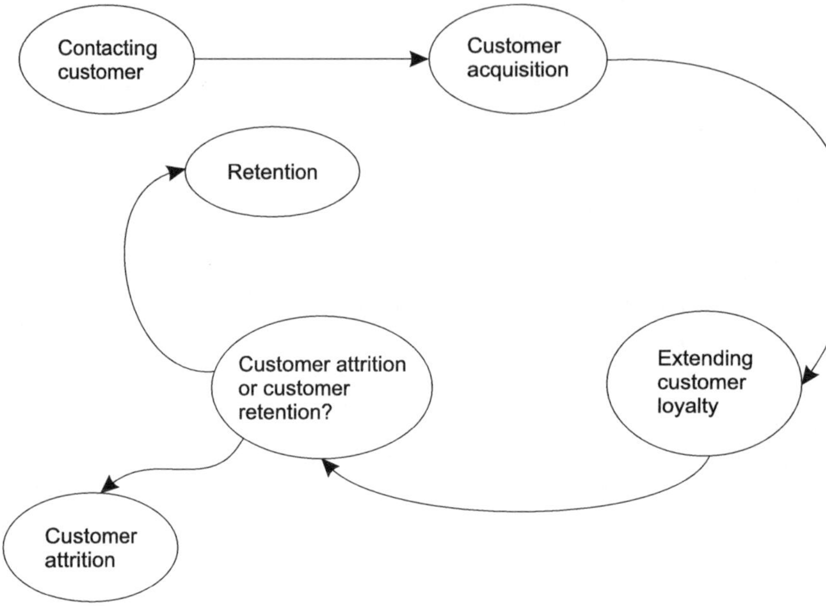

Fig. 1.1 *Customer life cycle managment*

A brief description of all these stages and activities focused during each of them is mentioned below:

1. **Contact a customer:** This stage includes activities to contact a customer. These activities include advertisement, marketing, mailing, face-to-face selling, and promotions.
2. **Customer acquisition:** This stage includes activities to increase customer involvement. It includes collecting as much customer details as possible, his wants and expectations, and promoting price–value relationship, which ultimately result in a strong base for a strong customer loyalty.
3. **Customer retention:** This stage involves activities that are focused on retaining an acquired customer. It includes increasing customer responsiveness and getting their regular feedbacks on products and services, along with the measures to maximize customer satisfaction and rewarding positive customer behavior.
4. **Extending customer loyalty:** This stage involves steps to extend loyalty of a customer. It involves focusing on cross-selling and up-selling, analyzing customer needs and expectations, working on their feedbacks and comments, and provide them best possible service and support.

5. **Customer attrition:** This is the stage where organizations may face customer defection. In this stage, the prime focus is on the steps to minimize the customer attrition by analyzing and identifying the vulnerable customers and designing schemes and programs to increase their satisfaction. The following figure illustrates various stages of CLC:

Management of CLC is called CLM. At this point, it is important to note that CLM is different from CRM. CLC has an added factor of time. According to Salesboom.com [6], "Customer Life Cycle Management, or CLM, is often misunderstood to be the same principle idea as Customer Relationship Management, or CRM. Customer Lifecycle Management, however, has a key difference from CRM - the added factor of time. A fast approach and very brief definition of CLM is simply the measurement of your CRM program's success over time - providing you have CLM metrics from before and after your CRM implementation."

The main idea behind CLM is to manage the CLC to maximize customer retention, thereby maximizing the profits, as the cost to acquire a customer is far more than the cost to retain an existing customer. As discussed above, CLM has an added factor of time. It is a slow process, as it includes examining of various matrices, such as purchase history, gross amount of money spent on customer acquisition, and retention over a period of time, on individual customer or against a mean average, along with post sales services and analysis of duration of relationship between customer and business.

1.3.5 Customer Value Management

Customer value management includes the activities to profitably manage the relationships with each customer, resulting in maximizing the lifetime profit and revenues from entire customer base. It helps organizations to plan strategies and programs to increase customer retention and loyalty, thereby minimizing customer acquisition costs, over an extended period of profitable relationship.

Each customer that belongs to organization's customer base is not necessarily profitable. The main goal of CVM is to manage each customer in such a way that maximizes the overall profit. CVM is basically a customer-focused activity. In spite of focusing on marketing, advertising, or product management to increase the profit, it focuses on maximizing the profits from each individual customer from organization's customer base, over an entire period of relationship. Customer value managers always focus on gathering more and more details of each individual customer, and plan their offerings to get maximum profit from that customer, throughout the period of relationship.

According to Jeffrey Pease [6], there are three "Rs" of the CVM cycle. They are as follows:

1. Right customers (acquisition)
2. Right relationship (development)
3. Right retention (keeping valuable customers)

Figure 1.2 explains this.

A brief description of all the above-mentioned stages is mentioned below:

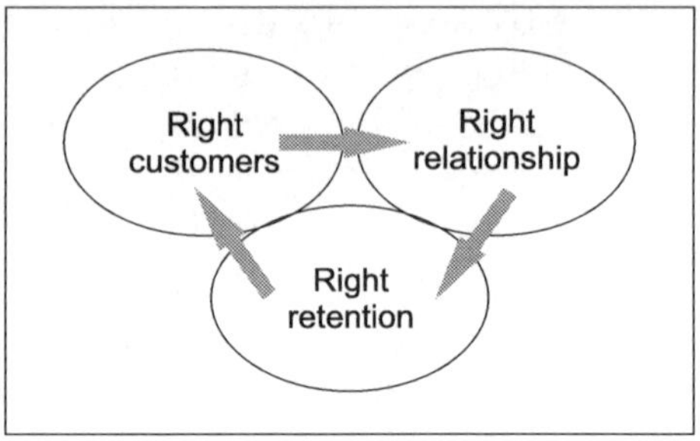

Fig. 1.2 *CVM cycle*

1. **Right customers**: This is the stage of identifying the potentially beneficial customers for the organization. Beneficial customers are those customers who remain loyal to the organization, and do repeated purchases for a long period of relationship. In this context, all customers are not equal. Those who will remain loyal and beneficial for the organization are given more focus in this stage, as compared to potentially less beneficial ones. The cost of acquiring a new customer is always huge, and a customer who will do fewer purchases, or is expected to have a short relationship term, will not be beneficial for the organization. Hence, at this stage, organizations should try to separate potentially beneficial customers, from the group of potential customers. One of the most crucial factors to recognize such customers is the analysis of the behavior of existing customers, as the organizations have sufficient amount of data about them. This analysis can reveal a lot of hidden factors, such as purchase frequency, value-affecting trends, and customer's reactions and expectations from organization's products and services. All these factors form a strong base to find and acquire potentially most beneficial customers.
2. **Right relationship**: This stage includes developing relationships with acquired customers. Acquiring profitable customer is not sufficient to earn profits. Organization also needs to develop a long lasting relationship with these customers. Customers always choose to leave the organization if they do not get the desired "touch." For instance, a customer who gets a lot of product offerings that he does not need would get irritated and will break the relationship. Similarly, a customer who gets very less options from organization as compared to his needs would prefer to go for some other organization. All the acquired customers, who leave at earlier stages, result in a huge loss to organization. Hence, it is necessary for managers to analyze the wants and expectations of each individual customer, and give him the offers based on that. A customer with high "lifetime value (LTV)" always results in huge profits. Jeffrey Pease [6] gives a simplified view of customer LTV as follows:

$$\textbf{LTV} = \textbf{purchase size} \times \textbf{frequency} \times \textbf{duration}$$

In words, the above relationship states that customer's LTV depends directly on purchase size (the amount of product purchased), frequency (the repeating nature of customer), and duration (the duration for which customer remains loyal to organization and do repeated purchases). Hence, in this stage, managers should focus on the following:

- Providing offerings and benefits that encourage the customers to purchase more.
- Understand customer needs and respond to their changing needs, to increase the frequency with which customer purchases from organization.

- Provide best product offerings, customer service, and support to increase the duration of organization–customer relationship.

3. **Right retention:** This is the stage of making the retention strategies that target on "right" customers, not every customer. In this stage, strategies targeting the customers with highest LTV are developed by managers. Hence, the most crucial part of this stage is to determine "right" customers, before making strategies. Spending time, money, and resources on less profitable customers result in huge loss to organization. If the strategies targeting wrong customers get successful, the whole customer base of organization gets affected.

Right retention strategies help managers to estimate the customers who are not significant today, but will be profitable tomorrow. Knowing this, managers can target these customers and provide them the same level of services that they provide them for their most valuable customers. This results in enhanced customer loyalty, by most profitable customers.

1.4 BENEFITS OF CRM

After the discussion on various definitions of CRM and concepts related to it, let us have a quick discussion on the benefits that an organization gets by using CRM. The following section provides some of the benefits of CRM:

- By using CRM strategies, an organization can personalize the relationships with its customer by knowing them and their preferences. This will result in better customer service, resulting in more customer loyalty.
- By using CRM strategies, an organization can keep track of customer preferences and his previous purchases. This will be helpful in targeting specific customers in marketing of products, avoiding the customers who would not prefer the product or who have already purchased it. This will result in huge saving of marketing cost, ultimately aiding in company's profit.
- Adopting CRM strategies also enable organizations to effectively cross-sale and up-sale the products. By cross-selling, we mean selling a complementary product to the customer, based on his past purchases. For example, a customer who has purchased a laptop may purchase a laptop bag, USB devices, or software CDs.
  By up-selling, we mean offering customers the same product that he purchased, in higher categories. For example, a customer taking a trial package for some product may need to get a full package later.
- By keeping track of existing customers and their preferences, an organization can easily find out its potential customers. For example, a book seller can keep track of students of a particular university, and can target other students of same university based on the preferences of its existing customers.
- CRM strategies simplify the management of customer life cycle. A CLC encapsulates all the steps from contacting a customer till providing the customer service. By knowing a customer better, organizations can serve them better. Most of the CRM solutions available today provide a centralized database that stores the customer

information, obtained from various customer facing departments and partners. This makes it easy for various departments across an organization, such as marketing department and customer service department, to gather customer information. This significantly reduces the time and effort to gather the required customer information across various departments of an organization.

1.5 GARTNER'S EIGHT BUILDING BLOCKS OF CRM

For an efficient implementation of CRM, an enterprise-level strategy spanning across whole business is indispensable. Implementation of an enterprise-level CRM requires a strategic framework to guide through the CRM process, a proper leadership to focus more on customers, and a big vision to see everything at enterprise level. According to Gartner, "Executing enterprise-level CRM is not easy. It requires board-level vision and leadership to drive a 'relentless focus on the customer'. It involves learning new customer management skills, potentially difficult changes to processes, culture and organization, and grappling with the technology challenges of multichannel alignment, systems integration, and data quality."

Although organizations agree with the importance of CRM implementation in their growth, it does not get the importance it deserves, typically, due to lack of proper leadership, more focus on revenue, profit targets, and quick wins.

With a deep analysis, Gartner created a framework, consisting of eight building blocks of CRM, to guide organizations to see the big picture, make their business cases and plan their implementation. These are shown in Fig. 1.3.

The following section provides a brief discussion on all the above-mentioned building blocks. It provides the importance of eight building blocks in the successful implementation of CRM framework [7]:

- **Vision:** A vision comprises of defining a CRM keeping the organization in mind. It involves figuring out the reasons to do CRM and the ultimate goals that the organization wants to achieve from CRM. According to Gartner, "Successful CRM demands a clear vision so that a strategy and implementation can be developed to achieve it. The CRM vision is how the customer-centric enterprise wants to look and feel to its customers and prospects — the customer value proposition (CVP) and the corporate brand values are key to the CRM vision. Without a CRM vision, the enterprise will not stand out from the competition, target customers will not know what to expect from it and employees will not know what to deliver in terms of external customer experience. A successful CRM vision is the cornerstone to motivating staff, generating customer loyalty and gaining a greater market share."
- **Strategy:** A CRM strategy provides the direction to target the potential customers, acquire them, develop, and retain them. According to Gartner, "A CRM strategy is not an implementation plan or road map. A real CRM strategy takes the direction and financial goals of the business strategy and sets out how the enterprise is going to build customer loyalty — that „feel-good factor" of customer connection with an enterprise that means customers stay longer, buy more, recommend the enterprise to

others and are more willing to pay a premium price. The objectives of a CRM strategy are to target, acquire, develop, and retain valuable customers to achieve corporate goals."

- **Valued customer experience:** When customers interact with the enterprise, their experiences play a valuable role in making an opinion about the enterprise among them. According to Gartner, "Customers' experiences when interacting with the enterprise play a key role in shaping their perception of the enterprise — the value it provides and the importance it places on the customer relationship. Good customer experiences drive satisfaction, trust, and long-term loyalty. Poor customer experiences have the opposite effect and, because bad news travels faster and further than good news, they harm the enterprise's ability to create new relationships with prospects. No amount of internal, second guessing" can simulate what it's really like to be a customer."

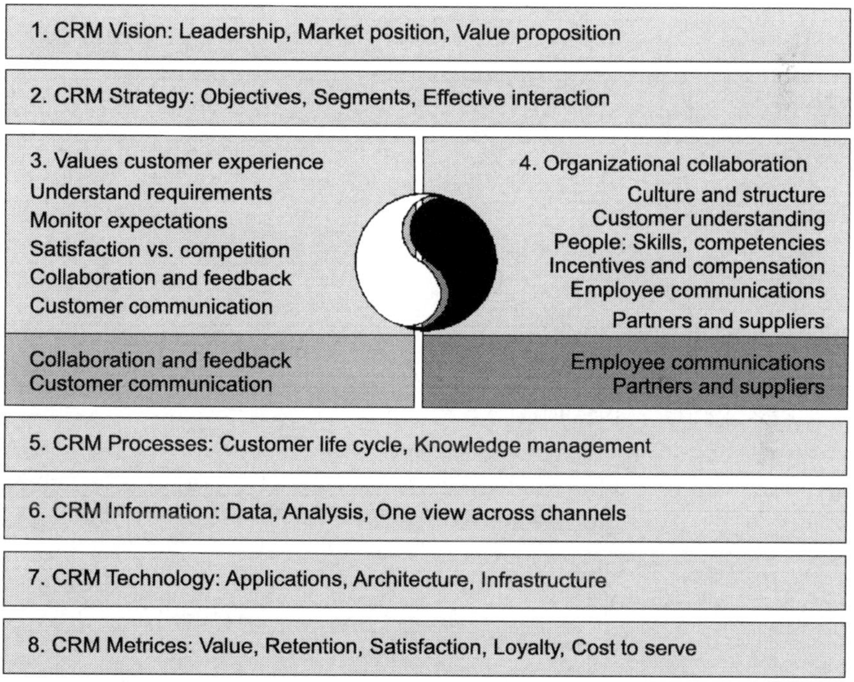

Fig. 1.3 *Building blocks of CRM. (Source: Gartner Research)*

- **Organizational collaboration:** For organizations trying to become customer centric, it is very crucial to do some enterprise-level changes to focus more on the needs and wants of customer, along with implementing CRM technologies. According to Gartner, "Many enterprises believe that implementing CRM technologies makes them a customer-centric organization. They forget, ignore or deliberately avoid the necessary changes to the enterprise itself. True CRM means that individuals, teams and the whole enterprise must become more focused on the needs and wants of the customer. As a critical part of a CRM program, it will involve changing organizational structures, incentives and compensation, skills and even the enterprise culture. Ongoing change management will be key."

5. **Processes:** Process re-engineering should create processes that should meet customer expectations, along with providing competitive differentiation to the enterprise. According to Gartner, "Past efforts to re-engineer processes were primarily driven by the desire to improve the efficiency of an enterprise and reduce costs. The beneficiary was the enterprise, not its customers. The rise in CRM has led to a focus on reworking key processes that touch the customer and asking customers which processes matter to them. We call this customer process re-engineering. Enterprises frequently do not realize that their functionally fragmented processes often mean that the customer has a poor experience and receives less than the expected value. Successful re-engineering should create processes that not only meet customers' expectations, but also support the customer value proposition, provide competitive differentiation and contribute to the desired customer experience."
6. **Information:** For a successful management of relationships with customer, a lenient stream of customer information across the organization, along with a firm integration between operational and analytical systems, is very crucial. According to Gartner, "Successful CRM requires a flow of customer information around the organization and tight integration between operational and analytical systems. Having the right information at the right time is fundamental to successful CRM strategies, providing customer insight and allowing effective interaction across any channel. Unfortunately, most enterprises' CRM information capabilities are poor — the result of numerous and fragmented departments, initiatives, databases and systems. Enterprises that establish a business plan for sourcing, managing and leveraging their customer information assets are more likely to achieve their CRM goals and objectives and gain a competitive advantage."
7. **Technology:** Any modern CRM initiative requires CRM technologies as its enabler. Gartner describes technology as follows: "For most technologists, CRM is all about technology. CRM technologies are an essential enabler for any modern CRM business strategy, but they are just one piece of the puzzle."

Also, Gartner's "Technology Decisions Are Key to Enabling CRM Strategies (DF-14-8082)" [8] highlights three areas where enterprises should take technology-related decisions, while enabling CRM strategies. These areas are : "CRM applications, architectural issues and integration." Typically, integration issues do not gain much relevance at the start. But as organizations start recognizing the importance of perfect customer-centric processes in true CRM Implementations, these issues gain prominence, both in cost and time.

8. **Metrics:** Metrics, along with efficient performance management, form the base for making a CRM strategy successful. To build a path for turning customers into assets, all the above-mentioned building blocks rely on an efficient performance management and metrics. Gartner's "Getting the Best Out of CRM Performance Metrics" (DF-13-1433) [9] introduces a framework for measuring an enterprise's success with CRM by creating a hierarchy of performance metrics with four levels, namely: corporate, customer strategic, operational and process, and infrastructure

input metrics. About these metrics, Gartner says that "These metrics have an internal and an external focus and link operations to strategy and corporate financial benefits. Each enterprise will have a unique set of metrics applicable to their situation."

1.6 CRM SYSTEMS

As the name suggests, CRM systems are the systems used by organizations to manage the relationships with their customers. It is a generic term used for software suits and methodologies that are used to automate all customer-centric activities of an organization. These systems are designed to be flexible and reconfigurable, based on organization's specific needs. They provide a common platform for all sorts of customer communication resulting in a broad view of entire CLC, which in turn improves organization's customer responsiveness. Some of the advantages of implementing CRM systems for carrying out CRM activities are as follows:

1. As CRM systems are software based, they ensure consistency in the quality of delivered service.
2. The single platform for all customer communications provided by CRM systems results in integrated and unified information system architecture.
3. Using front-end, user-friendly GUI, CRM system ensures improved validation of user requirements directly by the users.
4. As they are flexible and reconfigurable, they can be configured and customized on the basis of organization's specific needs.
5. CRM systems also ensure a reliable documentation throughout the CRM process.
6. CRM systems enable lenient information flow throughout the organization, thereby converting it into an "information-driven, real-time enterprise."

1.7 TYPES OF CRM SYSTEMS

Based on the functionalities and type of applications, CRM systems can be classified into the following three types [10]:

1. Operational CRM systems.
2. Analytical CRM systems.
3. Collaborative CRM systems.

1.7.1 Operational CRM Systems

Operational CRM systems include the applications that are used to collect and represent the data from various disconnected data sources in an organization. Their main focus is to help business's employees to provide a better and faster service to customers, as they do not need to collect the data themselves from various data sources. Operational CRM systems improve organization's customer responsiveness and save a lot of time and efforts in providing rapid customer service.

1.7.2 Analytical CRM Systems

Analytical CRM systems also integrate the data from numerous disconnected data sources across organization. The difference between analytical CRM systems and others is that analytical systems use and analyze the data, using techniques, such as data mining. These systems track the patterns and trends, and based on that, they highlight the problems that are quite widespread across customers, but are not evident, or are unknown, to the individual customers, and helps organizations to work upon them before they get worsen.

1.7.3 Collaborative CRM Systems

Collaborative CRM systems work as a bridge between business and various external entities, such as its vendors, distributors, or customers. These systems focus on making organization more customer-centric by providing an interactive platform between business and its customers, such as dedicated Web sites or instant messaging tools. Unlike the other two types of CRM systems that primarily focus on data integration within the organization, collaborative CRM systems focus on bringing additional data to business from external entities, which can be used to make organization's customer service more efficient.

1.8 ELECTRONIC CUSTOMER RELATIONSHIP MANAGEMENT (eCRM)

eCRM means implementing all forms of managing relationships with customers using Information Technology (IT). Just like e-mail means using IT for sending and receiving mails, eCRM enables practicing CRM over Web. It is a practice where all the CRM-related stuffs, for example, internal organization's resources and external resources, such as marketing strategies, are integrated by using IT, forming a virtual centralized repository, which helps organizations to understand customer's needs better and provide them efficient and faster service. eCRM has enhanced the process of customer communication. Most of the organizations today provide the facility of placing orders, checking the order status and contacting organization via mails and feedbacks to their customers by using a dedicated Web-based window. This makes it easy for the customer to get his queries resolved irrespective of organization's working hours, along with freeing organization from providing a live contact at other end to resolve customer queries and requests. At this point, it is important to understand the difference between CRM and eCRM to get a clear picture of advantages of eCRM over CRM. Following section gives some of the differences.

1.8.1 Difference between CRM and eCRM

With the proliferating popularity of Internet among crowds, it became crucial for the organizations to use IT in their CRM activities. Some of the points are highlighted in Table 1.2 [11]. Explanation of terms marked * is given in subsequent section.

Table 1.2 Technical Differences between CRM and eCRM

Serial number	*CRM activity*	*CRM*	*eCRM*	*Benefits of eCRM over CRM*
1.	Contacting customers	Done through retail stores, phone, and fax	Done through Internet using dedicated browser-based windows and mails, along with the traditional approaches used in CRM	Efficient customer contacting
2.	System interface	Uses ERP system* on client–server architecture, which focuses more on back-end operations	ERP systems, data warehouses* and data marts* are used for the interaction between front end and back end. More emphasis is on front end	Use of data warehouse and data marts supports organizations in the process of business intelligence*. Also, eCRM expands customer "touch points"
3.	Application and menus customization	Any change in application configuration and menus by the user (organization's employees or retail personals) required significant changes at organization level	Web-based user interfaces make it easy for the users to customize the application based on their needs	Application customization is easy, without the overhead of significant changes at organization level
4.	Client–application interaction	Applications are designed giving more emphasis on back-end functionality, such as data collection and maintenance. Web enabling these applications for client interaction gives a burden of downloading applets at client side, and they may have to be rewritten in different platforms	Accessing applications by the client in eCRM is as easy as accessing different Web pages using browser. These applications are designed to be optimally implemented over Web, and there is no burden of any additional download or installation by the client	Client-application interaction is easy and faster

Serial number	*CRM activity*	*CRM*	*eCRM*	*Benefits of eCRM over CRM*
5.	System focus	Main focuses of system design are products and internal job functions. Web-enabled applications are designed around one department or business unit	Main focus of system design is "customers," not the products or job functions. These are designed for external use. Web applications designed in these systems span across organization, and are not limited at department level	Enterprise-wide Web-enabled applications make customer communication efficient and faster
6.	System maintenance and modification	As the system is located on servers distributed at various locations, the implementation and maintenance is costly and burdensome	System expansion and maintenance can be done at one location and on one server	Reduced time and cost for implementation and maintenance

** **ERP:** ERP stands for Enterprise Resource Planning. ERP is basically a term that integrates various internal and external management activities of an organization by using automated software applications. It helps the organizations in achieving a seamless flow of information across various departments, both internal (departments inside the boundary of organization, such as finance, manufacturing, marketing, etc.) and external (departments outside the boundary of organization, such as organization's partners, stakeholders, etc.). CRM and ERP work in close collaboration. CRM is used to identify, target, and retain the customers, which requires a continuous flow of information across various departments of an organization. This seamless and continuous flow of information is done with the help of ERP systems.*

** **Data mart**: Data mart is a specific purpose-oriented subset of organizational database. It may be specialized to fulfill specific business needs, such as department-oriented data mart, or specific user group oriented data mart. This distribution makes data access and manipulation easy and efficient.*

** **Data warehouse**: Data warehouse is an integrated repository of electronically stored data, collected across various sources (departments, user groups, etc.), which is designed to facilitate reporting and analysis.*

1.9 MYTHS ABOUT CRM

After going through the content presented throughout the chapter, it is quite natural to develop a picture about CRM is minds. But, before making any picture, we should be clear on what "IS" CRM, and what it "IS NOT." After going through various concepts and methodologies of CRM, readers typically develop certain myths about it. In this section, we will have a look on some of the myths about CRM, along with the explanation of what is "wrong" in them.

Most of the organizations spend millions of bucks on purchasing the CRM software and its implementation. Yet, they face failure in successfully implementing CRM, as their expectations and planning are based on their myths about CRM, not the reality. In an article by Richard F. Gerson [12], there are following seven common myths about CRM among organizations:

1. **CRM is about managing customers**: CRM is basically the management of customer's relationship (by managing customer's data), and not the customer. Managing a customer simply means that you are controlling them, and telling them what they should do. It is practically impossible to ask customers to do what organization wants. Customers manage themselves, and purchase the products and services that they want. Hence, organizations should focus more on managing relationships with customers, and not on managing customers.
2. **Analytics is the key to success**: Analytics is just a way to analyze the data and work upon it. It should be treated as a "help" to reduce human efforts in data analysis. Analytics can tell the purchasing behavior of the customer, and his possible expectations and future purchases, but that is not sufficient to design and target campaigns for customers. The results from analytics require a human touch to be implemented successfully. Organizations can reduce human analysis efforts by using analytics, but cannot avoid it completely. In the words of Richard F. Gerson, "It has been my experience that the customer still wants the human touch. They still want to talk with a person, interact with a „warm body", and get their problem resolved or purchase confirmed by a real person. Analytics are important to CRM success, but anyone who thinks that constantly gathering more data, and that slicing and dicing that data takes the place of caring people who communicate with customers is sadly mistaken."
3. **Technology breeds/builds relationships**: Most of the organizations believe that if they spend more on purchasing new and compact software and technologies, they will achieve more market share. Here, it should always be remembered that a customer wants relationship, personal attention, and not the technology. Purchasing a technology never guarantees that you will know your customers better than if you had a lesser technology. Along with purchasing technology and working with it, organizations should also focus on building individual relationships with their customers. According to Richard F. Gerson [12], "Having great technology does not guarantee that customers will buy from you, nor does it guarantee that you will truly know your customers any better than if you had a lesser technology. Always remember that technology has nothing to do with relationships; people do."
4. **CRM success comes from full-scale implementation:** This is not the case. CRM implementations can be started at small level, say departmental level, and can be spread gradually at organization level. It is not mandatory to implement CRM solutions at full-scale level, right from the start. In fact, a lot of CRM experts suggest

that starting CRM implementation at small scale and gradually increasing its scope and functioning area is a good practice.

5. **People (employees) will always adapt to and adopt the new technology**: It is assumed by organizations that its employees will easily adapt to the new technology. But, unfortunately, this is not the case with everyone. Before changing a technology, or adopting a new technology, a change in mindset and corporate culture is mandatory. In order to achieve a successful CRM implementation, organizations must ensure that their corporate culture suits the CRM solutions, and all their employees are comfortable with this new technology and environment.
6. **CRM is on downswing due to high failure rates**: Currently, a lot of industries across the world are joining their hands with CRM. CRM systems of today are actually the old CRM strategies, implemented by using modern technologies. Modern CRM systems are doing the same work that any small shopkeeper of old times used to do to manage his customers, or what any small shopkeeper at your locality would do to retain you as his customer. Right from its evolution, CRM is on upswing, as it is considered as the best way to maximize organization's overall profits and revenues.
7. **CRM, as we know it today, is for everybody**: Here, we will again go to the example of a small shopkeeper at your locality. Does he use CRM software to manage his customers? Obviously not. But, he efficiently manages his customers and relationships with them. CRM products are available and can be customized for small as well as large-sized companies, but it is not actually needed by a lot of companies. Many companies can achieve a significant increase in their profit and revenues just by focusing on customer service, retention, and loyalty.

1.10 SUMMARY

CRM is one of the most crucial part in the success of organization. It encapsulates the strategies right from contacting the customer till the retention and repeated selling to customer. An efficient CRM strategy build with proper planning ensures the success of organization. On the other hand, lack of proper planning results in unexpected results.

REFERENCES

1. Gray, P. and Byun, J. (2001). *Customer Relationship Management*, Center for Research on Information technology and Organizations, University of California, Irvine, CA.
2. Thompson, B. (2002). *What is CRM*. Available from: http://crmguru.custhelp.com/app/answers/detail/a_id/416/~/what-is-crm.
3. (2008). *Introduction to Customer Relationship Management*, p. 4. Published in 2008 at Elsevier's website www.elsevierdirect.com

   Available from: http://buttleassociates.com/doc/Chapter1CRMbook2e.pdf.
4. destinationCRM.com (2010). *What is CRM*. Available from: http://www.destinationcrm.com/Articles/CRM-News/Daily-News/What-Is-CRM-46033.aspx.
5. Bosworth, M.T. and Holland J.R. (2004). *Customer – centric selling*, **26** (6).

6. Pease, J. *Customer Value Management: New Techniques for Maximizing the Lifetime Profitability of Your Customer Base.* Contributors: Marfise, S. and Wright D. Available from: http://www.docin.com/p-59597024.html.
7. Radcliffe, J. (2001). *Eight Building Blocks of CRM: A Framework for Success*, Gartner. Available from: http://www.gartner.com
8. Radcliffe, J. and Comport, J. (2001). *Technology Decisions Are Key to Enabling CRM Strategies (DF-14-8082)*. Available from: http://www.gartner.com/id=350572.
9. Jennifer Kirkby, Ed Thompson and Frank Buytendijk (2009). *Getting the Best Out of CRM Performance Metrics" (DF-13-1433).*
   Available from: http://www.gartner.com/id=350574
10. Austin, S. N. *The Types of CRM Systems.* eHow.com. Available from:
    http://www.ehow.com/list_6684022_types-crm-systems.html.
11. Chandra, S. and Strickland, T.J. (2004). *Technological differences between CRM and eCRM.* Vol. **V** (2).
12. Gerson, R. F. *The Seven Myths.* destinationCRM.com. Available from:
    http://www.destinationcrm.com/Articles/Web-Exclusives/Viewpoints/The-Seven-Myths-45358.aspx.

PART II

SIEBEL APPLICATIONS AND TOOLS

This section provides a first look and feel of Oracle's Siebel CRM 8.1 applications and tools. Till this point, our main area of focus was Customer Relationship Management. We have discussed various aspects of CRM, its' significance in industry and its advantages. Now we'll take a next step towards achieving our mission. We'll discuss about various Siebel applications, which include Siebel Enterprise Applications, Siebel eBusiness Applications and Siebel Tools. We'll also discuss the navigation in Siebel Applications and tools.

This major topics covered in this part are divided into four chapters:

- Siebel Enterprise Applications
- Siebel eBusiness Applications
- Siebel Tools
- Navigating Siebel Applications

Chapter 2

SIEBEL ENTERPRISE APPLICATIONS

Siebel Enterprise Applications suite is a suite of various applications, required by various Business Units of numerous organizations across world. In this chapter, we'll discuss about some of the major Siebel Enterprise applications, their role and significance in various business units of organizations and functional advantages of these applications. Major topics in this chapter are:

1. Siebel Marketing Enterprise
2. Siebel Service Enterprise
3. Siebel Call Center
4. Siebel Sales Enterprise
5. Siebel Field Service

While discussing about these applications, we'll also look on various benefits that an organization gets by adopting them.

2.1 INTRODUCTION

Siebel Systems was founded in 1993. Its main aim was to address the need of organizations of all sizes to achieve a better CRM, which includes better customer acquisition, better customer retention, and better customer service. Siebel Systems was taken over by Oracle in 2005. Today, Oracle's Siebel CRM is world's leading CRM solution, on which more than 4700 organizations are working in more than 100 countries across the world. Siebel enterprise applications suite is used by more than 8000 employees, whereas Siebel eBusiness applications suite is a leader in Internet-driven markets of today's world.

Siebel CRM is a CRM solution that caters to all the customer-related functions within an organization. It is an integrated suite that comprises of various application modules designed to cater the customers' needs in specific area. In this chapter, we will have a brief discussion on some of the major enterprise application modules provided by Siebel, along with their functional importance.

Before we dig more into various types of Siebel marketing applications, let us first discuss about the classification of Siebel applications. Siebel business applications can broadly be classified in the following two types:

- **Employee facing applications**
- **Customer or partner facing applications**

Employee facing applications are designed to be used by internal employees. They run in high interactivity mode and use Microsoft Internet Explorer as browser. The advanced capabilities provided by Microsoft Internet Explorer such as enabling users to select specific fields or rows (in list) by clicking anywhere in the element, column setting via drag and drop, are crucial for running Siebel applications in high interactivity mode. Examples of High Interactivity applications are Siebel Loyalty and Siebel Marketing. Various requirements for High Interactivity framework are discussed in section "Installing Siebel Web Client and Tools."

Customer or Partner facing applications run in Standard Interactivity mode. They do not require the advanced features provided by Microsoft Internet Explorer. They utilize the base features provided by all the browsers to carry on the required interaction. Examples of Standard Interactivity applications are Siebel eLoyalty and Siebel eSales. Various requirements for standard interactivity applications are discussed in Section "Installing Siebel Web Client and Tools."

Moving ahead, we will discuss about some of the important Siebel Enterprise applications along with various features provided by them and benefits that organizations get by using these applications.

2.2 SIEBEL ENTERPRISE APPLICATIONS

Various application modules in Siebel enterprise applications suite are designed to target various customer related activities for an organization. As Siebel is a complex integrated suite of modules, it is quite difficult to provide the overview of all its modules. Hence, we will discuss some of the major application modules and their functionalities. The modules to be discussed in this chapter are as follows:

1. Siebel Marketing Enterprise
2. Siebel Service Enterprise
3. Siebel Call Center
4. Siebel Sales Enterprise
5. Siebel Field Service

2.2.1 Siebel Marketing Enterprise

As the name suggests, this module focuses on various marketing tasks. It enables organizations to have a deeper customer analysis and insight, resulting in increased customer satisfaction and loyalty. Effective implementation of Siebel Marketing enterprise gives an organization a competitive advantage and enables it to carry out the best practices of marketing processes globally across the organization.

Siebel Marketing Enterprise provides a suite of tools and information, each of them helping marketing professionals in various activities. Table 2.1 shows some of them, along with their role in marketing-related tasks.

Table 2.1 Siebel Marketing Enterprise's Tools Suite

Serial number	*Tool/functionality*	*Benefits*
1.	Integrated customer data mart	Makes the entire data related to customers, products, sales, and services available for marketing professionals for a better analysis
2.	Online analytical processing (OLAP) server	Helps in digging out the hidden information from the data available in database, by using multidimensional analysis of data
3.	Work flow management tools	Enable efficient work flow across the organization to effectively carry out best practice marketing processes
4.	Built in marketing communications tool	Enables efficient communications related to marketing activities, such as pricing, competitive analysis, and product information
5.	Campaign management tools	Enables cheaper and effective campaign management activities including design and execution of personalized campaigns across all customer interaction channels, such as mails, telephone calls, and so on

Why Siebel Marketing Enterprise?

Siebel Marketing Enterprise helps marketing professionals to carry out a lot of core business processes. Some of them are mentioned below:

1. Siebel Marketing Enterprise allows organizations to automate, design, and target marketing campaigns and programs.
2. Siebel Marketing Enterprise enables organizations to effectively carry out marketing resource management activities including proposal definition, planning, and budgeting for marketing and setting goals for marketing plans, developing and managing funds, managing marketing assets and collateral.
3. Siebel Marketing Enterprise provides the facility to design single-stage and multistage marketing programs. The difference between the two is that single-stage programs target customers with individual campaign, with no follow-up campaigns after it, whereas in multistage programs, there are additional stages of follow-up campaigns planned for the contacts targeted in first stage.
4. Siebel Marketing Enterprise provides the facility to create offers and treatments as a part of campaign. Offers are the single messages to contacts, which motivates them to respond back. Offers are the part of campaigns, and one offer can be associated

to multiple campaigns. They are presented to the customers when the campaign is launched.

Treatments represent an instance of an offer, and are specific to a particular channel by which the offer is delivered to a customer. These channels may include e-mails, direct mail, or any other means by which you want to deliver your offer to the contacts. One offer can have multiple treatments, each specific to a particular delivery channel.

5. Siebel Marketing Enterprise provides the facility to plan, design, and launch campaigns to target one or more group of users. A campaign is basically an initiative, which enables organizations to target the existing customers to retain them, or potential customers to acquire them, by delivering promotional offers. A marketing campaign makes the target audience aware of the products and services provided by organization by promoting them, which ultimately results in increased sales and brand recognition.
6. Siebel Marketing Enterprise enables organizations to effectively create and manage the list of contacts and prospects to be used while targeting campaigns. The list management module is available to the users with a license of Siebel Marketing or Siebel campaigns, and it facilitates the grouping of contacts and prospects present in the Siebel database.

2.2.2 Siebel Service Enterprise

Siebel Service Enterprise is basically meant for customer service professionals. For a better customer service and maximum transparency, it is fully integrated into call center, marketing, field service and sales automation systems, and assists customer support professionals throughout the entire life cycle. Some of the comprehensive tools available with Siebel services enterprise include return material authorization (Commonly known as RMA in most of the organizations), service request management, computer telephony integration for comprehensive call management, and so on. The following diagram shows the login page for Siebel service enterprise.

Some of the salient features of Siebel Service Enterprise are as follows:

1. Siebel Service Enterprise enables organizations to provide efficient customer service and problems resolution. Some of the features of Siebel services that support this are as follows:
    - Siebel Services Enterprise provides efficient request routing and assignment. This ensures that each incoming service request from customer is routed to the customer support professional who is most suitable for it, based on the skills, expertise, certification levels, geographic levels, and availability. As a result, organization enjoys a better customer experience and feedbacks, and customers get optimal levels of service.
    - Customer support professional have easy and ready access to detailed customer and account profiles, which helps them to provide enhanced customer service.
2. Siebel Services Enterprise makes it easy for all team members to communicate directly with customer and other agents, along with keeping a full track of all the

communications with the customer related to particular case or service request. This keeps all the members in the team updated about the status of the case and customer requirements, enabling them to provide a solution that best suits the customer requirements.

3. It also enables organization to keep track of customer satisfaction level. With Siebel Service Enterprise, organizations can automate customer satisfaction surveys during or after the service event. Based on the customer satisfaction level, organizations can focus more on improving their customer service, thereby achieving better customer loyalty.
4. It also keeps a track of customer purchase history, full product information, and online knowledge base of solutions to prior problems to be used as reference, along with an easy access to this data whenever required.

2.2.3 Siebel Sales Enterprise

Siebel Sales Enterprise is basically designed to help sales professionals and managers to improve organization's sales revenues and profitability. Some of the benefits that organizations get by using Siebel Sales Enterprise are as follows:

1. **Efficient forecasting:** Siebel Sales Enterprise provides an accurate insight of customer's data, which helps sales managers to do efficient and consistent forecasting. This also reduces a lot of manual efforts required in forecasting. With efficient forecasting, organizations can plan and achieve their sales goals that ultimately results in increased revenues and profits. The predefined reconfigurable charts and reports enable sales managers to efficiently manage sales and revenues by Accounts, Opportunities, Partners, Employees and so on. It also facilitates real time revenue and profit analysis, along with automatic currency converter, which allows sales across multiple currencies.
2. **Comprehensive customer view:** With a centralized repository, sales managers and team get a complete view of customer base, which enables them to analyze customer's history before contacting them. This includes customers' past activities, purchase behavior, service requests, current orders placed by them, and so on. This analysis helps sales professionals to have a better communication with customers, which results in increased sales and better cross-sale and up-sale. Siebel Sales Enterprise also allows integration with Microsoft applications, which helps sales managers and teams to easily and effectively manage and access customer data.
3. **Increased sales and better alignment with customer expectations:** With continuously changing market trends, customer expectations and priorities change. Sales professionals and managers in organizations are supposed to remain aligned with these rapidly changing customer priorities in order to achieve continuous customer satisfaction. Siebel sales enterprise is equipped with efficient opportunity, lead, territory, and order management along with sales forecasting to help sales professionals and managers to achieve their goals. It also facilitates them to integrate with Microsoft applications to easily and quickly perform their jobs.

4. **Pipeline assessment:** Siebel sales opportunity management capabilities allow sales professionals and managers to have a complete transparent view at each stage of sales cycle. They can review the opportunities at various sales stages to analyze how the deals are closing. At each stage, the actual results can be compared with the expected targets and necessary steps can be taken to address concerns, instead of waiting till can be taken to the sales cycle gets completed.

To summarize, Siebel Sales Enterprise provide market leading tools to facilitate sales professionals and managers to efficient track and manage organization's sales. With Siebel sales enterprise, they can easily track changing market trends, customer priorities and expectations, and plan their strategies accordingly. This results in better customer satisfaction, which ultimately increases organizations revenues and profits. With efficient pipeline assessment capabilities, sales representatives and managers can review and track shortcomings at each stage of sales cycle and address them accordingly, which helps them to achieve the defined goals easily and comfortably.

2.2.4 Siebel Call Center

Siebel Call Center is basically designed for call center employees. It facilitates them with efficient functionalities to support a range of products and services and presenting tailored offerings designed to meet customer's needs, via a comprehensive integrated communication channels, such as Web, fax, phone, and interactive voice response (IVR). It provides them a comprehensive customer view by managing customer data, account profiles, purchase history, service-level agreements, service requests, and opportunities. Some of the important features of Siebel Call Center are discussed below:

1. **Account management:** The efficient account management capabilities provided by Siebel Call Center gives a broad and transparent picture of status and value of each account. An account can be the organization's partner, supplier, competitor, or a company representing a customer. With the account management capabilities, call center agents can associate contact and activities with account, along with a detailed analysis of service requests, account status, and product issues.
2. **Contact management:** Contacts are the individuals with whom the organization does business. Siebel sales contact management capabilities facilitate call center agents with a comprehensive contact data, enabling them to analyze previous activities and service history of a contact. It also enables them to create and analyze contact profiles to record and view relationships between two contacts, or between account and contact. They can also create and maintain contact profiles and associate activities with them.
3. **Household management:** A household is defined as a set of individual consumers who share common purchasing and service interests, and are economically affiliated. The household management capabilities provided by Siebel Call Center enables call center agents to track all the information associated with them and work accordingly. They can analyze contact (household members) information, their corresponding service requests, and activities along with the opportunities associated with them.

Typically, households share a common address, but due to their dynamic nature, if contacts leave household to join another one, their related details are also moved with them.

4. **Service request management:** Service requests are basically the requests raised by customers to get assistance with the products or services purchased from an organization. Service requests work as a central reference data while analyzing and resolving complex issues. The service request management capabilities provided by Siebel Call Center enable the agents to analyze service request details as reference. They can also create and update the service requests, log change requests associated with them, and update activity details related to service requests. They can gather customer feedbacks by conducting customer satisfaction surveys associated to particular service request, which results in improved customer service.
5. **Activities management:** Activities include all the tasks performed for, or required for a customer. Considering a call center agent's role, activities are the steps taken to resolve any particular issue associated with a service request. Siebel Call Center facilitates the activity management by tracking priorities, due dates, and completion dates for key activities, along with assigning and delegating the activities to organization's members automatically by using Siebel work flow manager and Siebel assignment manager.

2.2.5 Siebel Field Service

Siebel field service is basically designed to meet organization's field service activities. Field service targets on achieving better customer loyalty and exploring the opportunities of cross-sell. It starts with entering the service request raised by customer, followed by creating a return material authorization based on the problem analysis and service-level agreement, shipping of replacement parts, issuing invoice to the customer, updating service parts inventory, and updating the resolution in customer relationship database. Once the customer relationship database is updated with details, it can be used to figure out the possible cross-sell opportunities. Siebel provides the following features to manage field service cycle (Table 2.1):

Table 2.1

Serial number	*Name*	*Function*
1.	Siebel scheduler	• Appointment scheduling • Deployment schedule optimization • Updating already optimized schedule with service activities at high priority • Efficient assignment of work to engineers using Siebel assignment manager
2.	Dispatch board	• Enables call center agents to efficiently assign and delegate service activities to suitable engineers

Serial number	*Name*	*Function*
3.	Service part information	• Information includes installation instructions, operational constraints, and manufacturing data
4.	Service inventory	• Manages "real time tracked" service part inventory across locations and organizations
5.	Contracts management	• Supports contract life cycle
6.	Shipping and receiving	• Integrated with Siebel service inventory, and track customer's orders to shipment
7.	Oracle business intelligence	• Used to generate reports and charts in order to analyze large volume of data

2.3 SUMMARY

Siebel Enterprise Applications play a significant role in the success of organization's CRM strategies. They provide a comprehensive set of functionalities to support various tasks related to specific business units of various organizations across globe. Due to the large set of functionalities and flexibility provided by these applications, Siebel CRM solution is considered as world's leader in CRM solutions.

Chapter 3

SIEBEL eBUSINESS APPLICATIONS

Siebel eBusiness Applications facilitate organizations to run their business over web. In today's fast running world, an increasing number of customers are rushing towards web for their day to day needs. In this scenario, running business over web is slowly becoming an indispensable part of most of the organizations across globe. Siebel eBusiness Application suite addresses most of these requirements of various organizations.

In this section, we'll discuss about following applications from Siebel eBusiness Application suite:

1. Siebel eMarketing
2. Siebel eService
3. Siebel eSales
4. Siebel eChannel

While discussing these applications, we'll also discuss the role and significance of these applications in the success of organization's CRM strategies. Major topics covered in this chapter are:

- What is eBusiness
- Important eBusiness Models
- Siebel eBusiness Applications
- Features of Siebel eBusiness Suite
- Siebel eBusiness Application Components
- Optional modules of Siebel eBusiness Suite

3.1 WHAT IS eBUSINESS

In today's fast-running world, everyone wants the information quickly and easily. Most of the people rely on Internet as their first choice to gather any kind of details they require. Information about organizations and their products is not an exception. Most of the customers want the required details quickly and easily. With the increasing number of customers looking towards Internet as their way to get information, organizations also started relocating their internal and external business processes to Internet. Siebel, being the best CRM solution, provides eBusiness applications to help organizations to connect to their customers via Internet.

eBusiness is actually "Business on Internet," that is, the enterprises conducting their business via Internet and Web, in order to improve the productivity and profitability of their business by reaching more customers. By selling the products online, organizations can touch a much wider customer base regardless of their physical location. Along with buying and selling the products over Web, eBusiness also includes providing online customer service and receiving their feedbacks by conducting online surveys. Online customer service helps organizations to provide a more efficient customer service, both in terms of time and cost. Online feedback gathering enables organizations to get more customer inputs as compared to those who do not practice it, which helps them to align more with customer expectations.

Switching the business to Internet requires proper planning and re-engineering of the very nature of their business. One of the most significant steps in this planning is to decide the eBusiness model that best suites organization's goals. A business model is basically a model that is followed while shifting business to Internet, which involves organization's products, services, and information flows. Some of the most-adopted eBusiness models are listed in Table 3.1.

Table 3.1 Examples of eBusiness Models

Serial number	*Model*	*Description*
1.	E-commerce	Commerce on Internet. It includes buying and selling of products and services over Web, along with a complete online process from developing products and services till selling them and providing customer services and gathering their feedbacks
2.	Online shop	A type of e-commerce, where customers buy products and services directly from shop over Web in real time
3.	Online auctions	Auction over Web, where the supplier with lowest bid wins
4.	E-mails	The most familiar term of recent world. It refers to send mails over Web. Organizations use it to do various tasks, such as marketing, gathering customer feedbacks, launching campaigns targeted to specific customers, and so on
5.	E-procurement	Purchase and sale of supplies between businesses (B2B)*, business and consumer (B2C)*, or business and government (B2G)*

*** eBusiness classification based on consumers and suppliers:**

1. **Business to Business (B2B):** It refers to any type of commerce transaction between businesses. The business participating in these transactions may be partners, supplier–manufacturer pair, or retailer–wholesaler pair. With the increasing affinity of people toward Internet and a lot of benefits of eBusiness, most of the businesses prefer to do their B2B transactions over Web.
2. **Business to Employee (B2E):** It refers to all the commerce transactions and interactions of business with its employees. It happens over business's private network and is used to provide various benefits, which include products and benefits. B2E strategies facilitate organizations with a better employee insight and enhanced employee loyalty.
3. **Business to Consumer (B2C):** As the name describes, B2C includes all the activities that an organization do to serve their customers. It includes marketing, selling the

products, providing customer service, and encouraging them to provide their feedbacks on organization's products and services. A reverse model of this is Consumer to Business (C2B), where an individual consumer offers goods and services to business, and business pays to him accordingly. An example of this model is online data entry jobs, where an individual offers his services to organizations, and organizations pay him back accordingly. One more variation in this model is Consumer to Consumer (C2C), where the transactions happen between two consumers by using the services of some third-party organization. Typically, organizations charge some fee to consumers for each transaction. A very common example of this model includes the Web sites allowing consumers to sell their used items online. Various consumers bid on the items and the bidder having maximum bid wins and purchases the product. Web sites get their share as a flat fee for each transaction.

4. **Business to Government (B2G):** It is a form of reverse auction, where organizations bid on government opportunities that are present as solicitations in the form of Request for Proposals (REPs). A very common example of this model includes the tenders posted by public sector organizations, and suppliers respond to them with their proposals. A reverse model to this model is Government to Business (G2B), where businesses approach local and central governments for getting various details. This model is a kind of non-commercial model. One more variation of this model is Government to Government (G2G), which involves non-commercial interactions between various government departments. Another variation of this approach is Government to Citizens (G2C), which acts as a communication link between government and citizens. A very common example of this model is Indian Web site www.upsc.gov.in, which provides the details about various examinations held by Union Public Service Commission (UPSC), along with the results and due dates.

3.2 SIEBEL eBUSINESS APPLICATIONS

Siebel eBusiness is a comprehensive application suite that facilitates organizations by using Web as their platform to leverage their business by reaching a wider customer base, selling online products, providing online customer service, and gathering online feedbacks. The components in Siebel eBusiness suite discussed in this chapter are as follows:

1. Siebel eMarketing
2. Siebel eService
3. Siebel eSales
4. Siebel eChannel

Along with these components, there are certain optional modules present in Siebel eBusiness suite. Some of the important options are as follows:

- Siebel eBriefings
- Siebel eSearch
- Siebel eAuction
- Siebel eAdvisor
- Siebel eTraining
- Siebel eConfigurator

Before discussing these applications, their features, and their benefits, let us have a quick look on various features that are provided by Siebel eBusiness suite.

3.3 FEATURES OF SIEBEL eBUSINESS SUITE

Siebel eBusiness Application suite is a comprehensive suite of various eBusiness applications that address various requirement areas of organizations across globe. A lot of features provided by this suite provide all round benefits to organizations. Some of the salient features of Siebel eBusiness suite are as follows:

1. It is a comprehensive set of world's leading eBusiness applications that support easy and quick customization, configuration, and integration.
2. These applications are easily upgradable, supporting automated deployment strategies for continuous and quick customization of eBusiness sites.
3. It facilitates users at geographically dispersed locations to access a wide range of functionalities due to Web-based architecture. For accessing these functionalities, users do not need any additional installation. They can access all the functionalities by using their Web browser.
4. These applications support multiple environments, which makes it easy for users to select among a wide variety of environments available to access these applications.
5. These applications are easily scalable, due to which they can serve for organizations having small as well as large number of customers.
6. These applications support various backend tasks, such as data and information security, data synchronization, application integration, and supporting transactions done by a large number of customers concurrently due to a strong middle tier. It also helps to easily scale the application and makes it flexible based on the number of users and amount of data and information flow.

3.4 SIEBEL eBUSINESS APPLICATION COMPONENTS

In this section, we will discuss about some of the widely used Siebel eBusiness applications, along with their role and significance in the success of organization's CRM strategies.

3.4.1 Siebel eMarketing

Siebel eMarketing is designed to target customers by using personalized Web-based promotions or e-mails. These e-mails or promotions contain the URL that navigates the target customers to organization's Web site, where they can do online purchase of desired products and services, along with exploring various other related products and services. A clear benefit of this approach to customers is that they can purchase the desired products and services online without the headache of purchasing them directly at shop or outlets. They can explore through the wide range of products and services provided by organization and choose the one that best suits their requirements. Organizations get the benefit of wide customer base with minimal marketing and advertising costs. They can also view the statistical summary of revenues generated and return on investment (ROI).

3.4.2 Siebel eSales

Once organizations target the customer through Siebel eMarketing and navigate them to their Web sites, Siebel eSales comes into picture. It facilitates customers with the support throughout the process of buying or selling products and services. With a visual product catalogue, organizations can easily develop their Web-based outlet to provide the details about the products and services provided by them, and help customers to select one that best suits their requirements. It helps organizations to gather and store customer details in the form of profiles, which can be used for future reference while contacting the customer. This also helps organizations to do efficient sales forecasting based on the past purchases by customers. Along with Business to Customer (B2C) selling, Siebel eSales also supports Business to Business (B2B) transactions. Organizations can online collaborate with their partners and buy/sell the required parts from suppliers, which save a lot of time and cost incurred in these activities.

3.4.3 Siebel eService

After organizations attract customer toward their products and services by using Siebel eMarketing and sell them by using Siebel eSales, the role of Siebel eService starts. Siebel eService is basically designed to provide world-class customer service online and quickly. Providing an efficient customer service online significantly reduces the time to provide the service, which increases customer loyalty. It also cuts a major portion of cost incurred in providing such a high-quality service without Web. It assists customers while self-service, which saves a lot of manual effort for organizations, and reduces a lot of workload from customer support executives. It also facilitates organization's customer service with Web and e-mail interface to manage customer service requests and billing services.

3.4.4 Siebel eChannel

With an increasing customer base across diverse geographic locations, an increasing number of organizations started relying on channel partners to sell their products, along with providing customer service. This made channel partner management an important factor for organizations. Siebel eChannel is designed to support organizations in managing their channel partners, which includes routing service request and selling opportunities to most suitable channel partner by using configurable business rules, along with monitoring their performance over a period of time. It also ensures organization's data and information security when they send it to channel partners.

Along with enterprises, Siebel eChannel is helpful to their channel partners as well. It helps manage Contacts (by storing a list of Contacts, along with the capability to filter them based on Account or Opportunity), manage Accounts (by providing capability to view all assigned Accounts, along with creating new Accounts), manage Service Requests (by providing the capability to create Service Requests and assign them immediately to concerned resources) and manage Opportunities (with latest details about Accounts, Contacts and Activities).

3.5 OPTIONAL MODULES IN SIEBEL eBUSINESS SUITE

Along with various components, Siebel eBusiness suite provides some optional modules as well. In this section, we will discuss about these optional modules, along with the role played by them in various tasks done by organizations. They are listed in Table 3.2.

Table 3.2 Optional modules in Siebel eBusiness Suite

Serial number	*Module*	*Description*
1.	Siebel eBriefings	• Designed for organization's employees and partners to have a quick brief look on relevant and critical information about customers, competitors, and market • Makes them more effective and efficient in gathering customer and market data
2.	Siebel eSearch	• Designed for call center agents to do a full text search of data relevant to their job, which includes details about problem resolution strategies, product news, and other relevant documents • Makes it easier and faster for them to refer to search and refer the desired documents to resolve the specific problems
3.	Siebel eAuction	• Enables organizations to perform Web-based auctions • Helps them in real-time analysis of current demand and supply status by enhanced customer interaction to decide and vary product prices that best suit the situation
4.	Siebel eAdvisor	• Facilitates organization's customer acquisition strategies by providing online advice to customers • Provides instant personalized expert guidance targeted to specific customer based on his requirements
5.	Siebel eTraining	• Designed for creating and managing Web-based end user training
6.	Siebel eConfigurator	• Provides personalized guidance to customers while exploring through the organization's products and services catalogue, and helps him to make the best purchase that best suits his requirements

3.6 SUMMARY

With the growing number of organizations moving toward Web for proliferating their business, eBusiness is becoming crucial day by day. Siebel CRM, being the world's leading CRM solution, provides a comprehensive suite of eBusiness applications to meet requirements of various organizations across globe. The unbeatable features provided by the applications in Siebel eBusiness suite make them indispensable for guaranteeing the success of organization's CRM strategies.

Chapter 4

SIEBEL TOOLS

Let us now start the most crucial part in configuring Siebel Applications, i.e. Siebel Tools. Siebel tools provide a user friendly interface to configure various Siebel Applications. In this chapter, we'll concentrate on Siebel Tools client's user interface. We'll discuss about various menus, along with the options available in them. The process of configuring various Siebel objects using Siebel tools is covered in Part – 3, where we'll discuss about various Siebel object types. The main aim of this chapter is to make readers familiar with various menus in Siebel tools and options present in them. These options will be used in every Siebel Configuration activity. Major topics in this chapter are:

- Introduction to Siebel tools
- Details of Object Explorer
- Object List Editor
- Menu Bar and various menus present in it

4.1 SIEBEL TOOLS

Siebel tools client is used to configure Siebel applications. Using Siebel tools client, developers can create new objects (Siebel Objects are discussed in Part 3 "Configuring Siebel Applications"), or can modify the existing ones to meet the requirements. It is to be kept in mind that Siebel tools client provides a configuration environment, NOT a programming environment. In our mission of configuring Siebel applications, Siebel tools client will work as a Weapon Repository. Figure 4.1 shows the Siebel tools client's user interface. The various parts of this user interface are described below. We will discuss the use of Siebel tools while discussing the configuration of Siebel objects in Part 3.

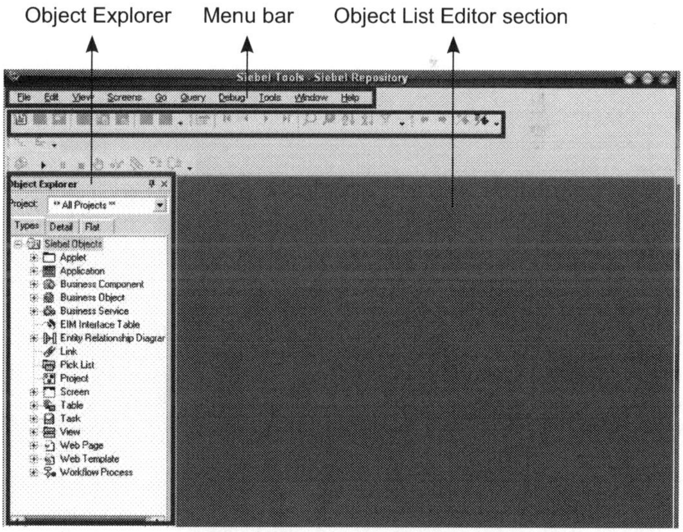

Fig. 4.1 *Siebel tools' client*

4.1.1 Object Explorer

Object Explorer actually contains a list of all Siebel object types, arranged in the form of a Tree, which arranges objects based on their parent–child relationship. The "+"sign on the left of an object type name shows that it has child objects. On expanding an object type, we can see their child objects. This is shown in Fig. 4.2.

As we can see in Fig. 4.2(a), the "Applet" Object type is expanded and its child objects are visible. Also, one thing to notice is that on expanding an object type, the "+" sign changes to "–"sign. On clicking this sign once again, the object type collapses, and the "–" sign gets converted to "+" sign. This can be seen in Fig. 4.2(b).

(a) (b)

Fig. 4.2: *(a) Object expanded (b) Object collapsed*

When we select any object type in Object Explorer, the Object List Editor at the right side gets populated with the list of that object type, available in the selected project. By default, "All projects" are selected in the drop-down list. In order to view the objects from a specific project, we will need to select the project name from the drop-down list. The drop-down list is shown in Fig. 4.3. Object list editor is discussed in the next topic.

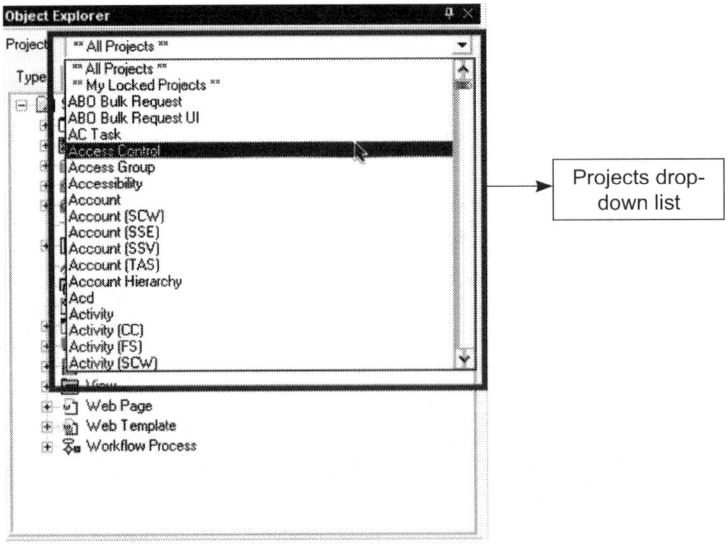

Fig. 4.3 *Projects drop-down*

There are three modes to view objects in Object Explorer: "Types," "Detail," and "Flat." We can select any one of these modes at the top of Object Explorer. Figure 4.4 shows these modes in an Object Explorer.

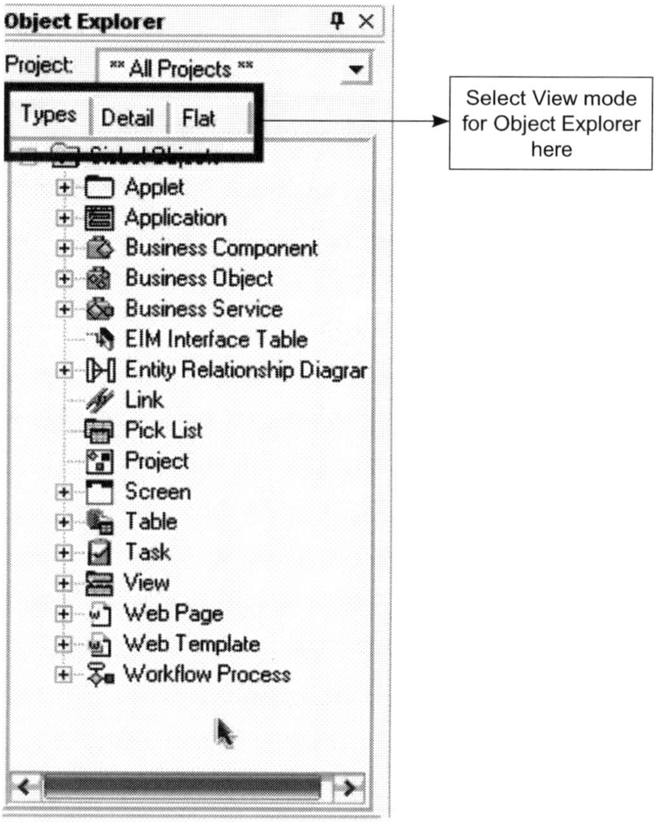

Fig. 4.4 *Modes in Object Explorer*

In "*Types*" mode, all the object types are represented in the form of tree, and the corresponding objects of that type are displayed in the Object List Editor at right side. By default, this mode is selected for viewing the objects. Figure 4.5(a) shows the objects represented in "Types" mode.

In "*Details*" mode, all the object types are represented in the form of tree. But, on expanding any object type, we will get the list of objects of that type. On further expanding these objects, we will get "Child Object Types" of parent Object Type. For example, in Fig. 4.5(b), on expanding "Applet" object type, we will get a list of all applets. On expanding any applet, we will get child object types of applet object type, that is, "Applet Web Template," "Controls," "Drill Down Object," and so on.

In "*Flat*" mode, object types are represented in form of list, instead of tree. Figure 4.5(c) shows the object types represented in flat mode.

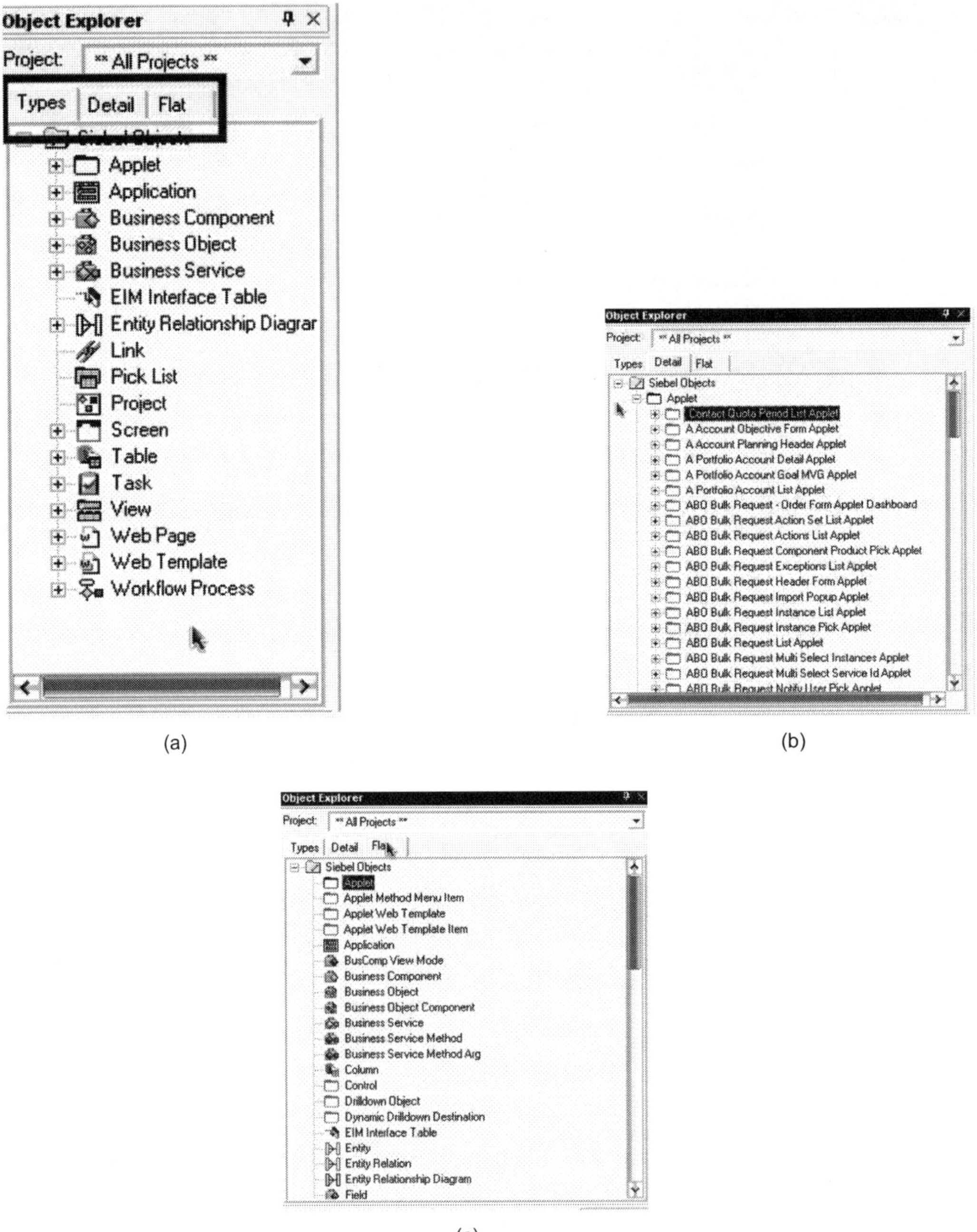

Fig. 4.5 *(a) Objects in Types mode (b) Objects in Detail mode (c) Objects in Flat mode*

While discussing configuration of various Siebel object types, we will discuss more about Object Explorer.

4.1.2 Object List Editor

Object List Editor is a list that shows all the Objects of the object type selected in Object Explorer. Figure 4.6 shows Object List Editor containing a list of all Applets.

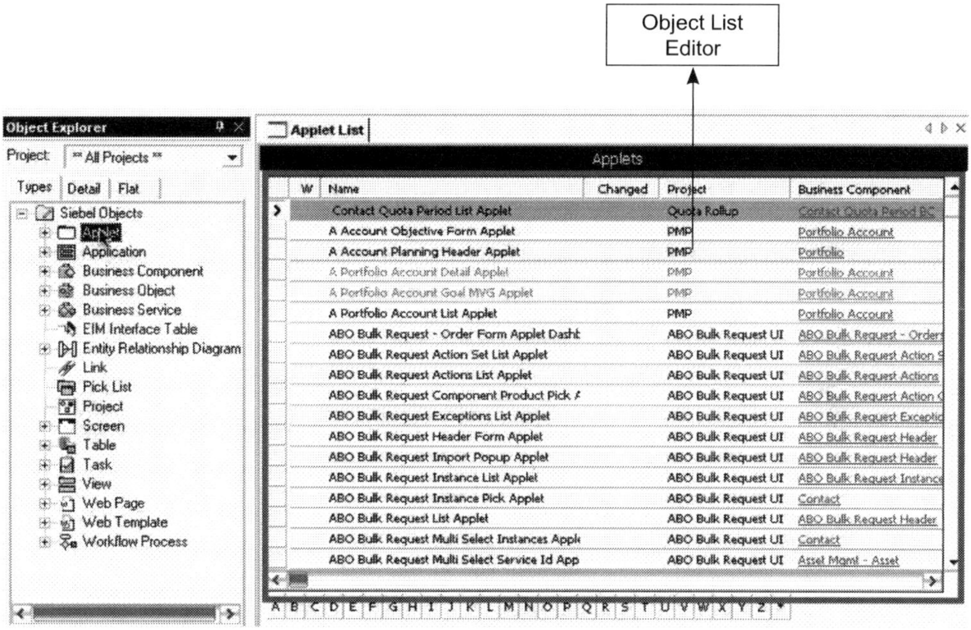

Fig. 4.6 *Applet objects in Object List Editor*

In Fig. 4.6, we have selected "Applet" object type in Object Explorer. Therefore, Object List Editor is showing the list of all the applets. If we want to select any other object type in Object Explorer, the Object List Editor will be populated with the list of objects of that type.

The columns present in Object List Editor are actually the properties of that object type. For example, in Fig. 4.6, the columns present are "Name," "Project," "Business Component," and so on. These properties are specific to the object type selected in Object Explorer. We will discuss the properties specific to an object type in detail while discussing its configuration.

4.1.3 Menu Bar

Menu bar, shown in Fig. 4.7, contains items that are common for whole application. The items present in this menu are "File," "Edit," "View," "Screens," "Go," "Query," "Debug," "Tools," "Window," and "Help." All the items present here are actually drop-down menus having various options. All the menus are shown diagrammatically in the corresponding sections. You will find some of the options missing in these menus. These options get activated only in certain conditions. For example, in Edit menu, the "Redo New Record" option gets activated only when an Undo command is executed on a new record before committing it to database.

Along with the diagrams showing the menus, you can also find the tables describing each option present in the menu (Fig. 4.7).

Fig. 4.7 *Siebel tools menu bar*

4.1.3.1 File menu

File menu contains options shown in Fig. 4.8. Table 4.1 contains the description of the options:

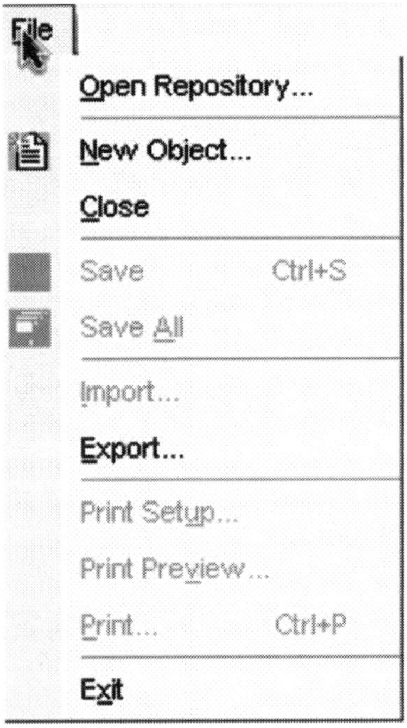

Fig. 4.8 *File menu*

Table 4.1 File Menu Options

Serial number	*Option*	*Description*
1.	Open Repository	Opens the "Open Repository Dialogue Box," which allows us to select the repository when multiple repositories are present in development database. We will discuss about repository and repository file later in this section

Serial number	*Option*	*Description*
2.	New Object	Opens "New Object Wizard." This wizard is used to create new objects and specify their properties. New Object Wizard is discussed later in this section
3.	Close	Closes Object List Editor
4.	Save	Saves the changes in current editing window
5.	Save All	Saves changes in all the open editing windows
6.	Import	Imports text from external text file (in SBL file format) into Siebel VB Editor window
7.	Export	Creates a text file with the list of property values for an object, or all objects displayed currently in Object List Editor. This file is in HTML format
8.	Print Setup	Allows us to edit printer or printing options
9.	Print Preview	Opens a window showing the preview of the Object Visualization view to be printed. It helps in verifying the layout of the item to be printed before printing it
10.	Print	This option is used to print the active object visualization view diagram. Print option can also be invoked by clicking CTRL + P
11.	Exit	Exit from Siebel tools

4.1.3.2 *Edit menu*

Edit menu contains typical record editing options. Figure 4.9 shows the Edit menu. Table 4.2 contains the description of all the options.

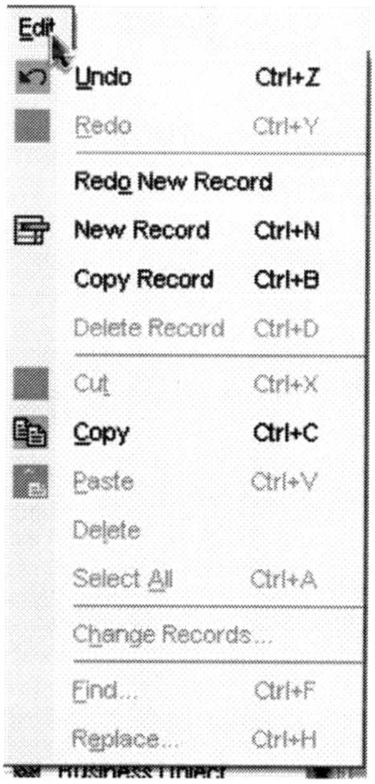

Fig. 4.9 *Edit Menu*

Table 4.2 Edit Menu Options

Serial number	*Option*	*Description*
1.	Undo	Reverts the most recent changes made to the property value of an object in Object List Editor before a commit is made. This option can also be invoked by clicking CTRL + Z
2.	Redo	After Undo is executed, we can re-apply the changes reverted by Undo command by using this option. This option can also be invoked by clicking CTRL + Y
3.	Redo New Record	This option gets activated when we create a new record, and Undo it before committing it to database. This option reverts the Undo command executed on the new record
4.	Undo Delete	This option gets activated when we delete any record. It is available before the changes are committed to database. Clicking this option undo the Delete command executed on the record
5.	Undo Record	This option rolls back any new record, or any modifications made to existing record, before the changes are committed to database
6.	New Record	Creates a new record in Object List Editor. This record belongs to the object type currently selected in Object Explorer. In the new record, the cursor is positioned in the first required property. This option can also be invoked by clicking CTRL + N
7.	Copy Record	Creates a duplicate record of the currently selected records. This duplicate record contains a copy of all the child record corresponding to copied record. This option can also be invoked by clicking CTRL + B
8.	Delete Record	Deletes the currently selected record. It also deletes all the child objects associated with the deleted object. This option can also be invoked by clicking CTRL + D
9.	Cut	Copies selected content to clipboard, and deletes the existing content. Content may be text (in text property) or a Control (in Applet Designer). This option can also be invoked by clicking CTRL + X
10.	Copy	Works like Cut option; the only difference is that it does not delete the existing content. This option can also be invoked by clicking CTRL + C
11.	Paste	Places the control from clipboard to the selected area. Content may be text (in text property) or a Control (in Applet Designer). This option can also be invoked by clicking CTRL + V
12.	Delete	Deletes the selected content. Content may be text (in text property) or a Control (in Applet Designer). This option can also be invoked by clicking DEL key

Serial number	*Option*	*Description*
13.	Select All	Select the whole content. Content may be text (in text property) or a Control (in Applet Designer). This option can also be invoked by clicking CTRL + A
14.	Change Records	Invokes a Change Record dialogue box that contains multiple field pairs with values "Field" and "Value." "Field" is a drop-down list, in which properties of selected records can be selected, and "Value" contains the new value to be entered in the corresponding property of all the selected records. Figure 4.10 shows the Change Record dialogue box
15.	Find	Used to search the specified text in Siebel script editor
16.	Replace	Replaces a particular text with the specified text in Siebel script editor window

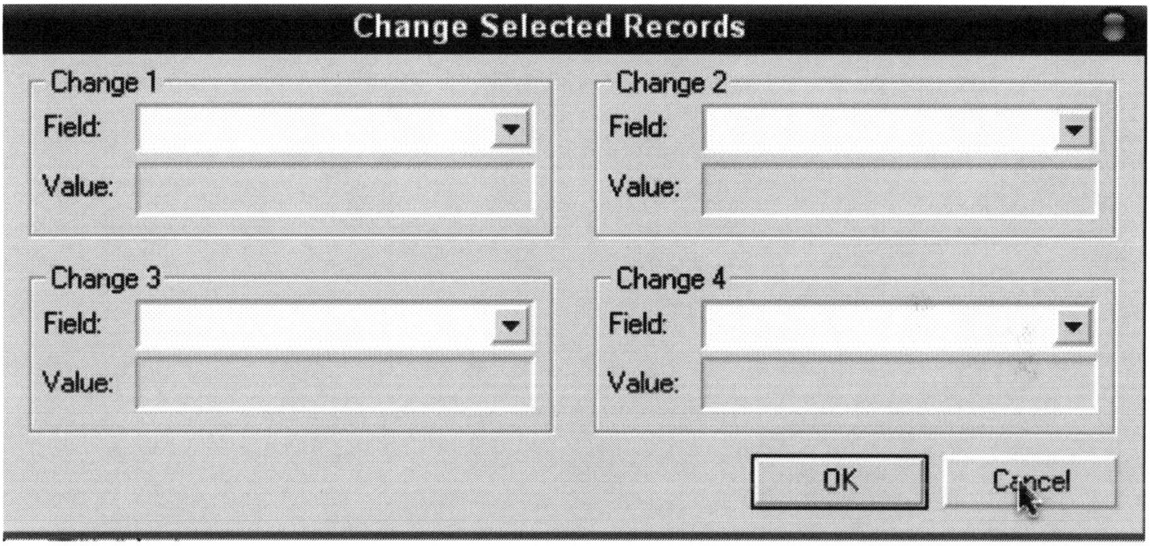

Fig. 4.10 *Change Selected Records dialogue box*

4.1.3.3 View menu

View menu basically contains the options specific to the display environment settings. Figure 4.11 shows a view menu, along with sub-options for "Windows" option in it. Most of the options present in this menu have sub-options. Table 4.3 summarizes all the options, along with the sub-options present for them.

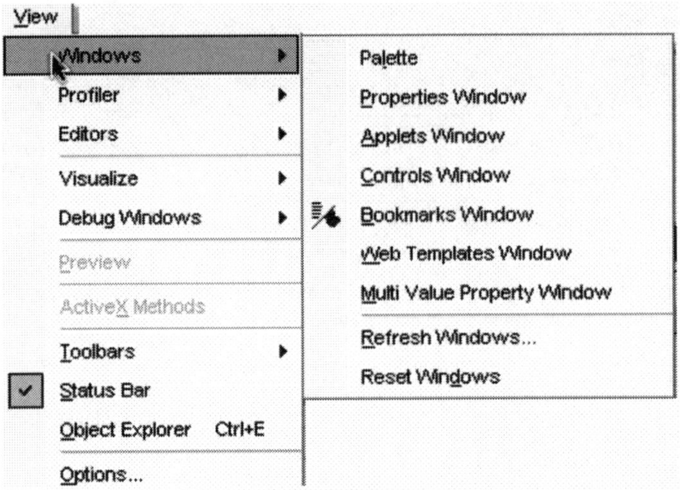

Fig. 4.11 *View menu*

Table 4.3 View Menu Options

Serial number	*Option*	*Description with sub-options*	
		Sub-options	*Description*
1.	Windows: Provides the options for opening and closing various windows discussed in sub-options	Palette	Opens Palettes window
		Properties Window	Opens Properties window
		Applets Window	Opens Applets window
		Controls Window	Opens Controls window
		Bookmarks Window	Opens Bookmarks window
		Web Template Window	Open Web Templates explorer window
		Multi Value Property Window	Opens Multi Value property window
		Refresh Windows	Refreshes current state of dockable windows by re-querying the data
		Reset Windows	Closes all dockable windows. Does not close editor windows and Object Explorer for the currently active editor
2.	Editors: Provides the options for opening various editor windows discussed in sub-options	Web Applet Editor	Opens Applet Layout editor including controls/columns and palettes window for the selected applet. We will discuss more about these windows while discussing the configuration of applet in Part 3

Serial number	*Option*	*Description with sub-options*	
		Sub-options	*Description*
		Server Script Editor	Opens server scripts editor
		Browser Script Editor	Opens browser scripts editor
3.	Visualize: Shows the relationship between objects	View Details	Generates and displays Details Visualization view, which displays the mapping of currently selected business component with its underlying base table (direct or join relationship) and other business components (through links)
		View Relationships	Generates and displays the Relationships visualization view, which shows the linking of currently selected business components with other business components via a multi-value link, or linking of table with other tables using Join
		View Descendents	Displays all the objects with the current object as their upgrade ancestor
		View Web Hierarchy	Shows a complete hierarchy of parent–child relationships of currently selected object. This hierarchy contains a parent–child relationship of current object with its parent and child objects, along with parents of parent object, and children of child objects
	Debug	Calls	For the Siebel VB or Siebel eScript currently being debugged, this option opens the Calls window to display the call stack
		Watch	While debugging Siebel VB or Siebel eScript, it is sometimes required to see the current values of local variables. This is done by using Watch option, which opens the Watch window with the current values of local variables
		Errors	Displays the errors window, which shows the runtime errors while debugging the Siebel VB or Siebel eScript
	Preview	Displays the preview of a Web view layout, which depicts the container page, screen bar, and view bar	
	ActiveX methods	Shows methods for the current ActiveX control in applet designer	
	Toolbars	Used to show or hide the various toolbars	
	Status bar	Shows or hides the status bar	
	Object Explorer	Shows or hides the Object Explorer	
	Options	Displays the development tools options dialogue box	

4.1.3.4 Screens menu

Screen menu is shown in Fig. 4.12. The options provided by this menu are listed in Table 4.4. Screens menu will display the below options only when we login to Siebel tools with System Administrator privileges. Otherwise, the menu will be empty.

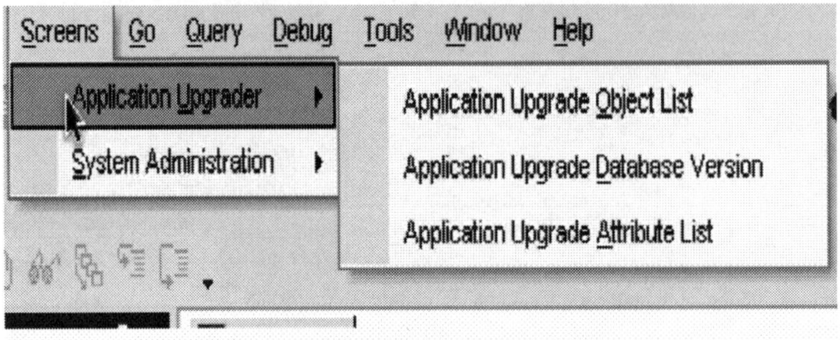

Fig. 4.12 *Screens menu*

Table 4.4 Screens Menu Options

Serial number	*Option*	*Description with sub-options*	
		Sub-option	*Description*
1.	Application Upgrader	Application Upgrade Object List	The Object List Editor gets populated with application upgrades, object differences, and attribute differences list
		Application Upgrade Database version	Reserved for internal use by Oracle
		Application Upgrade Attribute List	The Object List Editor gets populated with application upgrades and attribute differences list
2.	System Administration	System Preferences	System Preferences get displayed in Object List Editor
		Analytics Strings	Reserved for internal use by Oracle
		List of Values	List of values in Development Environment are displayed

4.1.3.5 Debug menu

Debug menu options allow users to control the script debugger, when Siebel VB or eScript is opened in Debug mode. Various options present in this menu are listed in Table 4.5. Figure 4.13 shows Debug menu.

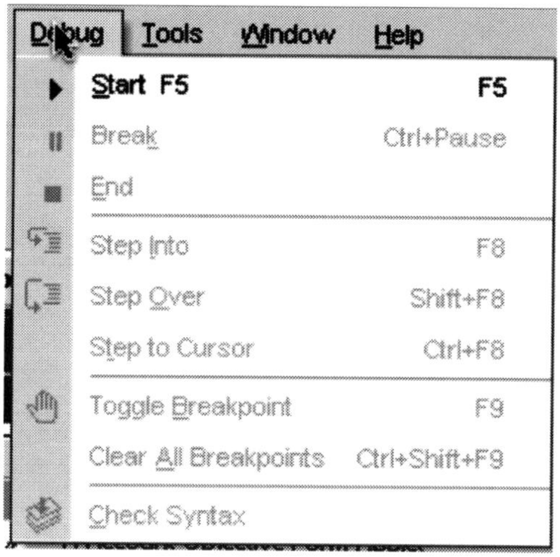

Fig. 4.13 *Debug menu*

Table 4.5 Debug Menu Options

Serial number	*Option*	*Description*
1	Check Syntax	Checks script's syntax and compiles it
2	Start	Starts the application allowing users to verify the changes made by them
3	Break	Stops the script that is currently executing
4	End	Stops application's execution and returns the control back to Siebel script editor
5	Restart	If any break has occurred during the application execution, it restarts the application
6	Toggle Breakpoint	Sets or removes a breakpoint at any particular line of code. The line on which breakpoint is set gets highlighted with a different color. This option is typically used to see the control flow while debugging the script, in order to check the proper functioning of code
7	Clear All Breakpoints	Clears all breakpoints from the current script routine
8	Watch	Displays the current values of variables used in script. This option is used to check the different values of variables during the control flow through the code
9	Calls	A list that contains the function and subroutine calls that were executed before to the current line of code. Clicking on any item in this list takes interpreter to that entry
10	Step Into	Executes the next line of code

Serial number	Option	Description
11	Step Over	Executes the line just after the current subroutine or procedure. It is different from "Step Into" option, because in "Step Into," the control navigates to subroutine or procedure if they are called, but in Step Over option, the control remains in same level of execution
12	Step to Cursor	All lines of code till the one selected by cursor are executed

4.1.3.6 *Go menu*

The options present in Go menu allow users to navigate through a set of records. Figure 4.14 shows the Go menu. Options present in Go menu are listed in Table 4.6.

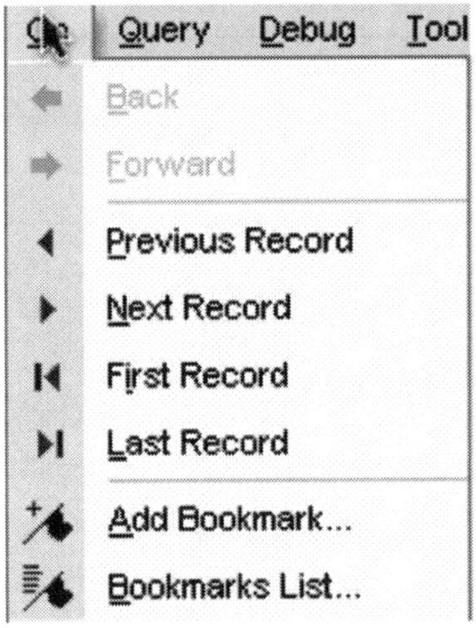

Fig. 4.14 *Go menu*

Table 4.6 Go Menu Options

Serial number	Option	Description
1.	Back	Returns to previous screen
2.	Forward	Returns to subsequent screen
3.	Previous Record	Selects the object above currently selected object
4.	Next Record	Selects the object below the currently selected object
5.	First Record	Navigates to first object in list
6.	Last Record	Navigates to last object in list
7.	Add Bookmark	Allows to add bookmarks in currently selected object by invoking Add Bookmark dialogue box
8.	Bookmark List	Shows the Bookmark dialogue box, from where we can select any bookmark to navigate

4.1.3.7 Query menu

Options present in Query menu allow users to create and refine the queries to restrict the records displayed in Object List Editor. Figure 4.15 shows the Query menu is Siebel tools. Various options in this menu are listed in Table 4.7.

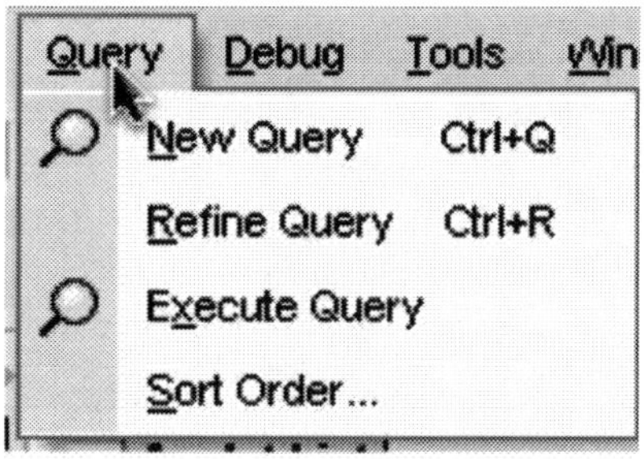

Fig. 4.15 *Query menu*

Table 4.7 Query Menu Options

Serial number	*Option*	*Description*
1	New Query	Allows to create a new query
2	Refine Query	Allows to refine the existing query to add more restrictions
3	Execute Query	Executes the query and displays the record that satisfies the restrictions specified in query
4	Sort Order	Allows to specify the sort order for the records displayed in Object List Editor

4.1.3.8 Tools menu

Tools menu options basically perform object and project-level tasks. They work as tools for developers to perform predevelopment and postdevelopment tasks. Figure 4.16 shows the Tools menu in Siebel tools. Various options in this menu are listed in Table 4.8.

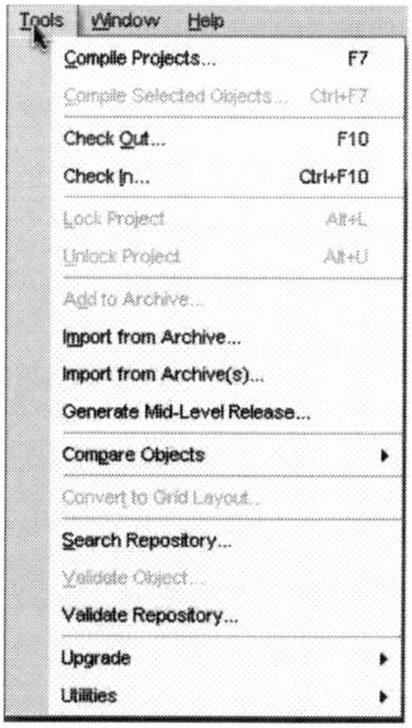

Fig. 4.16 *Tools menu*

Table 4.8 Tools Menu Options

<table>
<tr><th>Serial number</th><th>Option</th><th colspan="2">Description</th></tr>
<tr><td>1</td><td>Compile Projects</td><td colspan="2">Used to compile one or more projects into the Siebel repository file (SRF) file</td></tr>
<tr><td>2</td><td>Compile Selected Objects</td><td colspan="2">Allows users to do incremental compile, that is, compiling only the selected object where they have made changes</td></tr>
<tr><td>3</td><td>Check Out</td><td colspan="2">Allows users to check out and lock objects from server to local database. More about check-out and check-in process is discussed in Part 3</td></tr>
<tr><td>4</td><td>Check In</td><td colspan="2">Allows users to check in the objects from local database to server. More about check-out and check-in process is discussed in Part 3</td></tr>
<tr><td>5</td><td>Lock Project</td><td colspan="2">Allows users to lock the project corresponding to the currently selected object</td></tr>
<tr><td>6</td><td>Unlock Project</td><td colspan="2">Allows users to unlock the project corresponding to currently selected object</td></tr>
<tr><td>7</td><td>Add To Archive</td><td colspan="2">Allows users to archive the selected objects. The archived objects are stored in the form of a .sif file. They can be imported later to the repository</td></tr>
<tr><td>8</td><td>Import From Archive</td><td colspan="2">Allows users to import objects from archive, that is, .sif file</td></tr>
<tr><th></th><th></th><th>Options</th><th>Description</th></tr>
<tr><td>9</td><td>Compare Objects</td><td>Compare</td><td>Allows users to compare two selected objects by graphically showing the similarities and differences</td></tr>
<tr><td></td><td></td><td>Selected versus Repository</td><td>Allows users to compare the selected object with that in selected repository</td></tr>
<tr><td></td><td></td><td>Selected versus Archive</td><td>Allows users to compare the selected object with the corresponding object from an archive file</td></tr>
<tr><td></td><td></td><td>Archive versus Archive</td><td>Compares two selected archive files</td></tr>
<tr><td>10</td><td>Convert to Grid Layout</td><td colspan="2">Used with Form applets. Converts nongrid layout form applets to grid layout. (More about grid layout is discussed in Chapter 10)</td></tr>
<tr><td>11</td><td>Search Repository</td><td colspan="2">Allows users to search objects in repository based on their object types or some text in their names</td></tr>
<tr><td>12</td><td>Validate</td><td colspan="2">Runs validation on selected object based on rules and severity and lists errors. Also allows users to modify options for rules and severity</td></tr>
</table>

		Options	*Description*
13	Upgrade	Maintenance Upgrade	Not applicable to version 8.0
		Prepare Repository	Used while upgrading Siebel to version 8.0 from pre-7.x version
		Upgrade Application	Used to merge standard and customized repositories
		Migrate ICL Objects to Standard	Used to migrate Incorporate Custom Layout (ICL) objects to standard repository. This task is applicable only if during previous upgrade, ICL option had been chosen to preserve the layouts of customized objects, and should be done before performing a subsequent upgrade
		Generate EIM Processing Columns	Used to create missing EIM processing columns and indexes after the repositories are merged
		Web Client Migration	While upgrading from version 6.x to 7.x or higher, it is used to associate Web templates to applets and views to be used in Web Client
14	Utilities	Generate Help IDs	For Oracle's internal use
		Locale Management	Provides Locale Management Utility that facilitates us with the ability to import and export locale specific attributes and translatable text strings
		Map Fax Properties	Maps business component's fields to fax software property sheet properties
		Export View Previews	Used to export view's preview to HTML file. More about View and View preview is discussed in Chapter 13
		Case Insensitivity	This option opens the case and accent insensitive wizard, which facilitates us to perform case- and accent-insensitive search on columns in schema
		Build Patch	Used to create patch file by using Patch Builder wizard
		Apply Patch	Used to apply patch

4.1.3.9 *Help menu*

Help menu displays the options to help developers while configuring Siebel applications. Figure 4.17 shows Help menu in Siebel tools.

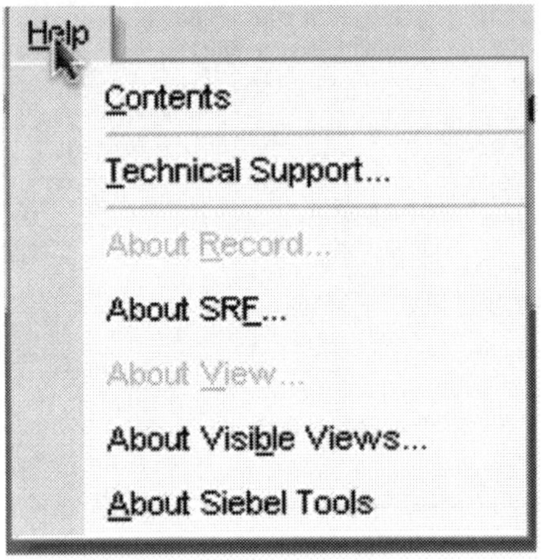

Fig. 4.17 *Help menu*

Table 4.9 lists various options available in Help menu.

Table 4.9 Help Menu Options

Serial number	*Option*	*Description*
1.	Contents	Opens Siebel tools online help
2.	Technical Support	Displays system information including schema version, user who is currently logged in, the connect string, table owner, repository file, and file system
3.	About Record	Displays detail about currently selected object
4.	About SRF	Displays details about the current Siebel repository file
5.	About View	Displays the details about the current view, which includes current screen, business object, and view
6.	About Visible Views	Displays the views along with their visibility details
7.	About Siebel Tools	Displays Siebel tools' version

After this discussion, we are left with following items about Siebel tools:

- Right Click menus
- Layout editors
- Script editors
- Toolbars

Out of these items, Script Editor is out of scope of this book. We will discuss about remaining parts while configuring Siebel Applications.

So, how do the changes made in Siebel Tools get reflected in Siebel Applications?

All the object-level changes made in Siebel tools are compiled to Siebel Repository File (SRF file with .srf extension). In the Configuration file (with.cfg extension) corresponding to the application, we provide the name of the .srf file along with its path. While opening, application uses this .srf file to display the objects in user interface. We will discuss more about objects in Part 3.

4.2 SUMMARY

Siebel tools is the most basic and crucial part of Siebel configuration. Before starting configuration tasks, it is quite helpful and beneficial to understand basic terminologies related to Siebel tools. In this chapter, we have discussed about some of the basic terminologies and functionalities provided by Siebel tools. At this point, it may be a bit difficult for everyone to understand each and every term used in this chapter. But, once we start and proceed with our discussion on configuring Siebel applications, these terms will gradually become clear to everyone. In next chapter, we will discuss about navigating Siebel applications. The aspects covered in Chapter 5 are very crucial before starting configuration. If you are already aware of Siebel Application navigation, you can skip Chapter 5 and jump directly to Part 3, which discusses about Siebel configuration.

REFERENCE

1. Siebel Bookshelf V8.0. Available from: www.oracle.com.

Chapter 5

NAVIGATING SIEBEL APPLICATIONS

Siebel navigation deals with logging into Siebel Application, accessing various screens and views and performing various available tasks at User Interface level. Also, we'll have a quick look on various elements of Siebel applications that form its User Interface. These elements include Screens, Views, Applets, Fields, Toolbars, Menus etc. While discussing the configuration of these objects, we'll discuss about their various important properties as well. Major topics in this chapter are:

- Entering into Siebel Applications
- User Interface Elements
  - Application Level Menu
  - Application Tool bar
  - Screen Tab
  - Link Bar
  - Screens
  - Views
  - Sub-views
  - View Tabs
  - Visibility Filter
  - List
  - Form
  - Branding Area
  - Explorer View
- Records
- Fields
  - Various Types of Fields in User Interface
- Record Tasks

5.1 ENTERING INTO SIEBEL APPLICATION

Navigation of Siebel Enterprise Applications starts with logging into the application. At organization level, we will need to access the URL given by organization using Internet Explorer (with all the essential settings discussed in Part 4). On accessing the URL, we will see the Login page of Siebel application, which will have User Id and Password fields. Here, we will need to provide the User Id and Password provided by organization to enter into Siebel application.

Since our discussion is more about getting the first look and feel of Siebel applications, we will concentrate more on locally installed Siebel Web client. For accessing Siebel application, double-click on the Siebel Web Client icon. This will open the Login page where we will need to enter User Id and Password. After entering these details, we will need to click on the Arrow button to login. This will open the Home page, which will contain the welcome message along with the items most important for us while using the application, such as Calendar to fix and display the important appointments. Here, we will be able to see various elements that combine to form the user interface for Siebel application. In next section, we will focus on these elements.

5.2 USER INTERFACE ELEMENTS

This section focuses on various elements that form Siebel application's user interface. Here, we will briefly discuss about the following elements:

1. Application-level menu
2. Application toolbar
3. Screen tab
4. Link bar
5. Screens
6. Views
7. Sub-views
8. View tabs
9. Visibility filter
10. List
11. Form
12. Branding area
13. Explorer view

Figure 5.1 shows these elements [1].

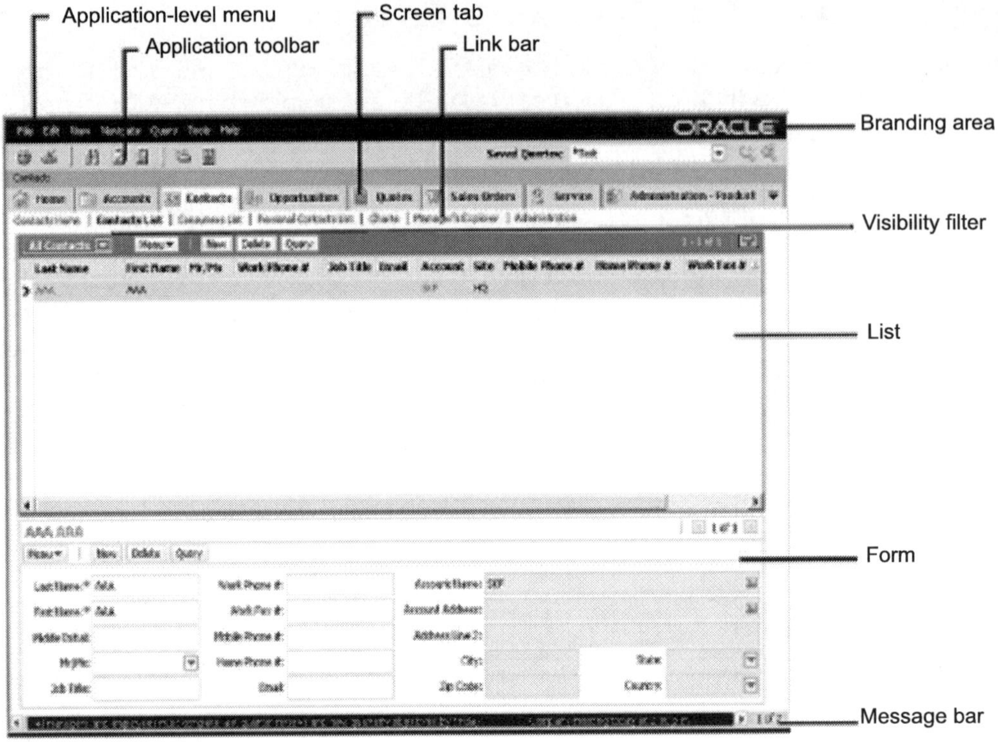

Fig. 5.1 *Siebel application screen*

5.2.1 Application-Level Menu

Application-level menu is present at the top left corner of application window and contains various menus specific to application. The menus present here facilitate us with various important tasks. Some of the typical menus present here are "File Menu," "Edit Menu," "View Menu," "Query Menu," "Tools Menu," and "Help Menu." Throughout our discussion about Siebel navigation and configuration in this book, we will use various options present in these menus.

5.2.2 Application Toolbar

Application toolbar is present just below the application-level menu. It provides various tools in the form of icons. We can click on these icons to access these tools. Oracle does not charge any additional bugs to click and access these tools; hence, I would suggest every reader to access all the tools while reading, so that you can have a clear picture of them. Table 5.1 provides a brief discussion about these the tools.

Table 5.1 Application Toolbar Options

Serial number	*Tool*	*Function*
1.	Sitemap 	Provides a hierarchical list of all the screens and views accessible to current user in the form of hyperlink. User can click on the link to jump to the screen or view directly
2.	Search 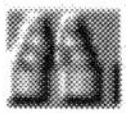	Activates the search center to allow users to search records without losing the data on current screen. We can also opt for advanced search options, listed in Table 5.2 Fig. 5.2 shows various steps that can be taken to perform search operation.
3.	How Do I 	Enables iHelp, a tool providing real time assistance to complete tasks. Once launched, iHelp remains active until we end it. It shows the steps related to currently running task, even if we navigate to another screen. For using iHelp, we just need to click on How Do I button, and drill down to an item in iHelp pane to launch it. After this, we need to follow the instructions provided in the iHelp pane to carry on with our task
4.	Tasks 	Activates Tasks UI, which provides step-by-step guidance to complete specific task
5.	Quick Print 	Using this button, we can print the data in current view
6.	Reports 	Lets us view all the reports corresponding to the currently active screen
7.	Saved Queries Drop Down List	Present at the right side of application toolbar. It lets us access the saved queries, which include queries created and saved by us and the predefined queries established by our organization
8.	New Query 	Allows us to launch new query, different from the predefined queries established by organization
9.	Execute Query 	Used to execute the query

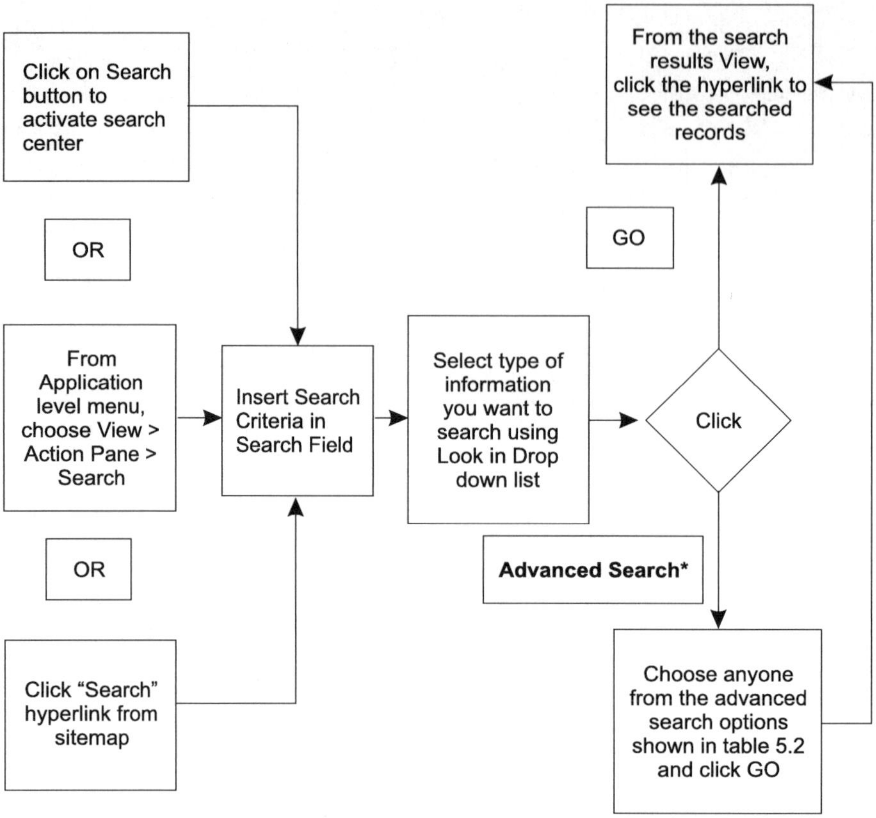

Fig. 5.2 *Steps to perform search*

Table 5.2 Advanced Search Options

Serial number	*Advanced search option*	*Function*
1.	Modified Between	Get results modified between particular dates
2.	Look In	Select categories from where you want to perform search
3.	File Format	File formats you want to display your results. File format is supported for integration with FAST but not with Oracle SES
4.	Data Source	You can opt to retrieve data from various data sources, for example, Siebel repository or any other application repository, such as Microsoft Exchange or an Intranet

5.2.3 Screen Tab

Screen tab is present below the application toolbar. It is a collection of tabs for the screens accessible to us. On clicking on any tab, we will be taken to that screen, which will show the views present in it. The Screen tab corresponding to the currently displayed screen in visible in different color, which differentiates it from other tabs. One thing to note about Screen tab is that it DOES NOT contain all the screens accessible to us. If we want to navigate to the screen that is not present in Screen tab, we will need to go to sitemap and click on the hyperlink corresponding to that screen. We can select the tabs that we want to display by default in the Screen tab. Figure 5.3 shows the steps to do this.

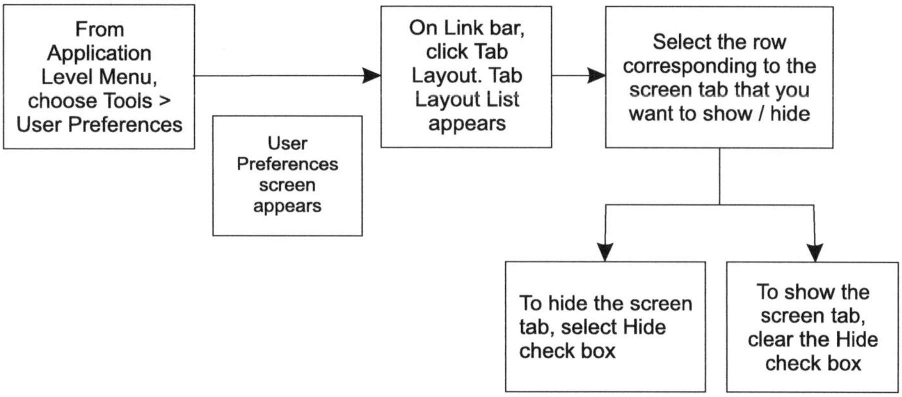

Fig. 5.3 *Steps to show or hide screen tabs*

Apart from showing or hiding the screen tabs, we can also edit the order in which they appear. Figure 5.4 shows the steps to change the order in which tabs appear in the Screen tab.

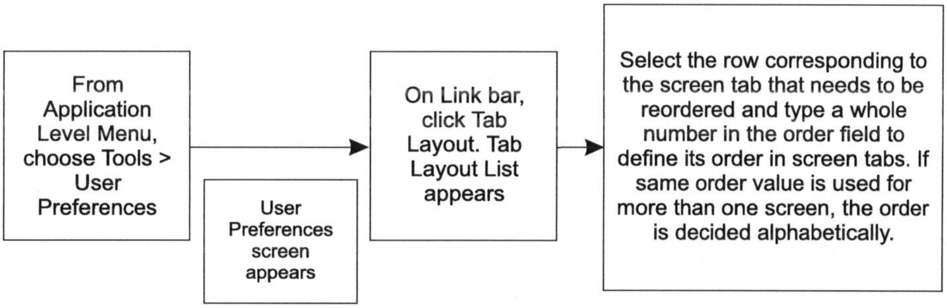

Fig. 5.4 *Changing screen tab order*

5.2.4 Link Bar

A screen is a collection of multiple views. While the screen gets loaded, the default view corresponding to it gets displayed. For accessing the additional views in the screen, we use

Link bar. It is a collection of links to the views corresponding to the currently active screen. Just like Screen tab, the selected link in the Link bar appears in a different color, which differentiates it from other links.

5.2.5 Screens

Screens collectively form an application. They are basically the collection of related views. Examples of screens are "Accounts Screen," "Contacts Screen," and so on. Screens can be accessed either by clicking the screen name from Screen tab, or by using sitemap. Here, we are basically concerned with the UI navigation of screen. The configuration of screens, its properties, and various objects related to it are discussed in detail in Chapter 14.

5.2.6 Views

Views collectively form a screen. They are the collection of related applets. We can navigate between multiple views by using Link bar, Visibility Filter, or View tabs. All the three options are discussed in next points. Configuring views, their properties, and various objects related to them are discussed in Chapter 13.

5.2.7 Sub-views

Sub-views are typically present at the bottom side of screen, and are used to display additional details about the record selected in the view. Navigation between sub-views is done through View tabs, which is discussed later. The block diagram shown in Fig. 5.5 describes the position of main view, sub-view, and view tabs.

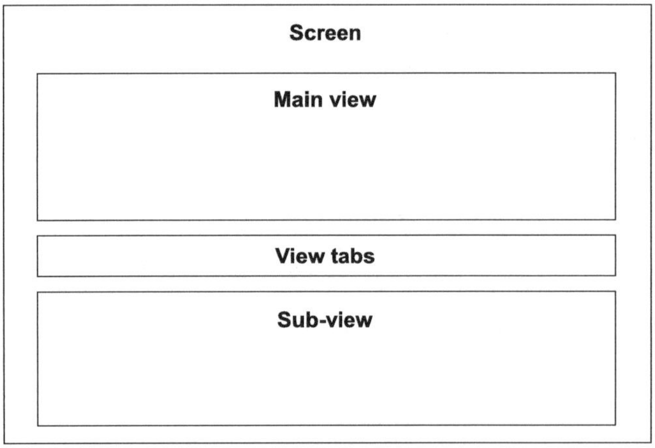

Fig. 5.5 *Positions of main view and sub-view*

5.2.8 View Tabs

View tabs look just like Screen tabs, and are typically present above the sub-view portion in a screen. View tabs are used to navigate between sub-views. We can directly jump to the desired sub-view to see the additional details about the record selected in the main view. The selected View tab appears in a different color, which differentiates it from other View tabs.

To understand the relation between Screen, View, Sub-View, and View tabs, let us take a simple real life example. Suppose our application is configured for a Super Store, having multiple branches across country. In our application, we will require screens to display data about branches, suppliers, customers, store representatives, and so on. Let us navigate to customer screen, which contains the views displaying data related to customers including their personal details (e.g., Name, Address, Contact Number, Email Id, etc.), purchase history (including product purchased, billing details, location, etc.), feedbacks (including their appreciation and complaints), and so on. For implementing this, we will require a view, displaying a list of all the customers, and one sub-view, each for customer's personal details, purchase history, and feedbacks.

Now, suppose we want to see the personal details of Mr. X, living in Mumbai. For this, we will navigate to Customers screen -> Customer List View. In this list, we will search for Mr. X with location Mumbai. Once we select Mr. X in this list, the sub-views present below will get populated with the relevant details of Mr. X. To view the personal details, we will select "Personal Details" view tab, which will load "Personal Details" view displaying the details about Mr. X.

5.2.9 Visibility Filter

Visibility filters are used to filter the data in main view. Access to this data is based on the responsibility of the person currently logged into the application. Visibility filter appears in the form of drop-down list at the top left corner of View. It is present in only those views where the data needs to be filtered based on the responsibility.

Let us understand this concept by elaborating the example of super stores discussed in previous point. For a chain of stores, there will be employees working in stores, a store supervisor, a manager for all the stores in a city, and a global head for all the stores across the country. All of the persons having these responsibilities will require viewing the data related to customers. The difference would be that the store employee would require viewing the customer details with which he interacted; a store manager would require all the customers of his store; a manager would require all the customers in all the stores in city; and a global head would require to view all the customers across country. Instead of making different views for them, we use visibility filters, with following four options in the drop-down list:

- My Customers
- My Store's Customers
- My City's Customers
- All Customers

The data in Customers View will get populated based on the option selected from the drop-down list. The access to these options will be based on the responsibility of the person who is currently logged in into the application. In Fig. 5.1, we can see the visibility filter for Contact screen at the top left corner "All Contacts" view, with the option "All Contacts" selected.

5.2.10 Applets

Applets together form a view. They are used by users to view and modify the data present in Siebel database. We can see many types of applets in Siebel application, but the most widely used applets are List Applets and Form Applets. We will discuss other applets in Chapter 10.

5.2.10.1 List applets

List applets show data in the form of list. The records in the list applets are shown in rows, with each column containing specific details about the record. We can select any record by clicking any field or column of that record. Selecting a record changes its color. Also, if record is editable, users can edit it directly in the list applet. Also, there is an arrow-shaped active record indicator at the left end of selected record.

Navigation in a list applet can be done by using vertical and horizontal scroll bars. Scroll bars are typically used when the data to be displayed requires more area than the available display area. Horizontal scroll bars are used to navigate through all the columns currently being displayed, and vertical scroll bars are used to navigate through various rows showing records in list.

Also, users can view more or less records in the list by using "Show More" and "Show Less Button," present at the top right corner of List applet. These buttons are displayed in Fig. 5.6. On clicking Show More button, more records get displayed in the list, converting the Show More button to Show Less Button. If we want to collapse the list again, we can click on Show Less Button.

To know more details about a record, typically drill downs are configured in List Applet records. Drill downs allow us to click on the record in List applet that takes us to a Form Applet showing more details about the selected record. The field on which Drill Down is configured appears in a different color from other fields. Form applets are discussed in the next point.

Fig. 5.6 *Show More and Show Less buttons*

5.2.10.2 Form applets

Unlike the List applet, which is used to display a list of records, Form applets display the details of one record. Typically, when we click on any record in list applet to drill down into it, a Form applet gets loaded with the details of that record. When we select another record, the details of that record get populated in the Form applet.

Whenever we step off a record in List or Form applet after making changes in it, the changes get automatically saved. Also, all the fields that are mandatory in Form applet are marked with asterisk (*).

Also, in the top right corner of most of the Form applets, we can find "Record Navigation Buttons" as shown in the Fig. 5.7 below. These buttons are used to navigate to next record or the previous record in the Form applet.

Fig. 5.7 *Record navigation buttons*

If we look closely at List and Form applets, we will find certain buttons that are common in both applets. Typically, these buttons are present at top left corner of applets. Some of the common buttons are "Menu," "New," "Delete," and "Query." Based on the applets, we can find some or all of these buttons. From their names itself, the functionalities provided by them might be clear to you to some extent. Table 5.3 summarizes the functions of these buttons.

Table 5.3 Buttons in Applets

Serial number	*Button*	*Functionality*
1.	Menu	Clicking on Menu button opens a list of actions that can be performed on a record, such as copy, edit, or undo the record. The same menu can also be accessed by right-click on the record in List or Form applet
2.	New	Clear from the name itself, this button allows us to create a new record. However, the effect differs in List and Form applet. In a Form applet, clicking on this button displays the form applet with empty field, allowing us to enter the required values in fields. In List applet, it inserts a new empty row, in which values can be filled by user
3.	Delete	After selecting a record, clicking this button deletes that record from database
4.	Query	It allows us to query the records in applets. In List applet, it provides an empty row, in which we can query the records by filling value in any field, or a combination of two or more fields. For example, if you want to search for all the accounts having status "Active," you can click on Query button, and in the empty row displayed, you can enter "Active" in the status field and click enter. It will display all the records with "Active" status. Similarly, in the Form applet, it displays an empty form, in which we can perform the search based on any field, or a combination of fields

5.2.11 Branding Area

Branding area is located at the upper right corner of the UI. The user interface used in Fig. 5.1 shows "Oracle" in branding area. This name can be changed to reflect specific organization's name that owns the software.

5.2.12 Explorer View

Explorer Views facilitate us with hierarchical navigation through a set of records. This view can be accessed by clicking the Explorer View link corresponding to a screen from Link bar. Explorer view typically contains a Tree Applet*, which is basically a list of records displayed in tree form, and a Detail Applet, which is typically a list or form applet showing the details about the record selected.

* Tree Applet displays the records in parent–child form. Every parent record in a tree applet has a + sign, clicking on which expands the elements and displays its child record. During this course, most widely used parent–child relationship is the one present in Siebel tools object explorer, where clicking on the parent object type expands it and displays its child objects. We will discuss about this in detail while discussing the configuration part.

5.3 RECORDS AND FIELDS

In our discussion till this point, we were limited till screen, views, and applets level. Now, we will dig it more to discuss about record, fields, and controls associated with them.

A record is basically a group of values assigned to related fields. Considering the scenario of a typical primary school admission procedure, student's "First Name," "Last Name," "Address," and so on, will be the required fields and the set of values given to these fields will form a set of records. For example, ("Mike," "Thomson," "201, New Street") and ("George," "Savariar," "10," "Old Street") will be two records stored in the database. In a list applet, we will find a list of records, whereas in form applets, we will see one record at a time, with the values of all the required fields populated.

Also, in most of the List applets, we will find some of the fields, whose values are in different color, and they appear just like a hyperlink. These fields are called as "Drill Downs," and they provide the facility to view additional details specific to the selected record. Before moving ahead, let us have a quick look on various types of fields in applets.

5.3.1 Different Types of Fields in Applets

This section discussed about various fields available in applets. While discussing about these fields, we will also look on the significance of these fields at application level.

5.3.1.1 Text fields

Text fields allow us to enter the values directly from user interface. To enter a value in a text field, we just need to click on the field and start typing. Some text fields also contain a text editor attached with them. We can simply click on the text field to enter the data. But typically in cases where the amount of text to be entered is large, Text Editor is used to enter the data. In Form applets, the text editor button is available almost every time, but in List applet's fields, the button appears only when we click on the field.

5.3.1.2 Read-only fields

Certain fields in user interface are noneditable, and they appear with gray background. These fields are the read only fields. We can only view the values in these fields, but cannot edit them from user interface. In case of read only fields having text editor attached, clicking on the text editor button launches the text editor with the data present in the field. We can view this data, but cannot edit it.

5.3.1.3 *Mandatory fields*

There are certain fields in the user interface marked with red (*) sign. These fields are the mandatory fields. To enter any record in database, these fields cannot be left blank.

Apart from entering the data directly in the fields by using text fields, there are certain field controls that help user to enter data. Table 5.4 lists some of these controls, along with their importance and uses.

Table 5.4 Field Controls

S. No.	*Field control*	*Significance/importance/use*
1.	Drop Down Lists	Drop-down lists are basically used when user is required to select any one value from predefined list of values. Drop-down lists show one value at a time, along with an arrow button at the right corner. Clicking on this button drops a list, containing some values. User can select any value from these values. Also, user can type initial characters of the option that he wants to select, and all the options starting with those characters are shown automatically in the list. We will discuss more on drop-down list while discussing the configuration of pick lists
2.	Check Boxes	Check boxes allow users to select or reject any option. Clicking on an empty check box fills a tick mark, or a X mark in it. Clicking it again empties it again
3.	Currency Calculator	Currency calculator allows users to indicate various financial transactions in different currencies. Currency calculator can be accessed by clicking the calculator field that appears in currency fields. A currency calculator has the following three fields: 1. Currency Code: Allows a user to select the country and corresponding currency code 2. Exchange Date: Allows a user to select a date by launching a calendar control 3. Amount: Allows a user to enter amount. User has an option to type the amount directly in the field, or to use pop-up calculator
4.	Option Buttons	Option buttons allow users to select one of various options. The difference between a check box and an option button is that users can select more than one option in case of options button
5.	Calendar Control	Just like a currency calculator, a calendar control appears at the right corner of date fields, and allows users to pick a particular date. Calendar controls allow users to select month, year, and date, along with the time and time zone

5.3.2 Records

After discussing about fields, we will now divert our discussion to focus on records and various tasks related to records. Records tasks start with creating a new record, followed by editing them and saving them. After these basic activities, we will discuss about other activities, such as searching records, identifying new records, flagging records, freezing and resizing the columns, sorting records, performing spell check, and so on.

5.3.2.1 *Creating records*

Records can be created anywhere in the Siebel application by using several approaches. Table 5.5 lists the common methods used to create records in Siebel application.

Table 5.5 Creating Records in Siebel Application

S. No.	*Method*	*Steps to create the record*
1	**Use Application-Level Menu**	1. In your applet, from application-level menu, select New Record from Edit menu 2. A new blank record appears. Fill the appropriate values and save it
2.	**Use Menu Button in Applet**	1. Click on the Menu button on the top of applet. This will open a drop-down menu with various options. Select "New Record" from the menu. (This menu can be opened by using a right-click in the applet) 2. A new blank record appears. Fill appropriate values and save it
3.	**Use New button in Applet**	1. At the top of List or Form applet, you will find a "New" button. Clicking this button displays a new blank record 2. Fill appropriate values and save the record

5.3.2.2 *Quick fill templates*

In certain cases, it is required to give same values for one or more fields in many or all the records. In such a scenario, for every new record, users have to provide same values for a particular field, which is merely a waste of time and efforts. Consider a situation in which for a field "XYZ" of an applet, all the records should hold a value "ABC." Now, whenever users create new records, they have to fill the value "ABC" for every record.

This task can be automated by the use of quick fill templates. Quick fill templates are used to store default values for the fields that need to be set while creating new records. In our example above, if we set the default value for the field "XYZ" to be "ABC" in our quick fill template, that value will be set every time when a new record will be created. Flowchart in Fig. 5.8 shows the steps to create a quick fill template:

After creating the template, the next step is to use this template while creating new records. The following flowchart describes the steps to use the template while creating new records. Figure 5.10 shows the steps to use a quick fill template while creating new records.

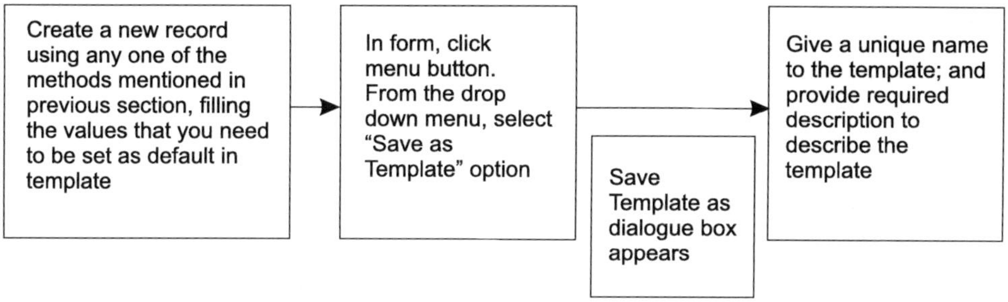

Fig. 5.8 *Creating quick fill templates*

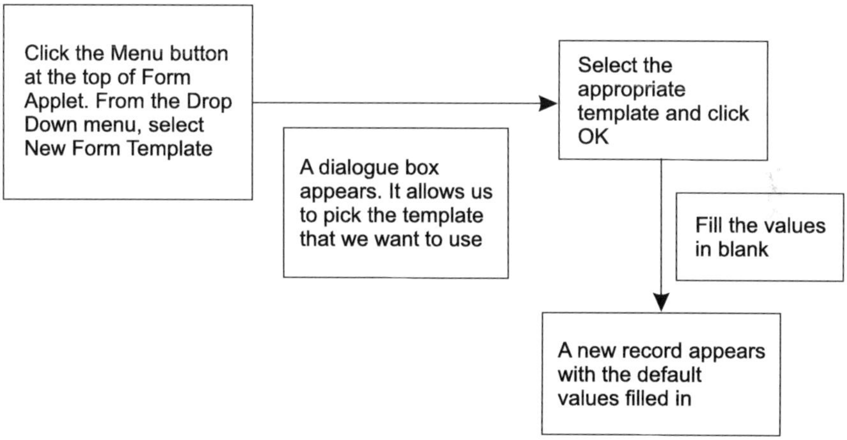

Fig. 5.9

Along with creating a new record by using a quick fill template, we can also apply a quick fill template to a new record. The following flowchart shows the steps to do this.

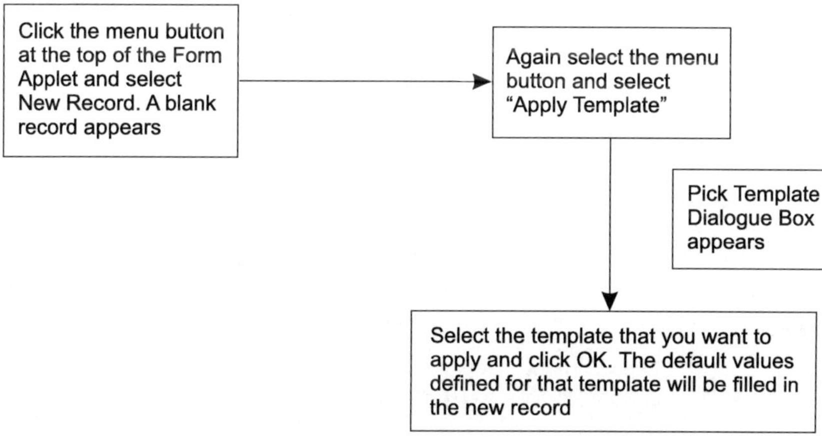

Fig. 5.10 *Steps to use quick fill templates*

5.4 RECORD TASKS

Till now, our discussion was focused mainly on the creation of a new record. Now, we will look at various tasks related to the existing record. The flowchart shown in Fig. 5.11 covers these tasks and steps to fulfill these tasks.

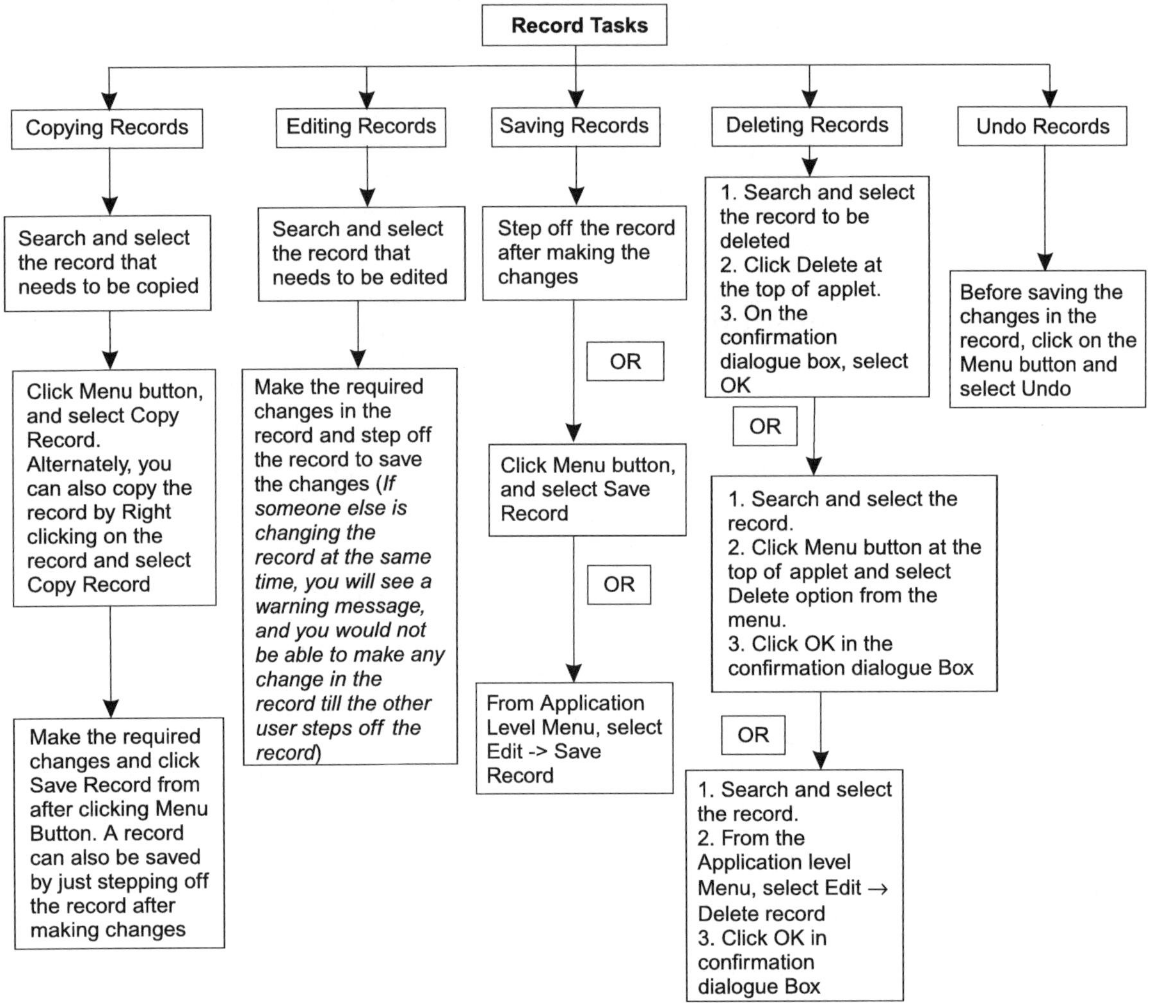

Fig. 5.11 *Common record tasks*

Apart from the basic tasks discussed above, there are some other important tasks related to records. In next section, we will discuss some of these important tasks. This discussion will include tasks, such as merging duplicate records, finding record count, associating records, flagging records, attaching files with record, and sorting and freezing records in list.

5.4.1 Merging Duplicate Records

Merging duplicate records is the process to merge records that contain same information. To keep database accurate, it is sometimes required to find and merge all the records that contain same information into one record. While merging, a user needs to select which record will survive. All the other records (selected as Source records) will be merged to surviving record. One thing to be noted here is that the field values of source records will not exist after merging records. All the records that are associated to source records get associated with the surviving record after merging. The flow diagram shown in Fig. 5.12 shows the steps of the merge records.

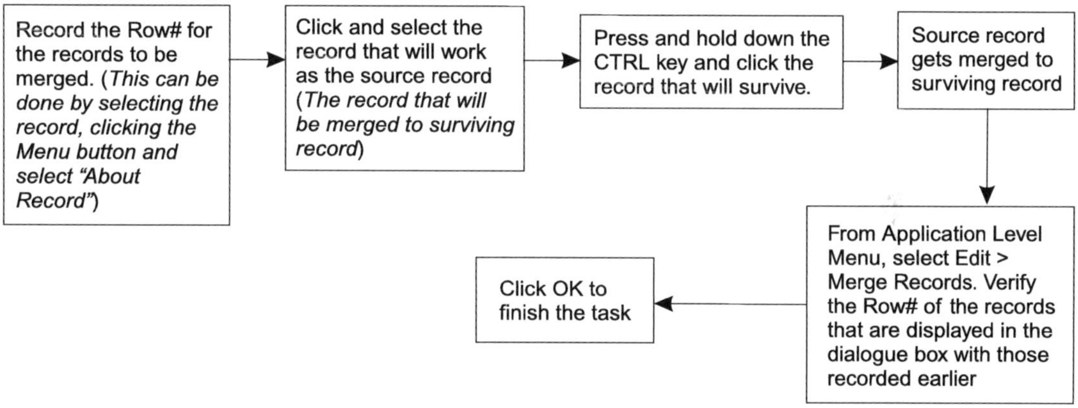

Fig. 5.12 *Steps to merge records*

5.4.2 Finding Record Count

Sometimes it is required to find the number of records. In Siebel, this is done by using "Record Count." To count the records, user just needs to right-click on the list, and select "Record Count." Record count gets displayed in Record Count dialogue box. Alternately, this can be done by using Menu button. From the drop-down list, click on Record Count to get the count.

5.4.3 Attaching Files and URLs to Records

Siebel provides the facility to attach files with records. These files can be the ones created in other applications. Attachments can be done by using attachments view. As attachments are not required in every screen, this view is available only in those screens where it is actually needed. Attachments view displays all the previously attached files to a record in the form of a list, and allows user to attach more files to the record.

To attach a file with a record, there are three ways. The flow diagram in Fig. 5.13 displays them.

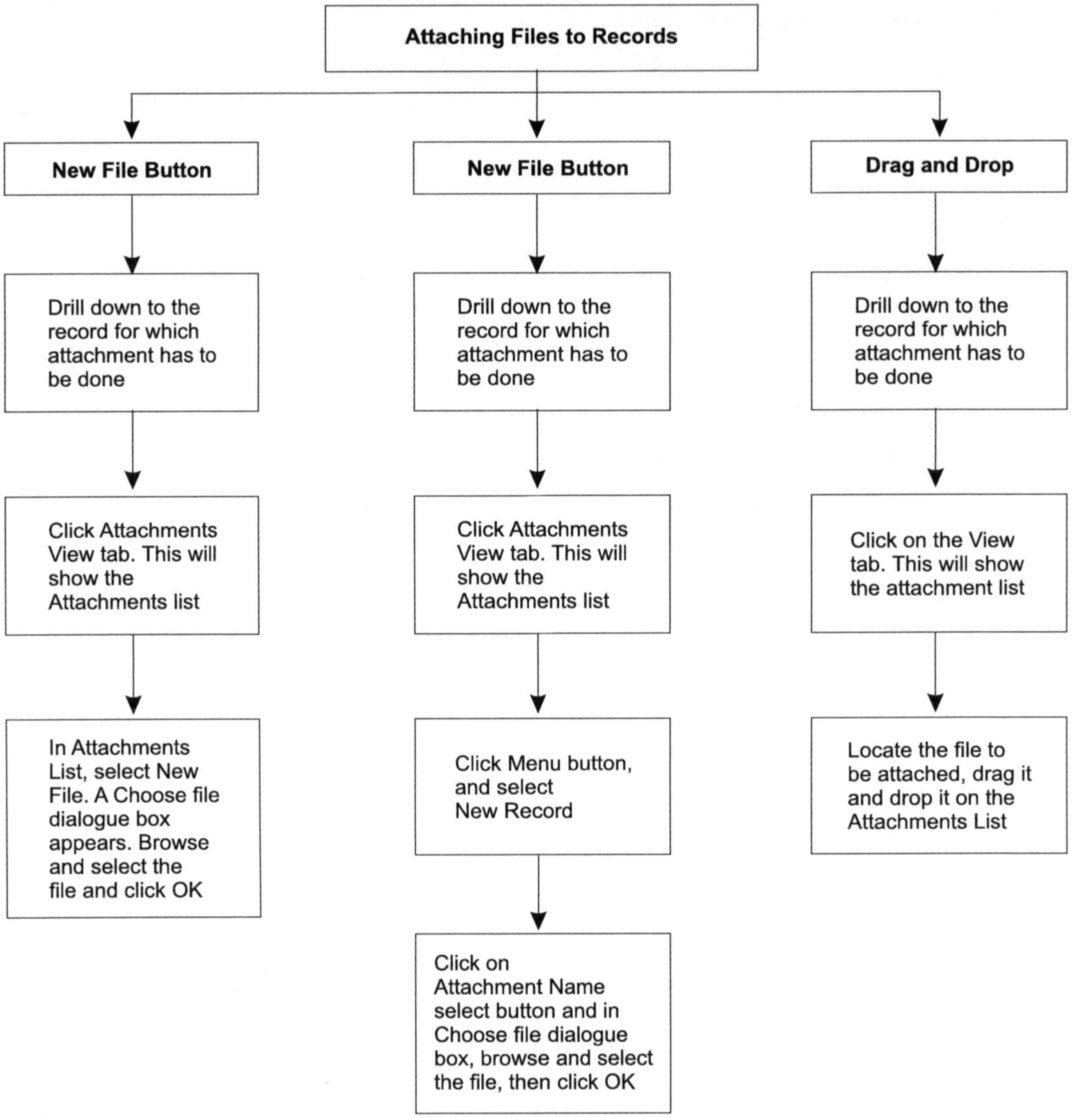

Fig. 5.13 *Attaching files to records*

Similarly, in some cases, it is required to attach URLs with the records. For attaching URLs also, we need Attachments view in the screen. Following are the steps to attach a URL to the record:

1. Select and drill down to the record to which URL has to be attached and click on Attachments view tab.
2. Select New URL and enter the URL in the URL dialogue box. Click OK. The URL appears as the hyperlink in the Attachments list.

5.4.4 Sorting Records in List

Sorting records refer to arranging records in a list in ascending or descending order. For sorting records, we actually perform sort operation on any column (column should be sortable) in the list. Based on the values of records in that column, they get sorted. Using advanced sort operation provided by Siebel, we can sort a maximum of three columns at once.

If a column is sortable, we will see an arrow (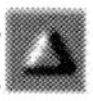) with the name of that column in tooltip. On clicking this arrow, all the records get sorted in ascending order based on their values in that column. On clicking it once again, they get sorted in descending order.

For sorting records in ascending order based on one column, we just need to click the header of that column. To sort them in descending order, just click on the header again.

Sorting records based on multiple columns, we will need to perform **Advanced Sort** operation. For doing advanced sort, we will need to navigate to Menu -> Advanced Sort option. This will open Advanced Sort window. Here, we will need to select the columns from sort drop-down based on their priority, along with the fashion (ascending or descending) in which we want to sort the records.

5.5 SUMMARY

Navigating Siebel applications make us familiar with them. Before we start configuring Siebel applications, we should be handy with the navigation aspects of them. This will make it easy for us to understand the significance of object types while configuring them. Also, if we are familiar with Siebel application's user interface, we can easily map the client's requirements to configuration requirements while preparing the technical design. With this chapter, we will wind up our discussion on introduction to Siebel applications and tools. In Part 3, we will focus on configuring Siebel applications.

REFERENCE

1. Siebel Bookshelf V8.1, Nov, 2008. Available from: www.oracle.com.
   Pdf name: Siebel Fundamentals
   Page 18, Figure 2.

PART III

CONFIGURING SIEBEL APPLICATIONS

Now we look on configuring Siebel Applications using Siebel tools. Here, we'll look on various Siebel Object types, their properties, steps to configure them and their use in Siebel Applications. In order to make it easy to understand these objects, this part contains a separate chapter for each object type.

This part contains following chapters:

- Siebel Object Types
- Tables and Columns
- Business Components
- Business Objects
- Applets
- Joins
- Links
- Views
- Screens
- Pick lists
- Multi Value Groups
- Toolbars and Menus
- List of Values
- Applications

Chapter 6

INTRODUCTION TO SIEBEL OBJECTS

From this chapter, we'll start our discussion on Configuring Siebel Applications. Siebel Applications stand on the base of Objects. Various Siebel objects combine to form a Siebel Application. Configuration of Siebel Applications basically means configuring the object required in it. In this chapter, we'll start with a brief discussion on Siebel Objects, followed by basic definitions of some of the important Siebel object types. Moving ahead, we'll have a look on Siebel Object architecture, along with classification of various objects in Siebel Object Architecture. Towards the end, we'll discuss about some of the best practices which should be remembered while configuring Siebel Applications.

Major topics covered in this chapter are:

1. Siebel Objects
2. Siebel Object Architecture
3. Best Practices for Configuring Objects
4. Summary

6.1 INTRODUCTION

Till now, our discussion was limited mostly on application-level navigation. In this part of book, we will concentrate mainly on the configuration of Siebel applications. But, before proceeding further, we will need to know some basic terms. Siebel applications stand on objects. Siebel objects form the backbone for Siebel applications. The configuration of Siebel applications is basically the configuration of these objects, which collectively form the application.

The following section provides brief definitions of Siebel objects. At this point, you would not be able to understand most of the terms, hence, just go through following and keep them safe for future reference. The purpose of providing these definitions here is NOT to describe these objects in detail. These definitions will give the first introduction of various Siebel object types, so that when you move ahead, you should not be SHOCKED by new terms used. We will discuss about each of them in detail while configuring them.

6.2 SIEBEL OBJECTS

Siebel object definitions are actually the metadata (data related to data) defining Siebel business application. These definitions form the backbone of the user interface, business entities, and database organization of Siebel applications. These definitions are stored in a set of database tables, called as Siebel repository. All the definitions that we are going to discuss below are actually the Siebel object types.

Before moving into the details of Siebel object types, I would suggest all to login into the Siebel tools with sample database. On logging in, you will see Siebel tools' home page. On the left hand side of this page, you will see something like the one shown in Fig. 6.1. This is called as Object Explorer. In Object Explorer, you can see a list of various items, with most of them having a "+" sign at their left. On clicking this + sign, you will be able to see a list of some other items.

All the items present in Object Explorer are the Siebel objects. Siebel objects represent **parent–child relationship**. Clicking the + sign at the left of an object type expands the list of its child objects. Most typical use of parent–child relationship can be defined be the term "*is a collection of*." For example, on expanding the Table object type in Object Explorer, you will see "Column" object. It shows that Table *is a collection of columns*.

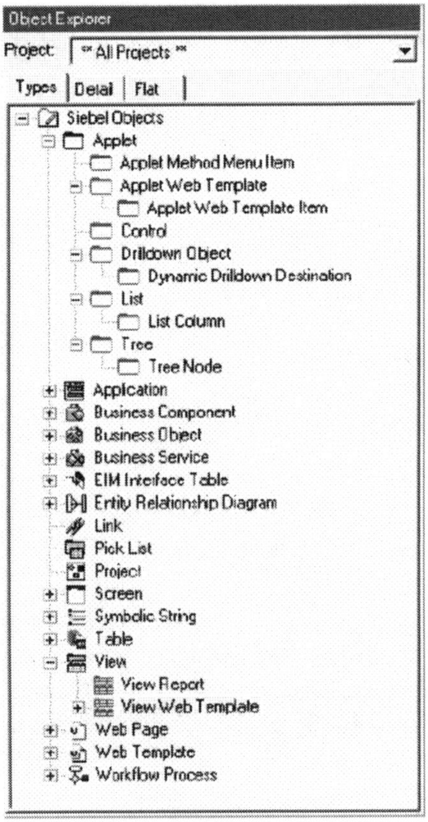

Fig. 6.1 *Siebel tools object explorer*

6.2.1 Siebel Object Types

In this section, we will discuss about various Siebel object types. The purpose of this section is to introduce these object types and providing their high-level significance in Siebel applications. At this point, you may not get the exact meaning and role played by each of them. We will elaborate our discussion on these objects while discussing their configuration. Some of the important Siebel object types are as follows:

1. **Table:** Table object definition is the logical representation in the Siebel repository of the underlying physical tables in DBMS. We can extend the Siebel data model by using extension tables and extension columns to base tables but we cannot add new base tables, delete base tables and columns, or modify the properties of base columns.
2. **Column:** Column object definition is used to represent the columns in table. Siebel provides a set of vanilla tables and columns, which are sufficient for most of the tasks. If, in certain cases, it is required to add more columns in a table, we can go for extension columns. We will discuss more about columns and extension columns in Chapter 7.
3. **Business Component:** A business component logically represents one or more database tables. A business component's definition controls all sorts of data handling in underlying tables, such as insert, select, or update data. Typically, a business component is made to specify a particular functional area, such as contact and account. We can think of business component as a logical construct that takes the required data from one or more underlying tables to carry out some specific functionality. Business components can be treated as logical blankets over underlying database, which picks one or more columns from one or more tables, thereby abstracting users from underlying database tables and columns.
4. **Field:** A field object definition associates a column from the underlying base table or joined table to a business component. Value in a field can also be derived from other fields in the business component. Fields supply data to controls and list columns in the Web interface.
5. **Business Objects:** Business objects logically bundle the business components, and represents a major functional area of the enterprise. Examples of business objects are contact, service request, and activity. A business object typically maps to a screen in application, as all views in the screen are based on the same business object. We can also say that business objects provide a base for views and screens. In the later sections, we will drill-down into the business objects, but for the time being, I guess this much is sufficient for business object.
6. **Joins:** As the name specifies, a join object definition joins a business component to a table, other than its base table, by using a foreign key in the business component. Join allows a business component to use the columns from the joined table on a one-to-one basis, even though the two tables do not have one-to-one relationship with each other.
7. **Links:** As you guys are aware, a join creates a one-to-one relationship between a business component and a table. Links, on the other hand, create one-to-many (also known as master detail) relationship between two business components. This means

that with the help of a link, we can show a record (from master view) along with all the records that are associated to it (from detail view). For example, a contact may have bought multiple products from an organization. With the help of a link, we can view all the products (detail view) bought by a particular contact (master view).

8. **Applets:** Applets are the user interface objects, which allow a user to interact with the data (view, enter, or modify) from a single business component. As you guys have gone through the Siebel navigation, you must be aware of list applets, form applets, pick applets, and so on. The screen that is visible to us in the application contains multiple numbers of applets.
9. **Views:** View is a collection of all the applets that are visible at a given instance of time. The applets in a particular view are related to each other, which means that the data and relationships corresponding to the view are from same business object.
10. **Screen:** Screen is a collection of views. Screens reflect major functional areas of organization, such as accounts screen and contacts screen. As all the views in a screen are interrelated, we can say that all the views in a screen map to the same business object.
11. **Application:** Application is a collection of screens, for example, Siebel services or Siebel marketing. When we login to application, we can navigate through the screens by using tab bar or the site map.
12. **Toolbar and Menu:** Toolbar and menu object definitions represent a toolbar and menu at user interface, respectively. Toolbar and menu are basically a collection of various operations available to the user. The basic difference between these two is that toolbars represent the options in the form of icons, whereas menus represent the options in the form of a list.
13. **Pick list:** Pick list object definition represents a pick list at user interface. A pick list is basically a list of various values, from which a user can select any one value. Pick list are typically used where we want users to select any one value from the pre-defined values, instead of filling those values manually.

6.3 SIEBEL OBJECT ARCHITECTURE

Based on the functionality and use, Siebel objects are divided into four architectural layers:

- The logical User Interface Layer
- The Physical User Interface Layer
- The Business Objects Layer
- The Data Objects Layer

Let us take the analogy of a car, to understand the concept of these layers. The manufacturing of a car starts from warehouse, where all the spare parts of car are present. All these parts collaborate to form a car, but individually they are of no use. In the warehouse, there are various sections based on the parts stored. For example, there will be section having parts for gear box, one section having pistons and so on. This warehouse can be connected with Siebel database in analogy, and various sections can be treated as Siebel tables. Siebel tables and columns form data objects layer. Now, suppose one of the various car factories picks some parts required for production, from various sections of warehouse.

The factory will have different sections based on the car model, and each section will need a different set of parts, with a lot of parts common to all. This factory can be connected to business objects, various sections in the factory as business components and the parts required by individual section as the fields for individual business component. Together, they can be connected to business objects layer of Siebel object architecture.

Moving ahead, an individual car belonging to a particular model will have specific parts used from that model's section. This car is now acting as a Siebel view, and various parts, such as front window, front seat, breaks, diggy, and so on, are acting as Siebel applets, which together form the view. Collectively, they resemble the Siebel physical user interface layer. Finally, the car will be painted and fine-tuned to be presented in market. The color and various designs done on car can be connected with logical user interface layer of Siebel object architecture.

After our short journey from Car's warehouse to market, let us now discuss the formal definitions of various layers in Siebel object architecture.

6.3.1 Physical User Interface Layer

The objects present in this layer basically decide "how to present to user." Various types of physical files present in this layer, including Template files (.swt files which defines layout and formatting of UI elements. Examples of these elements are View and Applet), Siebel Tags (used in template files to specify the layout and formatting of Siebel objects in the HTML page rendered in the user's Web browser) and style sheets (.css files, specify the appearance of HTML or XML elements and their contents in the Web browser) collectively decide the "Look and Feel" of the application.

6.3.2 Logical User Interface Objects Layer

The objects present in this layer decide "what to present to user." These objects define the user interface to which a user interacts. These objects are responsible to expose the data from business object layer and to facilitate the user with controls to navigate, view, or modify the data. The object types that fall on this layer include applets, views, screens, application, page tab, and so on.

6.3.3 Business Objects Layer

The objects present in this layer are responsible to pick the specific data from database, based on its relevance to the context. The objects present at this layer are responsible for organizing data from underlying tables into logical units and determining the business logic. Some examples are business objects, business component, field, join, and so on.

6.3.4 Data Objects Layer

Object definitions in this layer are basically responsible for shielding the application and the developer from database administration and restructuring. It logically represents the underlying physical database, irrespective of installed database management system, providing a "Blanket of Abstraction" over the DBMS. The objects that fall under this layer are table, column, and index.

Table 6.1 classifies various objects into layers of Siebel object architecture. Some of the important object types mentioned in the table are discussed in previous section. We will discuss about the remaining object types later in the chapter specific to them, or their parent object. (As an exercise, try to find out the names of these object types in Object Explorer.)

Table 6.1 Layers in Siebel Object Architecture

Serial number	*Layer*	*Object types*
1.	Physical user interface layer	Applets, Views, Screens, Application, Page Tab, Screen Menu Item, Control, List, List Column, Applet Web Template, View Web Template, Applet Web Template Item, View Web Template Item
2.	Business object layer	Business Object, Business Object Component, Business Component, Field, Join, Join Specification, Link, Multi-Value Link
3.	Data object layer	Table, Column, Index

Moving ahead in this part of the book, we will discuss about configuring these objects by using Siebel tools. It should be kept in mind that Siebel Tools is a Configuring Environment, not a Development Environment. We will use above mentioned object types to configure the Siebel objects. Before starting our discussion on configuring various Siebel objects, it would be very helpful to first look on various best practices to be followed while configuring Siebel applications. Next section encapsulates them.

6.4 BEST PRACTICES FOR CONFIGURING SIEBEL APPLICATIONS

Before starting the discussion on configuring Siebel applications, it is very important to know and understand the importance of certain best practices to be followed while configuring applications. This section describes some of the common best practices. There are certain best practices that are specific to the object types. We will discuss them while discussing the configuration of those object types.

1. Object names should be descriptive, which should describe the context in which object is used. For example, suppose you have one applet "Dream Country Dream City Dream School List Applet," which displays various schools in a city. Now if it is required to create one more applet to display various schools that are English Medium, we should name it "Dream Country Dream City Dream School English Medium," instead of something like "Dream Country Dream City Dream School List Applet 2."
2. We should not add a question mark in the name of any Siebel object, as it creates problems while querying that object.

3. Never use reserved standard SQL keywords, such as update, select, insert in the names of Siebel objects.
4. Typically, there is a difference in the naming of data object layer objects and other objects. Data object layer objects are named in capital letters with underscores between them replacing the spaces. For other objects, initial caps format is used for naming, with spaces between two words.

6.5 SUMMARY

This chapter is designed to provide a brief definition of various Siebel object types. Siebel objects work as units to configure Siebel applications. Moving ahead in this part, we will look on these objects in more detail. It is suggested to everyone to open the Siebel tools and try to find out all the objects and their child objects, which will be very helpful to understand the topics discussed later in this part.

REFERENCE

1. Siebel Bookshelf V8.0. Available from: www.oracle.com.

Chapter 7

TABLES AND COLUMNS

In this chapter, we are going to discuss about Tables and Columns. Table object definition logically represents the data which is present physically at underlying database management system. Column object definition, which is child object of Table object, represents the columns from corresponding tables in underlying DBMS.

We'll start our discussion with introduction to Table object and its important properties. Moving ahead, we'll look at Column object definition and its important properties. This will be followed by a detailed discussion of various types of tables and columns, and their significance in Siebel Application configuration. We'll wind up our discussion with steps to create various types of tables and columns.

Various topics covered in this chapter are:

- Tables and Columns
    - Various properties of a Table
    - Column Object and its Properties
- Extension Tables and Extension Columns
- One to One Extension tables
- One to Many Extension tables
- Extension Columns
- Intersection tables
- S_PARTY table
- System and Index Columns
- Database Extension
- Standard Database Extensibility Options
- Advanced Database Extensibility Options

7.1 TABLES AND COLUMNS

Data used and stored by using Siebel applications physically resides in the underlying DBMS. Table object definitions logically represent this data and make it available to be used by Siebel applications. The base tables and columns provided by Siebel cannot be created or deleted, but we can extend them by using the concept of extension tables.

Before moving ahead with the details about table object and its child objects, let us have a look on basic properties of table object. In Object Explorer, if we click "Table" object type, the Object List Editor gets populated with the list of tables. In Object List Editor, we can see the following important properties of table object.

7.1.1 Important Properties of Table

1. **Name:** Name of the table. We always use the convention PREFIX_NAME_SUFFIX format to name a table.
   - PREFIX: It can have following values (Table 7.1):

Table 7.1 Prefix Values

Sl. No.	*PREFIX*	*Description*
1.	S_	This value is used for Siebel base tables. All base tables in Siebel start with this prefix. Tables of form S_<Name>_IF are obsolete interface tables
2.	EIM_	This prefix is used for interface tables for enterprise integration manager
3.	W_	Signifies Siebel data warehouse tables

   - NAME: A unique name for the table.
   - SUFFIX: It can have following values (Table 7.2):

Table 7.2 Suffix Values

Sl No.	*SUFFIX*	*Description*
1.	_X	Used for 1:1 extension tables
2.	_XM	Used for 1:M extension tables
3.	_ATT	Used for file attachment tables
4.	_SS	Used for tables that store Siebel-to-Siebel integration details
5.	_REL	Used for table supporting many-to-many relationship from an entity back to itself
6.	_XA	Used for table that stores extended attributes associated with an object class

2. **Type:** Specifies the type of table. This property can contain any one out of the following values:
   - Data (Public): The data present in these tables is fairly public. These are the tables whose data is made available to developers through business components. See Chapter 8 for details. These tables and their columns can be extended by using extension tables and extension columns.
   - Data (Private): The data present in these tables can be accessed by developers through business components, but cannot be extended by using extension tables and extension columns.
   - Extension: These tables allow developers to extend Siebel data model by adding new columns, based on the requirements. These tables logically extend a

particular table (referred as parent tables), and have implicit 1:1 relationship with it. (Tables having 1:M relationship with their parent tables have type as data (public), but they are referred as extension tables.)

- Data (Intersection): These tables are used to implement M:M relationship between two data tables.
- Interface: Interface tables are basically used by enterprise integration manager, while populating one or more Siebel base tables with the data from any external enterprise applications. This migration is done by using periodic batch jobs.

Other table types that include "Database View," "Dictionary," "Journal," "Log," "Warehouse Types," "Virtual Table," "Extension (Siebel)," and "Repository" are reserved for Oracle internal use.

3. **Base Table:** For all base tables, this property is left blank. For extension tables, this property contains the name of its base table, that is, the table that is extended by this extension table.
4. **User Name:** A descriptive name that helps in identifying the table while using it in configuration.
5. **Comments:** Comments can be added in this property that can be used as a future reference for anyone who uses this table.
6. **Status:** This value contains current status of the table.

7.1.2 Column Object

Column is the child object of table object. We discussed in previous section that table object is a logical representation of tables present in underlying database. In the similar way, column object definition is the logical representation of corresponding physical columns in underlying physical table. To represent a column, we need to map the properties of that column in our column object. These properties include "Name," "Data Type," "Length," "Precision," "Alias," "Primary Key," and so on. All these properties can be seen as object properties in Object List Editor on selecting "Column" object in Object Explorer. Out of these properties, some of the important properties are discussed below:

1. **Name:** This property identifies the name of database column.
2. **Physical Type:** This property identifies the data type of the underlying column. Table 7.3 lists various data types of column:

Table 7.3 Column Physical Types

Sl. No.	*Data type*	*Description*
1.	Varchar	Variable length text. Used mostly for alphanumeric columns including ID fields (ROW_ID, primary, and foreign key values)
2.	Number	Any numeric value. The allowed length for values is 16 digits without decimal points, or 15 digits before decimal point

Sl. No.	*Data type*	*Description*
3.	Character	Stores fixed length text. By default, the length of text is 1. We can change this value by navigating to View Menu -> Options -> Database tab. Check the box "Allow to create column of type 'Character' being greater than 1." One drawback with this data type is if we have to set variable length text; the data shorter than maximum length defined will be padded with blank spaces in database. Hence, it is always recommended to use varchar if length of data is not fixed. For storing Boolean values of type character, this type is mostly used
4.	Character large object (CLOB)	CLOB is used to store a large amount of text, even more than "Long" type. We can set the physical type to CLOB while creating a new column; an existing column cannot be changed CLOB
5.	Long	Used to store large text data. The maximum length allowed is 16 KB
6.	Date	Stores date values
7.	Time	Stores time values
8.	Date Time	Stores both date and time values together in one column
9.	UTC Date Time	Stores time in Greenwich mean time

3. **Default:** The value provided to this property works as a default value when a new row is added to a table.
4. **Precision:** This property is used with columns of type "Number." It identifies the maximum number of digits allowed in column. For integer columns, its value is 10. For non-integer columns, it is 22.
5. **Primary Key:** This property identifies whether the column is primary key or not. For a primary key column, this property is set to TRUE, that is, the check box under Primary Key property is checked for primary key column.
6. **User Key Sequence:** This property identifies the sequence in user key for this column.
7. **LOV Bounded:** This property identifies whether the EIM should check the values while importing, against the values contained in the list of values defined in LOV type. A TRUE in this property makes EIM to check the values. This property can be edited only in extension columns. It is read only for Siebel applications' standard columns.
8. **LOV Type:** This property identifies the domain in which the column is to be validated. A list of values domain are defined in Administration -> Data Screen -> List of Values view. This property is used in conjunction with LOV bounded property, and just like that property, it is also read only for Siebel applications' standard columns.

9. Nullable: This property identifies whether a null value can be stored in this column. A TRUE value indicates that this column can hold null value.
10. Foreign Key Table: This property identifies the table that uses this column as its foreign key.

7.2 EXTENSION TABLES AND EXTENSION COLUMNS

Let us now discuss about another type of table, that is, extension table. We need extension tables and extension columns as we cannot make any change in Siebel base tables and base columns. Extension tables provide additional columns to store custom attributes. These tables are connected to base tables via implicit 1:1 or 1:M relationship.

Siebel provides us the facility both to create a new extension table and use an existing one. The existing extension tables are provided by Siebel and are the part of a data model. These tables are called as static extension tables. They contain generic columns with prefix (ATTRIB_), which can be used to store custom attributes. As these tables are already a part of Siebel data model, we do not need to update the physical database on updating these tables.

Along with using existing (static) extension tables, we can also create extension tables. As these tables are not the part of a data model, we need to make corresponding changes in physical database.

- When columns on base tables are updated, the timestamps in corresponding extension table are not updated unless extension columns are not updated.
- When data in extension table is changed, the corresponding change is applied in its base table.

Based on the relationship with base table, extension tables can be classified in two types:

1. One-to-One extension tables
2. One-to-Many extension tables

7.3 ONE-TO-ONE EXTENSION TABLES

One-to-one extension table is basically the extension of base table's record. They are called one-to-one extension tables because rows present in these tables have one-to-one relationships with the corresponding rows in base table. The name of these tables has suffix _X.

The 1:1 relationship between extension table and base table is implemented by using implicit joins. Implicit joins are basically the hidden relationship between base table and extension table, which are responsible to provide extension table's rows on 1:1 basis to the business component that uses extension table. Implicit joins are different from the join that we define as join object definition. Table 7.4 provides the differences between the two.

Table 7.4 Difference between Join and Implicit Join

Implicit join	*Join object definition*
We do not have to configure implicit joins for getting the columns from extension tables. These columns are automatically available for use	Join object definition should be configured before using it. Based on the configuration of join object, we can get the data from joined table to be used in parent business component
Implicit joins allow the data to be updated in columns	Using join object definition, we can only display data, and cannot update the same in columns

7.3.1 Important Definitions for Implementing Implicit Join

The following definitions are required to implement an implicit join:

- Id Field: It is a system field representing the ROW_ID column in underlying base table.
- PAR_ROW_ID column: Column in extension table, which serves as a foreign key to the base table. PAR_ROW_ID stands for parent row Id.

7.3.2 Fetching Value from 1:1 Extension Table in the Field of Business Component

The following configuration is required to fetch the value of extension table's column into business component's field:

- Set the "Column" property of business component's field to name of the column from extension table.
- Set "Join" property to the name of extension table. The name of implicit join between an extension table and its base table is the name of extension table.

7.4 ONE-TO-MANY EXTENSION TABLES

One-to-many extension tables contain multiple rows corresponding to one row in base table. Unlike 1:1 extension tables, which are of type "Extension," these tables are of type "Data (Public)." The names of these tables end with suffix _XM. 1:M Extension tables also contain the generic columns (ATTRIB_xx) that can be used to store custom attributes. Unlike 1:1 extension tables that store data for one business component, 1:M extension tables store data for multiple business components. The data is grouped based on the Type column. Each business component can retrieve the data for specified type.

From configuration point of view, there are lot of changes between 1:1 and 1:M extension table's configuration. Important objects participating in 1:M Extension table are described in Table 7.5.

Table 7.5 Objects Participating in 1:M Table Configuration

Sl. No.	*Participating object*	*Description*
1.	Business component	A new business component is required, with its fields mapped to the columns of the 1:M extension table. Three important (Additional) fields required are as follows: PAR_ROW_ID: Mapped to foreign key field used in 1:M link NAME: A unique name for this record to make it unique for each parent record TYPE: As discussed previously, this value is used to group values in table, in order to be fetched by business components configured to fetch this type of records
2.	Link	In order to establish a master–detail relationship between the two business components. The new business component created in step-1 acts as a "Detail" business component in this relationship
3.	Business object component	In order to establish the master–detail relationship discussed in Step 2, we need a business object component defined with child business component as the new business component, created in Step 1

7.5 EXTENSION COLUMNS

Extension columns are used by developers to store custom attributes. They provide the facility to extend the data model in order to store additional details, along with whatever is provided by Siebel data model. Extension columns can be of two types:

1. Extension columns in extension tables
2. Extension columns in base tables

7.5.1 Extension Columns in Extension Tables

These are the columns present or added by developer in extension tables. They can be either already included with Siebel data model or can be created by developers. Those that are provided in Siebel data model are "Static Extension Columns," and are named in the form (ATTRIB_nn), where the value of nn may be from 01 to 47. Modifying or deleting these columns is not recommended.

Those columns that are added by developers in extension tables are "Customer Extension Columns," and are named with prefix X_.

7.5.2 Extension Columns in Base Tables

Extension columns can be added to base tables as well, provided the underlying relational database system supports the addition of extension columns to base tables. If it is allowed by database system, it is always recommended to add extension columns in base tables, instead of Extension tables, due to the impact on performance. If the extension columns are added in extension tables, then an additional SQL query is required to join the extension table.

7.6 INTERSECTION TABLES

In certain cases, the relationship between two entities is 1:M from either side. Consider the relationship between School and City. One City can have multiple schools, and one School can be present in multiple cities. Hence, both School : City and City : School are 1:M relationships. These kind of relationships are known as M:M relationships.

We use intersection tables to implement M:M relationships between two business components. Typically, at user interface level, M:M relationships are implemented by using two different master–detail views, showing the M:M relationship in the form of two 1:M relationships in either direction. This is illustrated in Fig. 7.1 [1].

Figure 7.1 shows 1:M relationship in Account : Contact, where one Account is associated with multiple contacts. Figure 7.2 [1] shows this relationship in opposite direction, that is, one contact is associated with multiple accounts (Contact : Account = 1 : M).

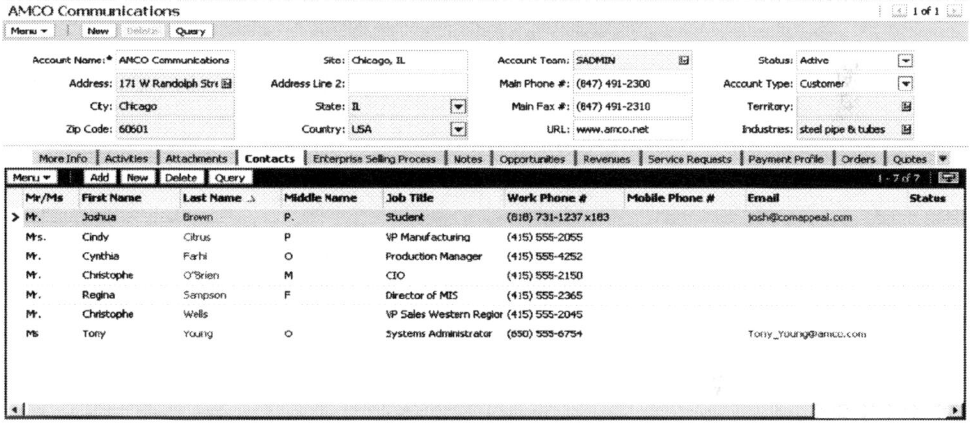

Fig. 7.1 *Account:Contact = 1:M (Source: Siebel Bookshelf V8.1)*

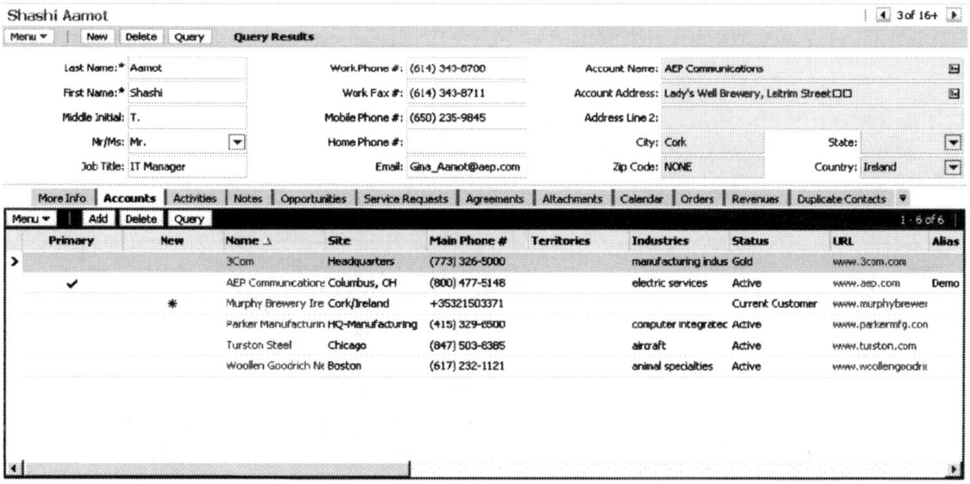

Fig. 7.2 *Contact:Account = 1 : M (Source: Siebel Bookshelf V8.1)*

Both the views, if seen together, depict M:M relationship between Account and Contact entities. But practically, it is not possible to implement M:M relationships between two tables directly, without data redundancy. Hence, we need a third table, working as an intermediary between the two tables participating in M:M relationship. It is implemented in the following way:

Suppose two tables, School and City have M:M relationship between them, such that City : School = 1 : M (i.e., One City can have multiple Schools) and School : City = 1 : M (i.e., One School can be there in multiple cities.). To implement this relationship, we will require a third table, say "School – City." This table will have 1:M relationship, both with School and City table. Consider Fig. 7.3 below.

Actual Relation:

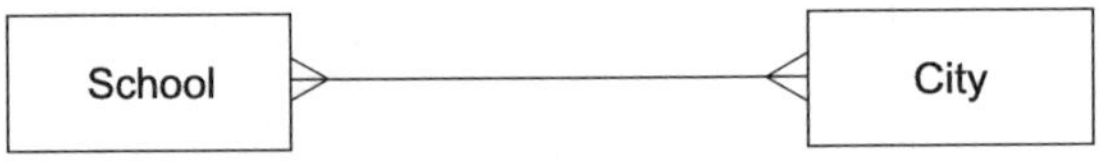

City

City_Id	*Name*
C_001	City-One
C_002	City-Two

School

School_Id	*Name*
Sch_01	School-One
Sch_02	School-Two

Implemented as:

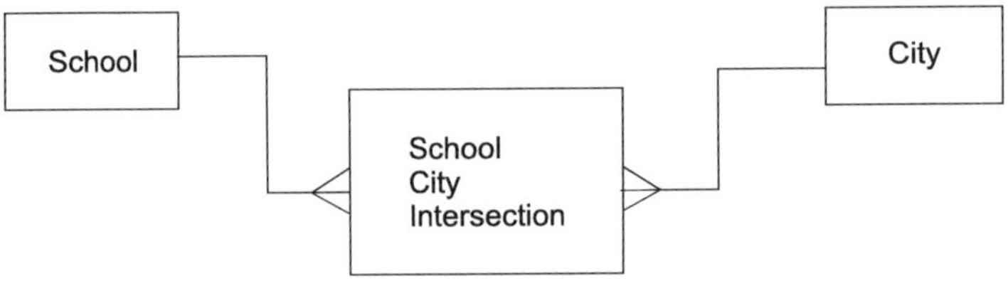

School–City (*Intersection table*)

Id	*School_Id*	*City_Id*
01	Sch_01	C_001
02	Sch_02	C_002
03	Sch_01	C_002
04	Sch_02	C_001

Fig. 7.3 *M:M relationship in the form of two 1:M relationships*

As we can see in Fig. 7.3, two tables School and City have M:M relationship between them. To implement this relationship, we have constructed a new table, "School - City," which serves as an intersection table between these two tables. Both the tables have 1:M link with the intersection table. Intersection table contains the records that associate the primary key fields of both the tables. As we can see the "School - City" intersection table, each record associates the records from School and City table. In this way, we can implement M:M relationship between two tables, without creating any data redundancy in tables.

Hence, we can say that for implementing M:M relationship between two tables, we need one intersection table, and two 1:M links. But apart from these two objects, there are several other objects involved in this task. The following section discusses about these objects.

7.6.1 Objects Involved in Implementing M:M Relationship

1. **Intersection Table:** Intersection table is used to associate records between the base tables of the two business components, participating in the M:M relationship. Each row in intersection table contains the association with one record each from both the base tables. This association is done by using two columns in intersection table, which serve as foreign key columns to both the base tables. These columns are identified in interparent and interchild properties of link (Discussed in next point).
2. **Link:** A link object is used to define the 1:M relationship between two business components. This relation is called as master–detail relationship, in which one business component acts as master, while the other one as detail. We will discuss more about Link object in Chapter 12. Three most important properties of a Link object used to implement M:M relationship are as follows:
   - Inter table property: This property holds the name of an intersection table between the two base tables participating in M:M relationship.
   - Inter parent column property: The intersection table's column identified by this property holds the ROW_ID values from the base table corresponding to master business component. In intersection table, this column works as a pointer to the associated rows in master business component's base table.
   - Inter child property: The intersection table's column identified by this property holds the ROW_ID values from the base table of detail business component. In intersection table, this column works as a pointer to the associated rows in detail business component's base table.
3. Business components: Implementing M:M relationship requires two business components, master business component, and detail business component. The applets that display data in master–detail view in user interface get data from these business components. These business components are specified in the link object definition as Parent (Master) and Child (Detail) business components. The important fields from these business components are their ROW_ID fields. These fields are specified in link object's inter parent column (master business component) and inter child column (detail business component) properties, and are used to establish the

relationship between them. We will discuss more about business components in Chapter 8.

4. Business object: Business object contains the two business components participating in the relationship, along with the link defined between them. Link is specified in the "Link" property of business object's child object "Business Object Components." We will discuss more on business objects and business object components in Chapter 9.
5. Business Object Components: "Business object components" is the child object of "business object" object type and contains a list of business components present in business object. Each business object has a "primary business component." All those business components in "business object components" list who have nonempty "Link" property are the child business components of primary business component. The link property defines the link used to establish the connection between the parent and child business component.

The flow diagram in Fig. 7.4 shows the implementation of master–detail relationship between two business components using a Link, and the role played by their corresponding base tables and intersection table. The diagram shows the implementation of 1:M relationship between the business components. For implementing M:M relationship, we will need just one more link with 1:M relationship in reverse direction of current link, that is, the master in first link should be the detail for second and vice versa.

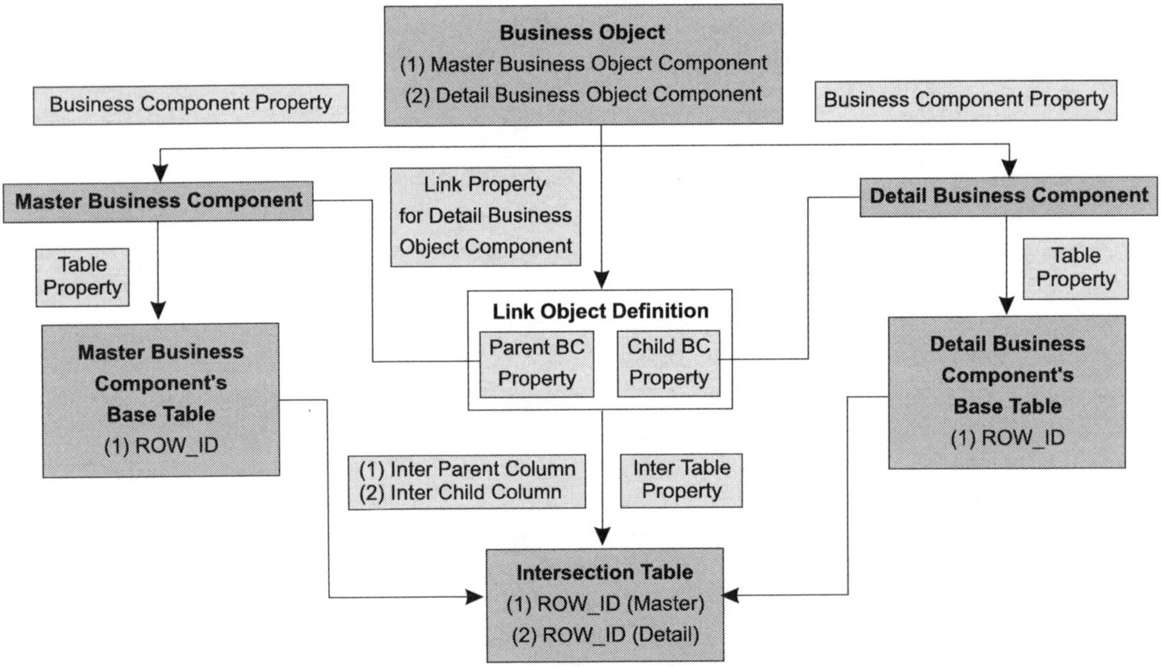

Fig. 7.4 *Master–detail relationship between two business components*

7.7 S_PARTY TABLE

The main aim of party model is to represent data in the form of a single set. This set can be a single person, or a group of persons, such as organization, company, and so on. The most common use of party model is to provide abstraction between various set of people, companies, and other legal entities. Siebel data access technology makes use of party model, and it is implemented by using a common base table for all such accesses, that is, S_Party table. All the related tables are implicitly joined as extension tables to S_Party table. Table 7.6 lists various extension tables of the S_Party table.

Table 7.6 Extension Tables of S_PARTY Table

Serial number	*Data type*	*Extension table name*
1.	Contacts	S_CONTACT
2.	Employees	S_CONTACT
3.	Accounts	S_ORG_EXT
4.	Users	S_USER
5.	Positions	S_POSTN
6.	Households	S_ORG_GROUP
7.	Business units	S_BU

7.8 SYSTEM AND INDEX COLUMNS

7.8.1 System Columns

System columns are special columns, as they appear in all the tables in Siebel database. Each table contains a subset of system columns such that the same subset of columns does not appear in every table. Table 7.7 lists some commonly used system columns.

Table 7.7 System Columns

Serial number	*System column*	*System field name*	*Description*
1.	ROW_ID	Id	• Present in all tables • Works as a unique identifier of each record present in the table • Mostly used for implementing joins with other tables • Business component's Implicit field "Id" is mapped to ROW_ID of its base table. Implicit fields are not displayed as child objects of business components in object list editor

Serial number	*System column*	*System field name*	*Description*
2.	LAST_UPD	Updated	• Stores the date when the record was last updated
3.	LAST_UPD_BY	Updated By	• Stores the user who updated the record most recently • Stores in the form of ROW_ID from S_USER table corresponding to the user who made the changes
4.	CREATED	Created	• Stores the date and time when the record was created
5.	CREATED_BY	Created By	• Stores the user who created the record • Stores in the form of ROW_ID from S_USER table corresponding to the user who created the record
6.	PAR_ROW_ID	–	• Present in all extension tables, _ATT and _T tables • Foreign key to the ROW_ID columns of corresponding base tables

7.8.2 Index and Index Columns

7.8.2.1 Index object

As discussed in previous sections, table and column object definitions logically represent the physical data present in underlying DBMS. In a similar way, index object definition logically represents the physical index present in underlying DBMS. Just like standard tables and columns, we cannot modify or delete standard indexes, but we can create custom ones, if required. The standard indexes present in Siebel are named with prefix S_.

Some important properties of index object are listed in Table 7.8.

Table 7.8 Properties of Index Object

Serial number	*Property*	*Description*
1.	Name	Stores the name of physical database index
2.	Unique	Stores TRUE or FALSE. These values decide whether multiple rows with the same value are allowed
3.	Type	Identifies the style that describe the index. It can have the following four styles: • Primary Key Value: Indexed on ROW_ID column • System Value: Standard Siebel indexes, which cannot be modified • User Key Value: Contains unique combination of columns, which is defined by developer • Extension Value: Creates by default when developer adds a new index

7.8.2.2 *Index column*

Index column object type is the child of index object. It is used to associate one column with its parent index object definition. Table 7.9 lists the important properties of index column object type.

Table 7.9 Index Column Object Properties

Serial number	*Property*	*Description*
1.	Column Name	Specifies the column object definition to be included in parent index object definition
2.	Sequence	It is mandatory property, which specifies the order of this column relative to others in the index. This value is mandatory. We must specify this value even if there is only one column in index
3.	Sort Order	Stores value either "Asc" or "Desc." The former sets the sort order for the index column as ascending, while the later sets it as descending

7.8.2.3 *Creating custom indexes*

The flow diagram in Fig. 7.5 encapsulates the steps to create custom indexes.

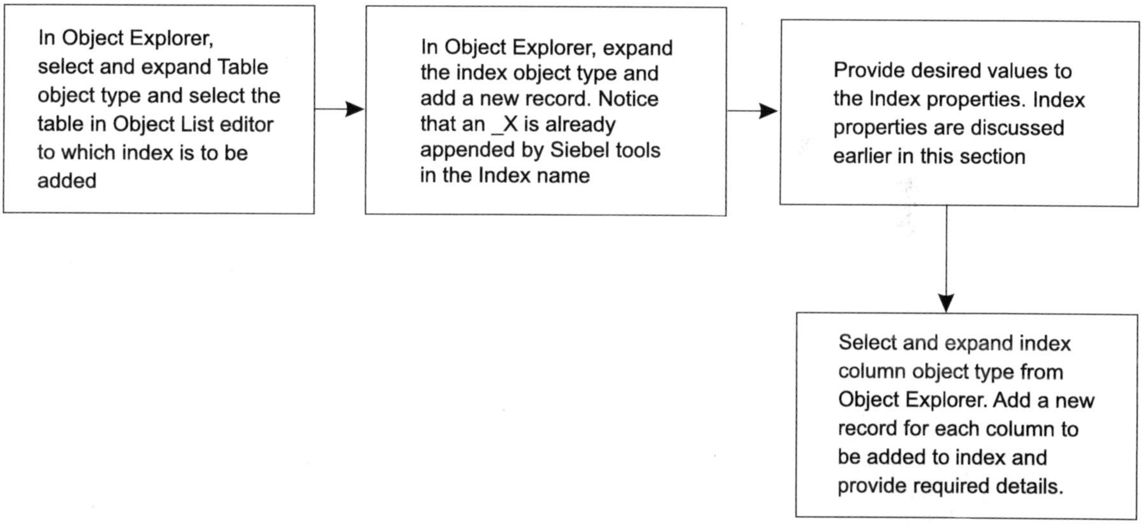

Fig. 7.5 *Steps to create indexes*

Things to remember:

1. Do not delete custom indexes from Siebel repository when they are no longer required. Just inactivate them by checking the "Inactive" property check box.
2. Generally, new indexes are required in new tables. After creating indexes, they should be thoroughly tested to ensure that they do not degrade the performance.

7.9 DATABASE EXTENSION

Siebel applications have predefined data model, which cannot be modified. To customize the environment, we have certain options for extending Siebel database. Chart 1 provides a high-level look on various database extension options available for developers. But before moving ahead with the discussion of these options, let us first understand various guidelines for extending Siebel data model.

7.9.1 Guidelines for Extending Siebel Data Model

1. Add extension columns to base tables (Fig. 7.6) when:
   - Data stored in extension columns is used very frequently. If we use a join to extension table in this scenario, it may result in the degradation of performance due to frequent execution of join.
   - Displaying additional attributes in list applet.

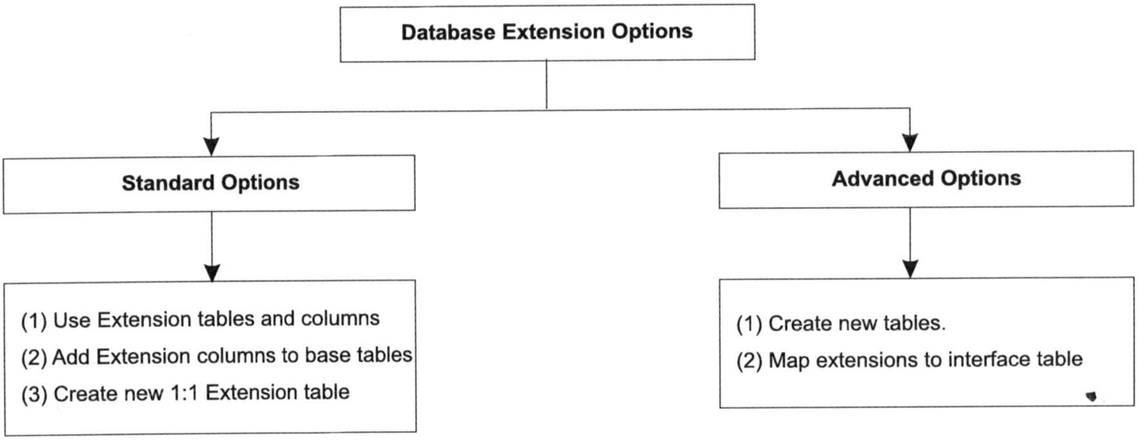

Fig. 7.6 *Database extension options*

2. Use columns from extension tables when:
   - 1:M relationship is required, and data is accessed very infrequently
   - Displaying additional attributes in form applets
3. Static extension tables and columns should be preferred over other options. Static extension tables and columns are the part of Siebel data model, and hence we do not require schema or physical database level changes.
4. Any bulk changes to schema should be planned and implemented at the beginning of the project, so that it should not impact any other developer's work. If bulk schema level changes are required in the midst of project, make sure that it is intimated and distributed to all mobile users to ensure proper synchronization in development.
5. Columns and indexes names should not be greater than 18 characters in DB2 environment.
6. Special attention is required while using extension columns as foreign key columns. They can be used while pointing to the business objects with enterprise-wide

visibility, but should be avoided for limited visibility business objects, such as service requests or account.

7. Data cannot be imported to foreign key columns using EIM, as some of the required EIM object types cannot be configured by customers.

7.10 DATABASE EXTENSION OPTIONS

In this section, we will have a brief discussion on various database extension options, represented in Chart 1. The guidelines discussed in previous section should be remembered and applied while implementing any of the options discussed here.

7.10.1 Standard Database Extensibility Options

7.10.1.1 Using static extension tables and columns

This includes the use of static 1:1 and 1:M extension tables.

1. **Using static 1:1 extension tables:** 1:1 Extension table is already discussed earlier in this chapter. Here, we will discuss some of the guidelines while using these tables and columns. A 1:1 extension table contains extension columns of various types. They are listed in Table 7.10. Before using these columns, we should ensure that they are not already in use by Siebel standard configurations. To ensure this, select the field object type in Object Explorer and search for following:
   - Enter the name of the column to be searched in column property
   - Enter the name of extension table in join property

If query does not return any record, the column is available to be used. If query returns any record, the column is unavailable. In this case, do not inactivate the existing field in order to use the column for other purpose.

Table 7.10 Available Extension Columns

Serial number	*Data type*	*Number of columns*
1.	Varchar(255)	1
2.	Number	12
3.	Date	10
4.	Varchar(100)	5
5.	Varchar(50)	10
6.	Varchar(30)	5
7.	Char(1)	4

2. **Using static 1:M extension tables:** 1:M extension tables have suffix _XM in their name. Just like 1:1 extension tables, these tables have generic columns that can be

used by developers. There are more than 20 predefined static 1:M extension tables. Using 1:M extension tables is discussed in detail in later part of the Chapter (section 7.4) " Using 1:M Extension tables."

3. **Adding extension columns to base tables:** Extension columns are added to base tables when the data access stored in these columns is frequent. Adding extension columns to base tables avoids the use and execution of join between base and extension tables, which may create performance degradation if executed frequently. Before adding extension columns to base tables, we should review and remember the guidelines to extend data model, discussed earlier in Section "Guidelines to Extend Siebel Data Model." Apart from them, other guidelines are discussed below:
   - All the extension columns should comply with the data type limitations of all DBMS types used in Siebel enterprise. This includes server, local, and mobile databases.
   - Always provide a default value to the extension columns added as mandatory columns to the tables having one or more rows of data.
   - Do not use the reserved key words in the names of the extension columns.
   - Once added in physical table, a column cannot be removed.
   - Extension columns cannot be added to tables of type Data (Private).

Figure 7.7 illustrates the steps required to add an extension column to base table.

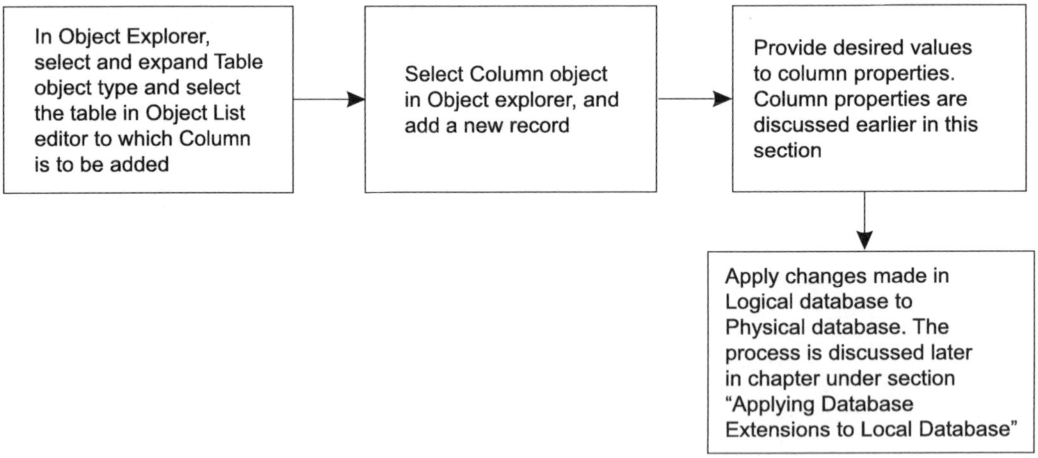

Fig. 7.7 *Steps to add extension columns to base table*

4. **Creating new 1:1 extension tables:** Custom tables should be created when the required goals cannot be achieved by using the existing standard extension tables and columns. Figure 7.8 illustrates the steps to create custom 1:1 extension table by using Object List Editor.

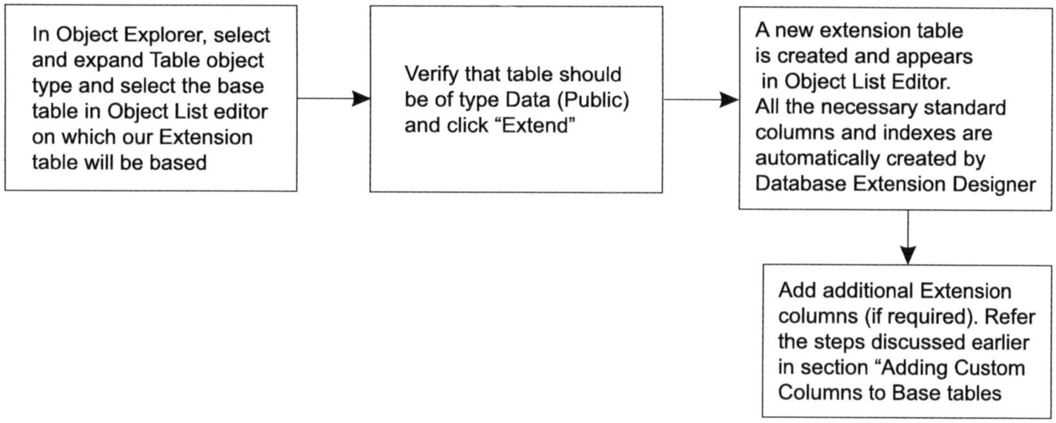

Fig. 7.8 *Steps to create new 1:1 extension table*

There are certain things to remember while creating new 1:1 extension tables. The first and most important thing is to review and follow the "guidelines for extending data model." Some additional guidelines are discussed below:

1. Do not extend the extension tables (tables of type "Extension" or Extension (Siebel)) directly if it is required. The suggested approach is to extend the base table of the extension table that is required to be extended.
2. New docking rules are not required for custom extension tables, as the data is routed based on the docking rules of their base tables.

All the three options discussed till here form standard database extensibility options. In next part, we will discuss about the advanced database extensibility options, where we will discuss about "Creating New tables."

7.10.2 Advanced Database Extensibility Options

7.10.2.1 Creating new tables by using new table wizard

New table wizard allows us to create new stand-alone tables, intersection tables, and extension tables of type Data (Public), Data (Intersection), and Extension. It is always suggested to analyze other options, such as using static extension tables to meet the required goals, before deciding to create a new table. Also, we MUST explicitly grant permissions on the tables that we create. Figure 7.9 illustrates the steps required to create new tables.

(Refer and Follow the "Guidelines for Extending Data Model.")

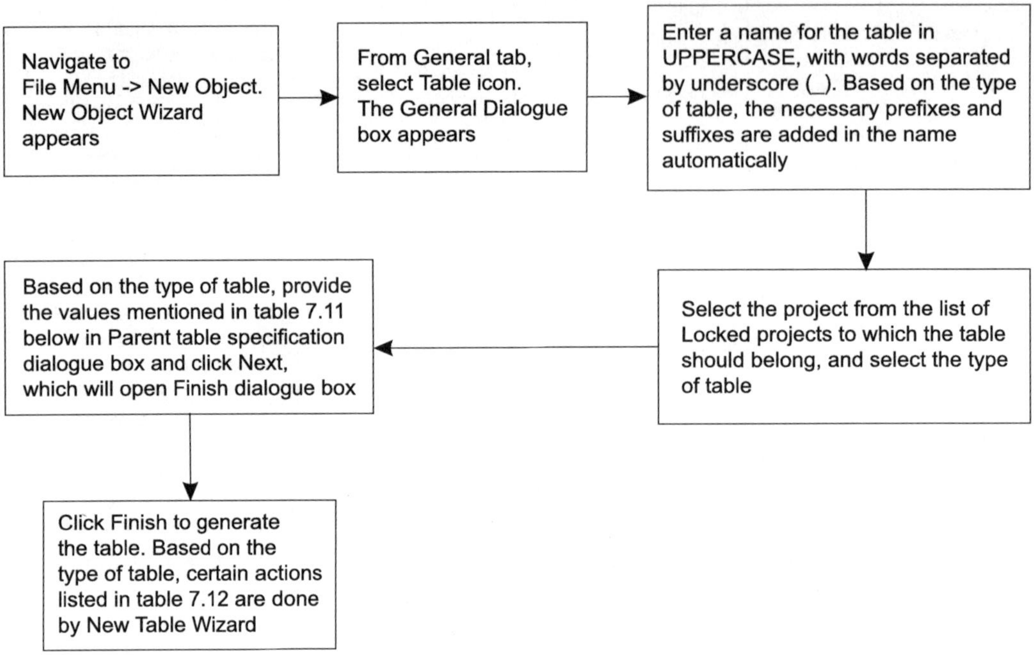

Fig. 7.9 *Creating new tables*

Table 7.11 Parent Specification Dialogue Box Values

Serial number	*Table type*	*Parent specification dialogue box value*
1.	Stand-alone table	Dialogue box is not visible
2.	1:1 extension table	Select the value from pick list. The pick list displays only the tables of type Data (Public)
3.	M:1 extension table	Select the value from pick list. The pick list displays only the tables of type Data (Public)
4.	Intersection table	Select the values of two parent tables from the pick lists. The pick lists display only the tables of type Data (Public). Also, we will need to enter the names of Foreign Key columns for both the tables

Table 7.12 Actions Performed by New Table Wizard

Serial number	*Table type*	*New table wizard actions*
1.	Stand-alone table	1. Generates system columns 2. Generates P1 index on ROW_ID column

Serial number	*Table type*	*New table wizard actions*
2.	1:1 Extension table	1. Generates system columns 2. Generates P1 index on ROW_ID column 3. Sets type of table = Extension 4. Generates PAR_ROW_ID column with base table's name as foreign key table 5. Generates U1 index with PAR_ROW_ID and CONFLICT_ID
3.	M:1 extension table	1. Generates system columns 2. Generates P1 index on ROW_ID column 3. Generates PAR_ROW_ID column 4. Generates U1 index with PAR_ROW_ID, TYPE, NAME and CONFLICT_ID 5. Generates M1 index with TYPE and NAME
4.	Intersection table	1. Generates system columns 2. Generates P1 index on ROW_ID column 3. Set s type of table = Data(Intersection) 4. Two foreign key columns for the two parent tables 5. U1 index with these two foreign keys, TYPE and CONFLICT_ID

7.11 SUMMARY

Table and column objects form the base for all the configuration work carried out by using Siebel tools. They represent the data from underlying base tables and make it available for other objects for accessing and modification. They form a layer of abstraction between the physical schema and Siebel objects by using the data from it. Moving ahead, we will look on business components, which makes the data from various tables available to applets.

REFERENCE

1. Siebel Bookshelf V8.1. Nov, 2008. Available from: www.oracle.com .
   Pdf name: Configuring Siebel Business Applications.
   Page 99, 100. Figures 12 and 13.

Chapter 8

BUSINESS COMPONENT

This chapter discusses about the most basic part of Siebel configuration; Business Component. Business Components can be considered as a logical blanket of abstraction over database tables, which present columns from various database tables to be accessed and modified. Every Business Component has one Base Table and one or more Joined Tables (If Required). Data from these tables is made available for applets to be displayed at User Interface. Every Applet has an underlying Business Component, from where it fetches the data to be displayed. Columns of tables used by a Business Component are mapped to it fields, which in turn map to Controls and List Columns in applet.

Major topics covered in this chapter are:

- Introduction to Business Component
- Important objects involved in configuring business component
- Steps to configure business components
- Important properties of business component
- Things to remember while configuring business component
- Business Component Fields
- Important properties of Field object type
- Special fields (System and Calculated fields)

8.1 BUSINESS COMPONENT

Business component is a blanket that logically represents one or more tables, providing a base for insertion, updating, and selection of data from underlying tables. Business components basically represent a specific functional area, such as Contact or Account. One advantage of business component is that they can be included and used in multiple object definitions. These business components may or may not be related to each other, based on the information present in them. While creating a business component, the user has to provide a base table for that, which is the source of its main data. Apart from base table, business components can access the data from other tables by using joins that we will discuss later.

Let us take an example to understand the significance of business component. Suppose our requirement is to show all the data related to schools in a city. This data should contain school details, information about its branches across various cities, students' details, and courses offered by it. Suppose, in our database, we have three tables; say SCHOOL_DTLS, CITY_DTLS, and STUDENT_DTLS containing data for schools, cities, and students, respectively. Since we want to access this data in same applet, we need a business component with one of these tables as its base table, and the other two tables Joined to it. An applet based on this business component (Applets are discussed in Chapter 10) will be able to access and display all the data from these three tables. Hence, we can say that our business component has taken all the three tables into a "Blanket," allowing applets to access data from all of them. Figure 8.1 shows this relationship.

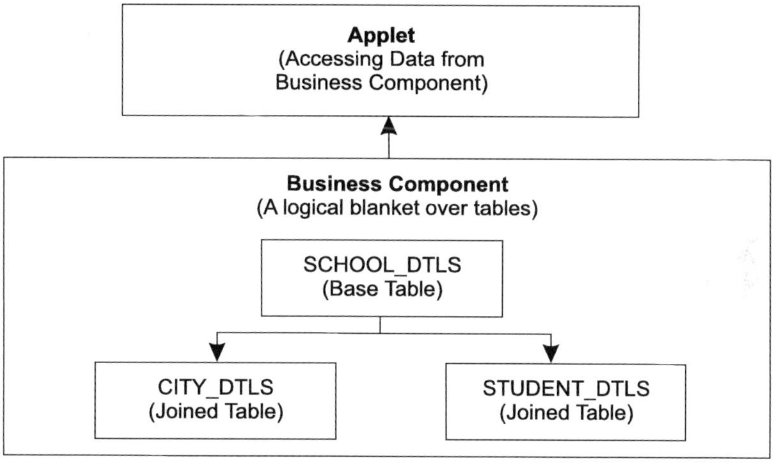

Fig. 8.1 *Table, business component, and applet relationship*

Before moving ahead with our discussion on configuring business components, let us have a quick look on various objects involved in the process.

8.2 IMPORTANT OBJECTS INVOLVED IN CONFIGURING BUSINESS COMPONENTS

Some of the important objects involved in configuring a business component are listed below:

1. **Table:** Represents the underlying base table of business component. Business component represents data from this table (along with the tables joined with it). The columns of this table are mapped to fields in business component.
2. **Column:** Column is the child object of table object. Columns are mapped to fields in business component.
3. **Business Component:** Business component is the logical representation of underlying base table and joined tables. It makes the data from these tables available for applets to be shown in UI.
4. **Fields:** Field is the child object of business component object. They are mapped to the columns from underlying base table. In case of join, fields represent the data from corresponding columns from joined table.

5. **Project:** Project object represents the project to which business component belongs.

After this brief discussion, let us move ahead to discuss the steps to configure a business component.

8.3 CONFIGURING BUSINESS COMPONENTS

This section focuses on the steps to configure a business component. We will need all the objects discuss in previous section to configure a business component.

For configuring a business component, navigate to Object Explorer and select the project name from the drop-down list, at the top. By default, we will see "All Projects" selected there. A project represents a collection of all the business object types, specific for a particular task, like the project FS Repair is a collection of all object types, such as business components, screens, views, and applets that are specific to service and repair functionalities of a business. After selecting the project to which business component should belong, do the following:

1. Click on Business Component from the Object Explorer. Object List Editor gets populated with all the available business components.
2. To create a new business component, choose New Object from File menu.
3. Select the BusComp icon, and click OK. The New Business Component wizard appears on the screen.
4. Select a Project, a Master Business Component, and click Next.
5. A Single Value Field dialogue box appears.
6. Select a column from base table and enter the desired name for the Business Component field, and click Finish.

On finish, we will find the newly created business component in the Object List Editor, where we can define the properties required for the business component. Some of the important properties of a business component are discussed in next section.

8.3.1 Important Properties of Business Component

Following are the key properties for the business component:

1. **Class:** This property represents the C++ class that implements the business component's functionality. There are certain functionalities that are common for all business components, such as sort, search, get or set field values in records, undo, redo, create and delete records, commit changes, and bookmark. By default, the class property of business component is having value of CSSBusComp or CSSBCBase. We can change this property by using the drop-down list available at the property field. CSSBusComp is at the top of the Siebel application's hierarchy of business component classes. All other specialized classes are derived from this class.
2. **Name:** This property represents a unique name for the business component.
3. **No Delete, No Update, No Insert Properties:** Obvious from the name, if these properties are set to TRUE, we cannot do any data manipulation operations.
4. **Table:** This property shows a list of SQL tables in a pick list. These tables are used to retrieve the records and populate the data in most of the fields.

5. **Search specification:** Search specification property is used to put a condition on the records supplied to an applet from a business component. If this property is blank, there is no restriction on the records being supplied to be viewed in applet. This property contains various fields of the business component, along with various operators, to impose a conditional expression. Records from business component that fulfill these conditions are allowed to be supplied to the applet.
6. **Sort specification:** This property is used to impose a sort order on the records being supplied to applet from a business component, based on the fields in business component. This property, if not blank, represents the name of the field in the business component, based on which the data represented in applet can be sorted.

8.3.1.1 Things to remember about sort specifications

There are certain rules that should be kept in mind while providing sort specifications:

- Field names in the sort specification should be separated by commas.
- The maximum length for a sort specification is 255 characters.
- If the sort specification is blank, the records are returned in the order in which they occur in the table.
- Include (DESCENDING) or (DESC) after the field name, as in "First Name (DESCENDING)," to indicate that a field in the list sorts in descending order. If we do not specify a sort order, ascending order is used.
- Never enclose a field name in square brackets (as in [First Name]).
- There are three values that are sorted {Y, N, and NULL} when we include a check box field in a sort specification. If descending order is specified for sorting, the order is NULL, Y, and N.
- If we include a multi-value field in a sort specification expression, the sorting is on the initial value of the multi-value field. This makes sense only if the multi-value group uses a primary foreign key. Also, this sort specification does not sort the underlying multi-value group (multi-value groups or MVGs are discussed in Chapter 16). If it is required to sort the underlying MVG, we will need to create a sort specification in the MVG's detail business component.
- In case of pick lists (discussed in Chapter 15), the sort specification property is left blank by default. If left blank, pick list uses business component's sort specification for sorting the records. In order to sort the pick list's records by using a sort specification other than business component's sort specification, we need to write it in the "Sort Specification" property of a pick list. The sort specification of a pick list overrides business component's sort specification while sorting the records in pick list.
- Calculated field cannot be sorted, as they do not have a fixed value.
- If a predefined query exists, it can potentially override a sort specification that has been defined as a property of the business component.
- Sort specifications can have a negative effect on performance. This is particularly true when the sorting is on fields based on joins or on fields based on new, non-indexed extension columns.

8.3.1.2 *Things to remember about search specification*

After sort specifications, we will now concentrate on defining search specifications in business component. Search specification property is used to restrict the records that are provided to an applet from this business component. Search specification basically uses business component's fields, along with various operators, to create a conditional statement. A set of records that evaluates the value of conditional expression to true is provided to the applet for displaying all other records being excluded.

While populating data in an applet, the data manager generates a SELECT statement, and uses the search specification as a WHERE clause. If two applets belonging to same business component appear in same view, then anyone of them should have search specification, as SELECT statement supports only one WHERE clause. If both of them have search specification defined, then it should be same for both.

Also, the search specifications should not be defined both for the applet and underlying business component. In case both the applet and business component have search specifications specified, then applet's search specification is appended to that of business component.

Syntax rules for search specifications: Following are certain syntax rules to be kept in mind while configuring search specifications (Table 8.1).

Table 8.1 Search Specification syntax rules

Operators/ constants	*Rules/comments*
Standard comparison operators (=, <>, >, <, >=, and <=)	Used to compare a field to a constant, or a field to another field. e.g., [TYPE] = "Mobile Device" • Fields name should be enclosed in square brackets
String constants	• Always enclosed in double quotes • String values are case sensitive e.g., [TYPE] = "Mobile Device" and [TYPE] = "MOBILE Device" are two different specifications.
Logical operators (AND, OR, and NOT)	Used to combine or negate expressions. Case is ignored in these operators. e.g., [NAME] IS NOT NULL and [NAME] <> "N"

In addition, the search specification expression should not be more than 255 characters.

It should be kept in mind to avoid using joined fields and calculated fields in search specification, as they may negatively impact the performance. Also, the operators NOT or OR should be used carefully, as they may force a full database scan while executing the search specification condition.

8.4 THINGS TO REMEMBER WHILE CONFIGURING BUSINESS COMPONENTS

Certain good practices should be kept in mind before creating a business component. They are as follows:

- Create a new business component if it is really needed. Always try to reuse the existing business component by modifying them. This will result in lesser number of business components, resulting in a small repository that will be easier to manage and update. Always try to create your application in a manner that it allows the maximum reuse of existing business components. For example, you can have an implementation where a particular group of users can create accounts, while the other may only view them. Instead of creating a new business component and setting the No Insert, No Delete and No Update properties to TRUE, you can define a new applet and set these properties to TRUE for the applet.
- If creating a new business component is really needed, avoid copying business components based on a specialized class, unless you intend to create a true clone of the original business component (with the same functionality), and then apply minimal changes. Also, if you clone a business component, copy the links used by that business component, and then update the copies with the new business component name.
- Always try to avoid parentheses in the names of business component's fields, as it may create SQL error while performing query on that field. An SQL query expects a valid SQL statement within parentheses.
- The field URL must be named URL and the class of the business component must be set to CSSBC Base for the hyperlinking functionality to work correctly.
- The names of business components that represent child entities should not contain their parent entity, for example, ABC Child Component instead of ABC FS Repair Child Component. Similarly, the applets that are based on these child business components should only reflect the name of the business component itself, for example, ABC Child Component Form Applet instead of ABC FS Repair Child Component Form Applet.
- The field URL must be named URL and the class of the business component must be set to CSSBC Base for the hyperlinking functionality to work correctly.

8.5 BUSINESS COMPONENT FIELDS

With a lot of discussion over business components, let us take one step ahead and start discussion on configuring business component's fields.

Fields are the child objects of business component. Data is provided to all the controls and list columns in applets from business component's fields. Fields represent data either from database table's columns (base tables, extension tables or joined tables of business component), obtained through a column object definition or the value calculated from the values of other fields. Such fields are called calculated fields and these fields are not stored in database.

While configuring field-column mapping, it should be kept in mind that we are not mapping multiple fields to same column of base table. This will lead to data integrity issues. The SQL query also fails as it tries to access the same column twice in one query. It can also lead to error messages while trying to update the data and data loss for denormalized columns that reference the column.

To identify the table and column name from where our field is getting data, we will need to look on the column and join properties in field's definition. The nonblank join property identifies the join object definition, through which our field is getting data from other joined table or extension table. A blank join property indicates that the field is getting data from business component's base table's column.

8.5.1 Field Data Types

Each field has a particular data type, which represents the data that can be retrieved from or sent to database server by using this field. All the data types available for fields start with DTYPE_. The appearance of field values of some data types, such as DTYPE_NUMBER and DTYPE_CURRENCY, can be controlled by using Windows Control Panel. Table 8.2 lists various data types for business component fields.

Table 8.2 Field Data Types

Data type	*Maximum length of data*	*Description*
DTYPE_NUMBER	22	Supports the data of type Number
DTYPE_CURRENCY	22	Refers to data of type Currency
DTYPE_INTEGER	22	Refers to data as Whole Number ranging from -2147483648 to 2147483647
DTYPE_BOOL	1	Refers the data of type Boolean, which is stored as Y or N. This data is often displayed as Checked/Unchecked or TRUE/FALSE
DTYPE_PHONE	40	Stores the data of type Number. Displays the Phone Number data. The displayFormat property is ignored for this data type
DTYPE_TEXT	2 KB	Stores to data of type VARCHAR. Refers data as string less than or equal to 4000 bytes. We can define certain text properties by using "ForceCase." ForceCase = "Upper" or Forcecase = "Lower" will force the text to all uppercase or all lowercase after the users tabs out of field. Similarly, ForceCase = "FirstUpper" forces the first letter of each word to uppercase. If we do not use any of above options, then by default, data will be stored in mixed cases, as it is entered by user

Data type	*Maximum length of data*	*Description*
DTYPE_ID	15	Stores the data of type VARCHAR. Refers to data as an autogenerated primary key
DTYPE_DATE	7	Refers to the data as a Date
DTYPE_DATETIME	7	Refers to data as Date and Time. We can use the properties called "Date" and "Time" to display the Date and Time portion of the value, respectively. The values are presented by using the format specified in Windows Control panel
DTYPE_TIME	7	Used for data of type Time, ignoring any additional information (e.g., Date)
DTYPE_ UCTDATETIME	30	Used where the mapped field represents date information, including both date and time components, which is stored in database in UTC time. UTC time is equivalent to Greenwich Mean Time without any adjustments of daylight saving. Fields of this type should correspond to database columns of type U, and the display values for these fields will be converted to/ from UTC based on the default time zone specified in the user's preferences
DTYPE_NOTE	16 KB	Refers to data as a long string <= 16KB
DTYPE_ID	15	Used to make a field a primary key, which is generated automatically by application
DTYPE_INTEGER		Field of physical type Number that can store whole numbers ranging from - 2147483648 to 2147483647

8.6 ADDING FIELDS TO AN EXISTING BUSINESS COMPONENT

One of the most important tasks in day-to-day configuration activities is to add fields in existing business component. For most of the change or enhancement requests, designers and developers prefer adding fields to existing business component over creating new business components.

Following are the steps to add a field in existing business component:

1. In Object Explorer, select business component object type. All the available business components in selected project get populated in Object List Editor.
2. Select the business component to which field is to be added and select its "Field" child object. All the available fields in this business component get populated in Object List Editor.

3. In Object List Editor showing the list of business component's fields, add a new record.
4. Provide the values to the properties and step off the record. The new field gets added in a business component.

While adding fields to business components, it should be kept in mind that all the required properties should be populated. The next section discusses about important properties of field object.

8.7 PROPERTIES OF FIELD OBJECT TYPE

Following are some of the important properties of the "Field" object type:

1. **Name:** A unique name for the field.
2. **Join:** The value of this property shows the column from the joined table from which field is getting data. If this property is blank, it shows that field is mapped to base table's column.
3. **Column:** This property represents the table column from which field is getting value. If the join property is nonblank, column property contains the name of joined table's column, else it contains the name of base table's column. (This property is left blank for calculated fields, which is discussed later.)
4. **Calculated:** If the property is checked, it shows that this field is a calculated field (Calculated field is discussed later.)
5. **Calculated Value:** If the "Calculated" property of field is checked, this property gets activated. It contains the expression from which the field derives its value.

8.8 SPECIAL FIELDS

Special fields are different from general fields, and are meant to serve some special purpose. In this section, we will discuss about these fields, along with their significance. The fields discussed in this section are as follows:

- System fields: These fields represent data from system columns. They are provided by default in all business components in standard Siebel business applications.
- Calculated fields: These fields are not mapped to any column. They derive their data from other fields in business component based on the expression provided in "Calculated Value" property of field. These fields have "Calculated" property set to TRUE.

8.8.1 System Fields

System fields represent data from system columns. They are provided by default in all business components. We do not need to explicitly add these fields, such as other fields. These fields are provided by default as they are crucial for almost all business components. Table 8.3 lists various system fields, along with their significance.

Table 8.3 System Fields

Serial number	*System field*	*System column*	*Description*
1.	Id	ROW_ID	Primary key for the table
2.	Updated	LAST_UPD	Contains the date when the row was last updated
3.	Updated By	LAST_UPD_BY	Contains the login Id of the person who last updated the row
4.	Created	CREATED	Contains the date and time when the row was created
5.	Created By	CREATED_BY	Contains the login Id of the person who created this record
6.	Last Updated – This Database	DB_LAST_UPD	Contains the date when the row was last updated in this database

8.8.2 Calculated Fields

Calculated fields derive their data from other fields in business component, based on the expression present in "Calculated Value" property.

Some of the important points about calculated fields are as follows:

- Calculated fields are not mapped to any column in base table
- Values of calculated fields are not stored in database
- Calculated fields have their "Calculated" property set to TRUE
- Calculated fields use the expression written in "Calculated Value" property to derive their value. This value changes with the values of fields for different records

The expression used by calculated fields to derive their value is built from field names, standard functions, and string, numeric and logical operators. Following is an example of such an expression:

IIf((([Member Id] <> NULL) AND ([Customer Id] = JHKQ84)), 'Y', 'N')

In this expression, we have put a condition that says "If Member Id is not null and Customer Id is equal to "JHKQ84," the value of field should be "Y," else "N."

Here, Member Id and Customer Id are business components.

8.8.2.1 Expression builder

We can create the expressions for calculated fields by using expression builder provided by Siebel. Figure 8.2 shows the expression builder.

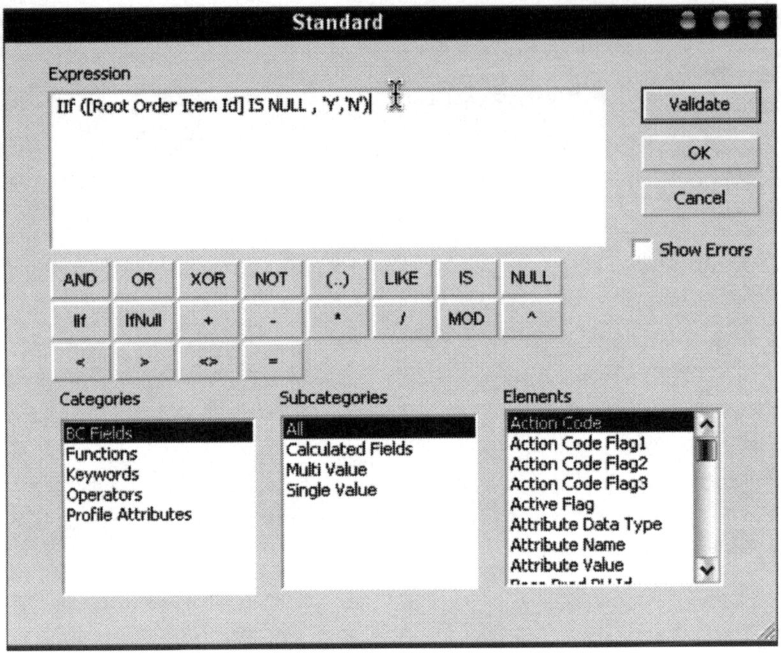

Fig. 8.2 *Expression Builder*

This expression builder can be invoked by clicking the control shown in Fig. 8.3. This button is present at right corner of "Calculated Value" property for a particular field.

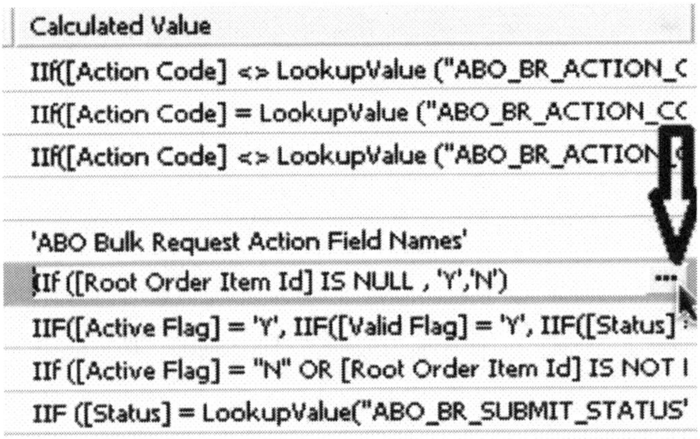

Fig. 8.3 *Control to invoke Expression Builder*

The expression builder helps us to create and validate the expression created by us. The "Validate" button present in it validates the expression and displays the error, if any, in it.

8.9 SUMMARY

Business components are one of the most basic and important part of Siebel configuration. They provide a base for developers to use the data in physical database. They work as single access points for the applets based on them to access and modify data from various database tables (Business Component's Base table and Joined tables). Also, they make it easy for architects to plan their strategy before starting the actual development work.

Chapter 9

BUSINESS OBJECTS

Business Objects represent a specific functional area of an organization. At User Interface level, they form the base for a View, which shows the data specific to a particular functional area. Business objects logically group all Business Components specific to that functional area. For a Business Component to display its data in a particular view, it should be added as the child of Business Object for that view.

In this chapter, we'll explore various details about Business Objects. Major topics covered in this chapter:

- Introduction to Business Objects
- Important objects involved in creating business objects
- Configuring Business Objects
- Things to remember while configuring business objects

9.1 BUSINESS OBJECTS

A Business Object is a logical group of related business components. It represents a specific functional area of an organization. In user interface level, business object forms the base for a view. Every view has a corresponding business object, whose data it displays. The applets present in the view get their data from their business component. Hence, it is mandatory that the business components corresponding to the applets that we want to show in our view should be added in view's underlying business object.

Every business object has a master business component. The business components working as child business component are linked to it by using "Link" object definition. Let us again take the example of "School" and "City" to elaborate our discussion. We will assume that in user interface, our view name is "City," and it contains two applets, one form applet showing the details of City and one list applet below it showing the list of schools present in city.

Here, we are trying to show many schools present in one city, that is, we need to implement a 1:M relationship between City and School. In our business object, "City" business component will be the master business component, and "School" business component will be its child business component. Both of the business components should be added in business object, along with their corresponding "Link" relationship.

To add a business component in a business object, we need to add it in its child object, "Business Object Component." If we select "Business Object Component" in Object Explorer, the Object List Editor gets populated with the list of business components added in business object. In order to add "School" business component as a child business component in our business object, we will need to create a new record for "Business Object Component" child object, and provide the link used between "School" and "City" here.

As business object provides data to a view, and related views group together to form a screen, we can say that a business object works as a foundation for providing data to screens. However, there is no direct relationship between a business object and a screen object. Their relationship is established via views. The business objects corresponding to the views in a screen get related indirectly to the screen. The relationship between any two business components is unique in a business object, but they can appear together in other business object. For example, in case of M:M relationship, there may be two different views showing 1:M relationship between two business components, but in reverse direction. Considering the example of "School" and "City" again, there may be one view showing 1:M relationship between "School" and "City" (i.e., One School can be there in multiple Cities), and another view showing 1:M relationship between "City" and "School" (i.e., One City can have multiple Schools). For both the views, there will be different business objects in which "School" and "City" business components appear in 1:M relationship in opposite direction, but they cannot appear in same business object with multiple relationships with each other.

9.2 IMPORTANT OBJECTS INVOLVED IN CREATING BUSINESS OBJECTS

In this section, we will concentrate on creating business objects. Before moving ahead with our discussion, let us first have a brief look on various objects involved in creating business objects.

Important objects involved in creating business object are as follows:

1. **Business Object Component:** Business object component is the child object of business object. It contains the business components that are included in business object. These business components may or may not be the detail business components for the master business component of business object. This can be identified by seeing the "Link" property. If Link property for a business object component is nonblank, it means that this business component is working as a detail business component for the business object's master business component.
2. **Master Business Component:** Each business object has one master business component, identified in its parent business component property. All the business components added in business object component child object typically work as detail business components for this business component; however, there may be certain business components (with blank Link property) that are not detail business components for it.
3. **Detail Business Component:** These business components have nonblank link property value in business object component child object's properties. They work as detail business components for business object's master business component.

4. **Link:** Used to establish the master–detail relationship between business object's parent business component and child business components. In business object component child object definition, all child business components working as detail business component for business object's parent business component contain the link that identifies their master–detail relationship with business object's master business component.
5. **Business Object:** Used to supply data to a view. For a business component to display its data in a view, it should be added to the business object component child object of view's business object. Every business object has a master business component, identified in its "parent business component" property. The other business components added in business object component child object typically work as detail business component for its master business component.

9.3 CONFIGURING BUSINESS OBJECTS

The flow diagram shown in Fig. 9.1 shows the steps for configuring business object. Refer to the points listed in Section 9.4.

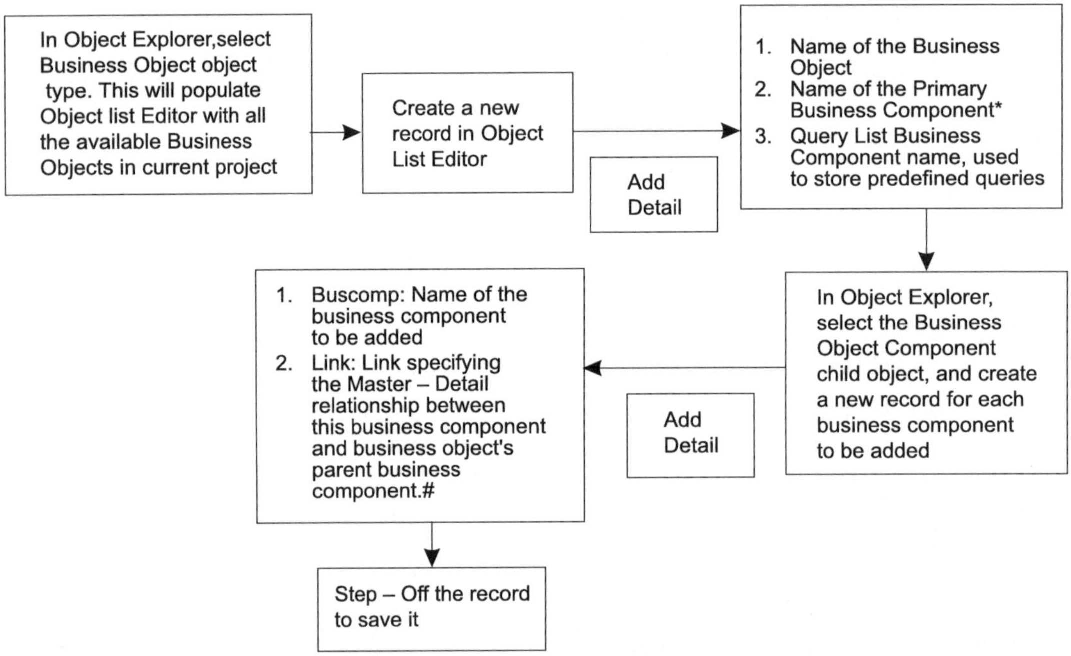

Fig. 9.1 *Steps to configure business objects*

* We cannot provide this value before adding records in business object component child object. Hence, after adding business components in business object component child object, provide this value.
# Links are provided for a business object component child record only when it has master–detail relationship with the business object's parent business component. For business components that are added in business object component but do not have master–detail relationship with business object's parent business component, this property is left blank.

9.4 THINGS TO REMEMBER WHILE CONFIGURING BUSINESS OBJECTS

1. Create new business objects only when it is the last option to fulfill our requirement. It is always suggested to use or modify the existing business objects as far as possible.
2. The relationship between any two business components is unique in a business object, that is, we can be added only once in a business object, and it can be linked to only one business component.
3. We have to add the business components corresponding to all the applets that we want to display in a view in its business object.
4. The applet based on master business component of a business object works as a driving or master applet in the view based on it. All other applets are the child applets of this applet.

9.5 SUMMARY

Business objects group related business components, and form the base for a view, which groups together related applets based on these business components. Hence, logically speaking, business objects allow the related applets to show their data together to the user. In Chapter 10, we will look on various types of applets, along with their significance, configuration, and use.

Chapter 10

APPLETS

In this chapter, we will discuss about various types of applets. Applets are the building blocks of user interface. They occupy a section in the view and provide a user-friendly environment to view and modify the data in underlying database. In Part 2, we have discussed about various navigation aspects of applets at user interface level. In this section, we will discuss about the steps to configure these applets, along with their various properties. Also, we will discuss about various types of special purpose applets and their significance.

Major topics covered in this chapter are:

- Introduction to Applets
- Creating List Applets
- Important Applet Controls
- Creating Form Applets
- Editing Applet layout
- Grid Layout
- Special Purpose Applets
  - Tree Applets
  - Pop Up Applets
  - Chart Applets

10.1 APPLETS

Applets occupy a section in the view and are the means by which a user can view, enter, and modify data from a single business component. Examples of applets are Form Applets, List Applets, Tree Applets and so on. They are basically the user interface objects that include data controls, such as fields, text boxes, and check boxes, as well as other types of controls, such as buttons that invoke methods and ActiveX controls.

Most of the actions performed by users at user interface using applets are already discussed in Part 2 of the book. In this chapter, we will concentrate on steps to configure them, along with their important properties and child objects.

We will start with list applets and then move ahead with other applets. During our discussion on configuring these applets, we will also elaborate their important properties, their role, and significance.

10.2 CREATING LIST APPLETS

List applets present the data in the form of a list of records. They allow us to view and modify the data in the list itself. Just like business component, a list applet creation starts from New Object Wizard. In this wizard, you will find an Applets tab. Click on this tab and double-click on List Applet icon, which will take you to List Applet wizard. In this wizard, you will provide basic details of List Applet.

On first page, you will find the following values to be specified (Table 10.1):

Table 10.1 Applet Properties

Field	*Comment*
Project	Select a project for the applet. Only locked projects will appear the drop-down list
Applet Name	Name of applet. This should be unique throughout the repository
Business Component	The name of business component to which the applet belongs. This will act as the parent business component for the applet
Display Title	The title for the applet that will be visible on user interface
Upgrade Behavior	Specifies the way the applet is handled during an upgrade. Let us select "Preserve" here

After filling these details, go to next page. This page will help you to specify a Web template for each mode of applet (Base/Edit/Editlist). The list of Web templates that you will see here will be filtered based on Web template type. To see all available Web templates, select "Show All Templates" check box. After selecting the appropriate Web template for your applet, click Next. This will take you to Web Layout – Fields page. From here, you can select which field from parent business component to be displayed in applet. By default, you will find all the fields selected. You can use all the fields, or can go for selecting specific fields based on need.

After selecting fields, you will need to select controls to be used for your applet. You can do this in next page. The selection process for controls is same as fields. Finally, review the information in final page and click on Finish. You can also go back and modify the information at any page.

The list of available controls that you will see to select from comes from Model HTML Controls applet. This applet specifies the available controls and to which template each control is mapped. You can modify the model applet if necessary by adding or removing controls from the applet.

A List Applet wizard performs the actions listed below. It takes the information passed by us as the base for performing these actions.

1. **Creates the list applet:** List Applet wizard creates the List applet based on the user's input, along with the other actions discussed next.

2. **Creates List Columns and Control:** These are the child objects of Applet object type and play a vital role in accessing and editing of data by user. Controls implement the user interface elements, such as buttons, check box, and text box. List columns implement fields in List applets. *In Form Applets, fields are implemented by using controls. We will discuss more on this while discussing form applets.*
   These are created by the List Applet wizard based on the information passed. Controls correspond to the controls added while creating the applet, whereas List columns correspond to Fields. Some of the important available controls are discussed in the next section.
3. **Creates the Applet Web Template for the applet:** Applet Web Templates are used to associate a Web template to an applet. Web templates determine how the applets look on user interface. They define the layout and format of applet. An applet can be displayed in five modes. They are as follows:
   - **Base:** This mode is used to make applet fields read-only. An applet, displayed in this mode, is a read-only applet and its fields can be modified only when user takes an action, such as clicking Edit button.
   - **Edit:** This mode allows user to edit, create, and query for the records. This mode is used with form applets. For example, Use Office system to give example of any editable form applet.
   - **Edit list:** Using this mode allows user to edit, create, and query for the records directly in the list applet. This mode is used with list applets. For example, Use Office system to give example of Editable list applet from application. You will understand it better while configuring a List applet in the next section.
   - **New:** This mode is used for creating a new record where the requirements for new mode are different from the edit or edit list mode.
   - **Query:** This mode is used for querying where the requirements for the query mode are different from the edit or edit list mode.

In a List applet, typically we define three modes: Base, Edit, and Editlist mode. If we want to define additional modes for an applet, we need to add templates in it. Following are the steps to manually associate an applet Web template to an applet. (These steps are common for all applet types.)

- Select our applet and expand the applet object in Object Explorer to see its child objects. Click on Applet Web Template object type.
- In the Applet Web Templates properties list, right-click and choose new record.
- Provide the following information to complete the record (Table 10.2):

Table 10.2 Applet Web Template Properties

Property	*Description*
Name	By convention, we use applet mode name in this property. For example, if we are using Edit Mode, the value of this property will be Edit
Type	This field is used to provide the Applet mode. (Base, Edit, Edit List, New, Query)
Web Template	This field names the Web template, used for the applet. We need to select the Web Template from the drop-down list, available in this field

4. **Creates Applet Web Template Items:** Applet Web Template Items, as clear from name, is the child object of Applet Web Template. They map the control (selected from the controls that you added while creating the applet) and list column (selected from the fields, that you added while creating the applet), to placeholder tags or locations on a Web template. Applet Web template items are automatically created when you drag and drop controls on to Web templates by using the applet layout editor or when you create an applet by using a New Applet wizard. (We will discuss more about applet layout editor in later sections). They contain the name of a control or list column as well as an identifier of a template placeholder. The placeholder determines its position of the control or list column in the Web page delivered at run-time.

Let us now discuss about how to create a new Applet Web Template Item and its properties. To create a new Applet Web Template Item, go to Applet Web Template object type (Applet -> Applet Web Template -> Applet Web Template Item), in the list, right-click and select New Record. Populate the following major properties:

Property	*Description*
Name	Name of the control or list item, which should be unique for the item
Control	Select any one control or field from those which you added in applet. Based on the selection you made in list applet wizard, it creates list columns and controls
Item Identifier	Provide an item identifier for this particular item. This should be a number only
Type	Specify whether this item is a control or a list item. If you have selected a field in "Control" property, this value should be a list item, and for controls, it should be control
Comments	Provide a brief comment to describe this particular item

10.2.1 Important Applet Controls

Some of the important controls available to be used with applets are discussed in this section. Most of these controls are common for all applets. For more details on various controls, refer to Siebel Object Reference Guide provided with Siebel Bookshelf.

1. **Button controls:** As the name implies, button controls are actually the various buttons that you will see on UIs. Button controls initiate an action when clicked. A button can invoke a built-in method or a custom method. The method that is invoked by a button control is specified in the Method Invoked property of a button. Following are the steps to associate a method with a button control:
    - In Object Explorer, select the applet object type and select the applet to which button control is to be added from Object List Editor.
    - In Object Explorer, select Applet User Properties, create a new record in Object List Editor, and provide the following values to the properties:

Name = CanInvokeMethod: <NameOfMethod>

Value = Y

2. **Combo box controls:** Just like VB, a ComboBox control consists of a field with a drop-down button attached at the right edge. A click to this drop-down button activates a selection list, from which we can select the appropriate value. The selected value replaces the previous value in the box. These controls are useful where we want user to select a value from the available values, instead of typing that value manually.
3. **CheckBox control:** A CheckBox control is used to check or uncheck a particular value. It is used to represent a TRUE or FALSE field with a data type of DTYPE_BOOL.
4. **ActiveX control:** This control allows to use an ActiveX control in the applet. Siebel tools do not support placing a frameless ActiveX control.
5. **Field and field label:** As you might have seen on UI, as fields display data in rectangular box. It has a native HTML type of TEXT. A field label specifies the label for the particular field in an applet.
6. **Drill down title:** This control represents the title for the applet, which can take a user to an appropriate view. (Use office system to provide a screenshot.)
7. **File:** This control provides a user interface element, which can be used to attach a file.
8. **FormSection:** A custom control, providing the capability to group the related fields in an applet. It can expand to fit the region where we place it. To set it apart, the label appears against the FormSection color defined in the cascading style sheet. (Use office system to provide an appropriate screenshot.)
9. **Link:** This control will create a HTML hyperlink in our applet, which will perform the specified task when clicked. In most cases, we use links to navigate between views. It is used with the controls that have "InvokeMethod" specified.
10. **MiniButtons:** As the name implies, these are the custom controls that appear as buttons in user interface. Examples of MiniButtons are MiniButtons, MiniButtonEdit, MiniButtonEditQuery, and so on. The look and feel of these buttons is defined in CCHtmlType.swf file. We can find this file in WEBTEMPL folder under our Siebel Installation folder. The .swf files are Siebel Web format files. These files are useful when we require additional HTML types along with the several control types supported by Siebel application. We can define our own HTML types by adding type definitions to the .swf file.

Just like Java, VB, or Dot net, whenever we click a button, a method is invoked. Hence, we have to define the method invoked property of the control, for which we want to use the MiniButton. This property can be a built-in method supplied with Siebel applications or a custom method programmed in Siebel VB or Siebel eScript. Also, to execute the method associated with the MiniButton, we should set the run-time property of the button control to TRUE.

11. **MailTo:** This is used with controls that contain e-mail address. Here, the control will appear as a link, and it will open the user's default e-mail program with the address filled in with the control value, when clicked or activated.
12. **Password:** As the name implies, it is a user interface element that is used to input a

password field, with the characters in the field masked by asterisk (*).

13. **RadioButton:** This control places a radio button control on UI. This is not used for custom configurations and is used for specialized applet classes.
14. **Text:** A text control is used to display the text in a rectangular box in UI. It displays data in a specific format, such as alphanumeric, date, currency, and so on, with or without the icons, such as calendar, calculator, MVG, and so on, based on the underlying business component field. This text can be editable/noneditable depending on whether text control is read-only or not. The HTML height property of this control determines the number of rows of text displayed in a text box.

10.3 CREATING FORM APPLETS

Form applets display the data in the form of a form. Unlike list applets, they display only one record at a time. They allow us to view and modify the data. We have already discussed about form applets during our discussion on navigating Siebel application. Here, we will concentrate more on configuring form applets.

For creating a form applet, do the following:

1. Go to New Object wizard and click on the Applets tab.
2. Now you can see all types of applets. Select Form Applet and click OK.
3. This will take you to Form Applet Wizard. Put following details in the wizard (Table 10.3):

Table 10.3 Form Applet properties

Field	*Comment*
Project	Select a Project for the Applet. Only locked projects will appear the drop-down list
Applet Name	Name of applet. This should be Unique throughout the repository
Business Component	The name of Business Component to which the applet belongs. Applet will use the data from this Business Component only
Display Title	The title for the applet that will be visible on User Interface
Use Grid Layout	Grid layout allows us to control the layout of Form Applet using Applet Layout Editor. By default, this check mark is selected. It is a good practice to configure Form Applets using Grid Layout

The information entered in wizard is used to create a new applet object and defining its properties.

- In the next window, if you have selected Use Grid Layout on the previous dialog, choose whether or not you want the applet to display in base mode. The appropriate Web template is automatically selected for edit mode. If you did not select the Use Grid Layout option on the previous dialog, select the Web templates you want to use for each mode. In most cases, using the Edit mode only is sufficient. However, you may want to use base mode too. For example, this is useful when you want the applet to be read-only until the user takes an action, such as clicking the Edit button. Or you may want to use base mode only. Only one mode is required.

- In the next layout, Web Layout – Fields Page, you will see the fields in underlying business component. You can select the fields that you require in your applet. You can select all the fields present.
- In second Web Layout – Fields Page, you can see the controls available for our form applet. *(These controls come from* ***Model HTML Controls applet****. This applet specifies the available controls and to which template each control is mapped. We can modify this applet by adding or removing controls from it)*. We can select which controls we want to use in our applet. We can select all the controls available.
- Click Finish on the final page after reviewing the information displayed there.

The Form Applet wizard creates the applet and supporting object definitions based on the selections we made. The Applet Layout Editor opens and displays the layout of the new list applet ready to edit. Based on the information we passed, the Form Applet wizard creates the form applet, creates the controls specified by us, and maps applet to the Applet Web Template and controls to Applet Web Template Items.

10.4 EDITING APPLET LAYOUT

The next step after configuring the applets is to edit the Web layout, that is, deciding the look and feel of applet on user interface. Editing Web layout basically means placing or replacing the controls and columns at desired places in applet, along with required buttons, menus, and other required user interface elements. Applet's Web layout is edited by using Applet Web Layout Editor. After creating the applet by using "New Object Wizard," the applet layout editor automatically opens to edit the layout. In order to edit the layout of existing applets, we need to right-click on that applet in Object List Editor and click on "Edit Web Layout" option.

Before we start editing Applet's Web layout, it is required to set the target browser in "Configuration Context" toolbar. If we do not set it, we will get an error message while opening the Web layout editor.

10.4.1 Editing Applet's Web Layout

1. Select the applet in Object List Editor whose layout we want to edit. Right-click on it and select "Edit Web Layout Option."
2. In Web Controls toolbar (typically appears at left hand side of Applet Layout Editor, shown in Fig. 10.1), select applet mode that needs to be modified (Base/Edit/Editlist/New/Query). The changes made in one mode are not navigated automatically to other mode.
3. In "Application" field of Configuration Context toolbar, choose the application for which the changes should be reflected.
4. Edit the applet layout. We can perform one or all editing tasks shown in Fig. 10.1.

Things to Remember

- *Typically, "Controls Window" opens automatically when we edit the applet layout with applet layout editor. If the window does not open, we can open it by navigating to Windows menu -> Controls window.*
- *If you are working to decide the applet layout for different configuration contexts, never change the context after the modification is started.*
- *In Language override mode, delete a control or list column only when it is required to be deleted from all languages. If it is required to remove the item from only one language, then just set its "Visible" property to "FALSE".*
- *Always avoid mapping nonbutton controls to applet's header and footer area, as they are designed to hold button controls.*

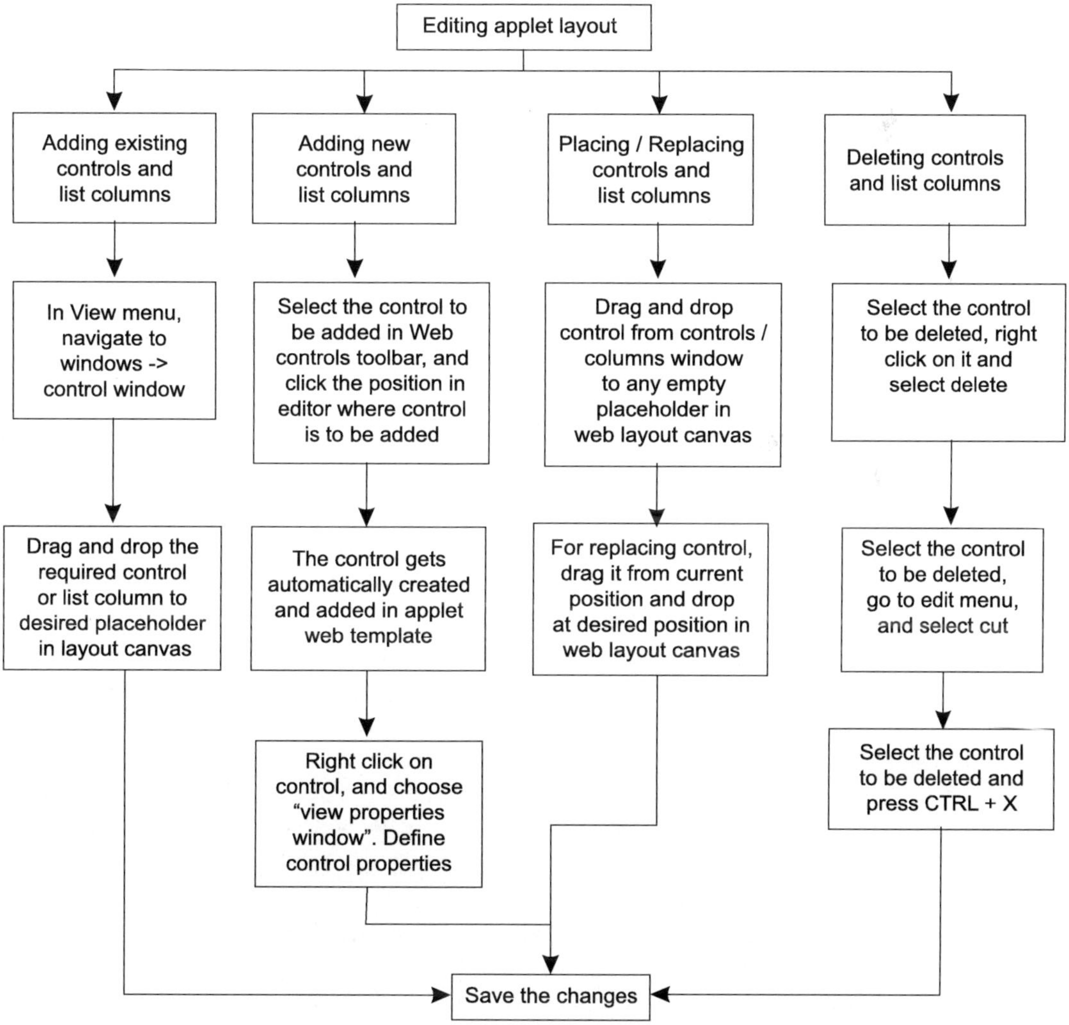

Fig. 10.1 *Tasks with Applet Layout Editor*

The tasks mentioned in Fig. 10.1 are the most basic tasks done while editing the applet layout. Apart from these tasks, there are some other tasks that can be done in applet layout editor. They are discussed in next section.

10.4.2 Other Tasks Done by Using Applet Layout Editor

1. **Preview:** We can also preview the changes that we made by using applet layout editor. Let us see how the applet will look in user interface. It does not give the exact look and feel of an applet, but shows a simpler and lighter version of it. To preview the changes made, right-click at any empty place on the applet layout editor and select "Preview" option. The "Preview" option gets checked in the list and applet preview opens. To come back to editing canvas, right-click on the preview and select "Preview" option again. This unchecks the "Preview" option and the applet layout editing canvas opens again.
2. **Editing display names of controls and list columns:** The captions of controls or display names of list columns can be changed directly in applet layout editor. For changing the names, we just need to double-click the control/list column in editor canvas, highlight the names and write new text. Once we navigate away from it, the new name gets assigned to it.

On providing a new name to control or list column, Siebel tools searches the symbolic string that exactly matches it. If a symbolic string is found that exactly matches the new name, it is associated with the control/list column. If there is no string that matches the new name, an error pops up telling to enter a new symbolic string in Object List Editor. We can also enter the value in "String Override" field in properties window. ***The new name is assigned to the control/list column only when either there is a symbolic string that matches with the new name, or we provide the value in string override field.***

3. **Displaying a control on the click of "Show More" button:** Siebel tools allow us to configure a control in such a way that it will be displayed in UI only when "Show More" button is clicked. For the rest of the time, the control is not displayed in UI. To configure a control in such a way, we just need to select the control in layout canvas, right-click on it and choose More option.
4. **Displaying a subset of controls or rows:** Siebel tools allow us to configure the applets in such a way that they will show a limited subset of controls (in form applets) or rows (in list applets) in user interface by default. To see other controls or rows, users have to click on Show More or Less button present at the top right corner of applet. For configuring the applets in such a way, Siebel tools provide two methods: ToggleLayout and ToggleListRowCount. The former is for form applets, whereas the later is for list applets. Following are the steps to do these changes:
   - In applet layout editor, drag and drop any one of the above-mentioned controls (Togglelayout for form applet, ToggleListRowCount for list applets) on the empty placeholder at top right corner of applet.
   - Set the following values to the properties in the Properties window (Fig. 10.2) [Ref. 1]:

Property	Value
HTML Bitmap	BTTNS_MORE
HTML Display Mode	EncodeData
HTML Icon Map	■ Form applet: ToggleLayout ■ List applet: ToggleListRowCount
HTML Type	Link
Method Invoked	■ Form applet: ToggleLayout ■ List applet: ToggleListRowCount
Name	■ Form applet: ToggleLayout ■ List applet: ToggleListRowCount
Read Only	FALSE
Runtime	FALSE
Show Popup	FALSE
Sort	FALSE
Visible	TRUE

Fig. 10.2 *Source: Siebel bookshelf*

- Close the editor after saving the changes and step off the applet to save the changes to it.
- Open the "Applet Web Template Item" grandchild of the applet to which we made the changes, and verify that it has an item with the name of the control added (Togglelayout for Form Applet, ToggleListRowCount for List applets).

10.5 GRID LAYOUT

Grid layout is basically a design technology that allows us to modify the form applet's Web layout without the need of directly modifying the underlying Web template. It is incorporated in applet layout editor, and provides a palette of layout tools for configuring the layout of form applets. Table 10.4 lists various tasks that can be done in grid layout, along with the steps to perform those tasks.

Only the applets based on grid layout applet Web templates support the features of a grid layout in Applet Layout Editor. Typically, grid layout applet Web templates have the name ending with "GridLayout," for example, "AppletFormGridLayout" template. The Web template for an applet can be seen by navigating to "Applet Web Template" child object of applet object. The "Web Template" property of this child object contains the name of underlying Web template used for the applet.

For performing these tasks, select the applet for which changes are required, right-click on it and select "Edit Web Layout." This will open the Web Layout Editor canvas. Choose the applet mode to be edited in Web controls toolbar's "Mode" field and move ahead to perform the following tasks:

Table 10.4 Tasks that can be done in Grid layout

<table>
<tr><th>Sl. No.</th><th>Task</th><th>Steps to follow</th></tr>
<tr><td>1.</td><td>Changing existing form applet's Web template to grid layout based Web template</td><td>1. Select View menu -> Toolbars -> Web Controls option. This opens the Web controls toolbar
2. Click "Change Template" button
3. In Choose Template dialogue box, select "Applet Form Grid Layout" for Form Applets and "Applet Popup Form Grid Layout" for pop-up form applets
4. Edit the layout based on requirement</td></tr>
<tr><td>2.</td><td>Converting existing form applets to grid layout based applets*</td><td>1. In Object List Editor, select the applet(s) to be converted to grid Layout, right-click, and select "Convert to Grid Layout"
2. Move the applets to be converted to selected window
3. Select Additional options# and click Next</td></tr>
<tr><td>3.</td><td>Placing or replacing the controls in grid layout</td><td>1. Do one of the following in editor canvas
• Drag and drop the control to desired location
• Move control to desired location by using arrow keys</td></tr>
<tr><td>4.</td><td>Aligning controls relative to selected control</td><td>In editor canvas, select all the controls to be aligned by holding the Shift key. All the controls are aligned to the last item selected in this selection</td></tr>
<tr><td>5.</td><td>Aligning controls</td><td>1. In editor canvas, hold the Shift key and select all the controls to be aligned. Then click any one of the following buttons based on the requirement:
<table>
<tr><th>Requirement</th><th>Button</th></tr>
<tr><td>Align left</td><td></td></tr>
<tr><td>Align right</td><td>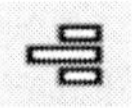</td></tr>
<tr><td>Align middle (horizontally)</td><td>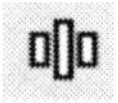</td></tr>
<tr><td>Align middle (vertically)</td><td></td></tr>
<tr><td>Align top edge</td><td></td></tr>
<tr><td>Align bottom edge</td><td></td></tr>
</table></td></tr>
<tr><td>6.</td><td>Aligning label text</td><td>In editor canvas, hold the Shift key and select the label text to be aligned. Press any one of the following buttons based on the requirement:
<table>
<tr><th>Requirement</th><th>Button</th></tr>
<tr><td>Align left</td><td></td></tr>
<tr><td>Align right</td><td></td></tr>
<tr><td>Align center</td><td></td></tr>
</table>
• If any of the item selected is not a label, these buttons will be disabled</td></tr>
</table>

<table>
<tr><th>Sl. No.</th><th>Task</th><th>Steps to follow</th></tr>
<tr><td>7.</td><td>Setting field tab order</td><td>1. Select Format menu -> Set Tab Order option
2. The Set Tab Order mode appears with all the controls having a sequence number next to them. This sequence number indicates the current tab order for the controls
3. Click on the controls in the sequence that should define the new tab order
4. Save the changes and select Format menu -> Set Tab Order option. The Set Tab Order mode disappears</td></tr>
<tr><td>8.</td><td>Copy and paste the items</td><td>1. In editor canvas, hold down the Shift key and select all the items to be copied. Then select Edit Menu -> Copy option
2. Go to the Web template where the copied items should be pasted. Select Edit Menu -> Paste
• If we paste to the same applet but in different mode, only Applet Web Template Items are created
• For all other scenarios (pasting to a different applet or pasting to same applet's same mode), new controls and Applet Web Template Items are created</td></tr>
<tr><td>9.</td><td>Resizing the controls relative to selected control</td><td>In editor canvas, hold down the Shift key and select all the controls to be resized. All the controls get resized to the last control selected</td></tr>
<tr><td>10.</td><td>Resizing the controls</td><td>In editor canvas, hold down the Shift key and select all the controls to be resized. Then press any one of the following buttons based on requirement:
<table>
<tr><th>Requirement</th><th>Button</th></tr>
<tr><td>Resize the controls to same height</td><td></td></tr>
<tr><td>Resize the controls to same width</td><td></td></tr>
<tr><td>Resize the controls to same size</td><td></td></tr>
</table></td></tr>
<tr><td>11.</td><td>Resizing the grid layout canvas</td><td>Place the cursor on any one of edges (right, bottom, or bottom right), drag it till the grid layout canvas resizes to desired size</td></tr>
</table>

* Before starting the conversion, make sure that Configuration Context is the same for which changes are to be made. Also, the tools language should be set to the language in which changes should be reflected in case of "Language Override Mode."

\# Good practice: Always backup the existing Applet Web Templates by selecting "Backup existing Applet Web Templates Option."

Things to remember about Grid Layout

- The position of a control or label in grid layout is identified by "Item Identifier" property of Applet Web Template Item object (grandchild of Applet object)

- Like Applet Layout Editor for other Web templates, the Grid Layout Editor does not compress the empty space in the applet. Hence, we should place all the controls at required location without leaving any empty space in grid layout.

10.6 SPECIAL PURPOSE APPLETS

Till now, we have discussed about the most widely used types of applets, that is, form applets and list applets. In this section, we will look on various special purpose applets. The applets that we are going to discuss here are as follows:

1. Tree applets
2. Pop-up applets
3. Chart applets

10.7 TREE APPLETS

Tree applets work quite similar to Object Explorer in Siebel tools. They present the records in the form of a tree, allowing us to navigate through them in hierarchical way. The records in tree applet have a "+" sign at their left, clicking on which the child records associated to them can be accessed. The details about the selected record get populated in the list applet at the right of tree. This view is called as "Explorer View." Figure 10.3 shows an Explorer View, with a tree applet at left, and a list applet at right.

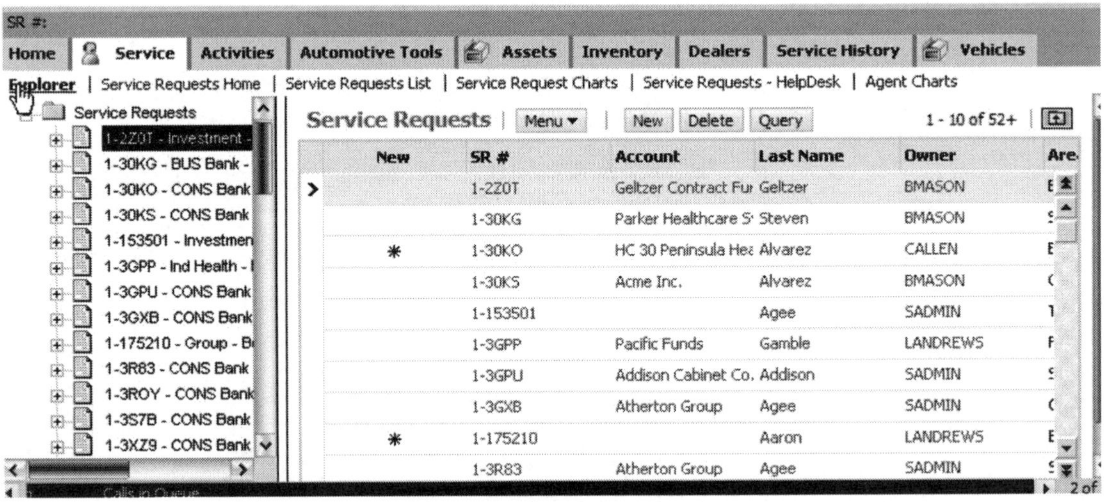

Fig. 10.3 *Explorer view*

10.7.1 Configuring Tree Applet and Explorer View

After a brief introduction of tree applet and Explorer View, let us now move toward the steps to configure them. Before starting our discussion, it is important to be aware of important objects involved in configuring a tree applet and Explorer View.

10.7.2 Important Objects for Configuring Tree Applet and Explorer View

Following are the important objects involved in configuring tree applet and Explorer View:

1. **Tree applet:** Tree applet is just a normal applet, with "Tree" child object defined. The configuration of a tree applet is similar to that of a normal applet, except that we have to define "Tree" child object definition for it. Also, the class of a tree applet should be set to CSSFrameTree. Tree object has one child object, "Tree Node." We will discuss about it in next points.
2. **Tree object:** Tree is the child object of applet object. It works as a join between applet and tree nodes, which attaches tree nodes to the applet. It is always named as "Tree." Its child object "Tree Node" contains the list of nodes that should be attached to applet.
3. **Tree node:** Tree node is the child object of a tree object, and contains the nodes that should be attached to applet. In a tree applet, all the folders present with a "+" symbol have a corresponding tree node defined. The hierarchical relationship presented in UI is implemented by using position property of a tree node object. A tree node object has following important properties:
   - **Display name:** Name of the folder displayed in UI.
   - **Applet:** Applet to be opened at right side when user selects the folder corresponding to this tree node.
   - **Position:** The hierarchical position of tree node in UI.
   - **Business component:** Should be same as the business component for the right side applet.
   - **Selected bitmap index:** Should have value 5, which corresponds to folder symbol.
   - **Label field:** Contains the field name that is used to populate the names in records list that gets displayed when the folder corresponding to this tree node is expanded by user in UI.
4. **View:** The configuration of Explorer view is similar to that of normal views. This view is different from other views as it has a tree applet mapped to it. Also, the list applet used at the right side is not mapped to this view. This applet is determined based on the tree node definition.

10.7.3 Configuring Tree Applet by Using Tree Applet Wizard

The flow diagram in Fig. 10.4 shows the steps to configure a tree applet by using Tree Applet Wizard:

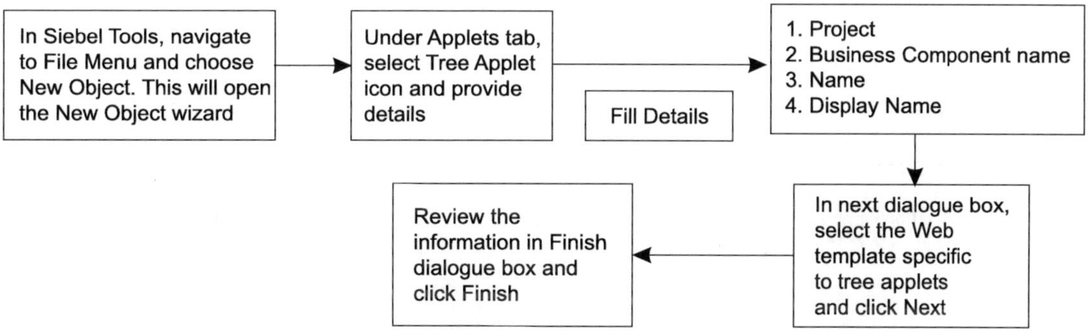

Fig. 10.4 *Steps to configure tree applets*

10.8 POP-UP APPLETS

Pop-up applets are typically used to implement dialogue boxes. In this section, we will discuss about configuring dialogue boxes and pop-up windows. The flow diagram in Fig. 10.5 presents the configuration steps for:

- Pop-up applets
- Pop-up views launched from pop-up applets

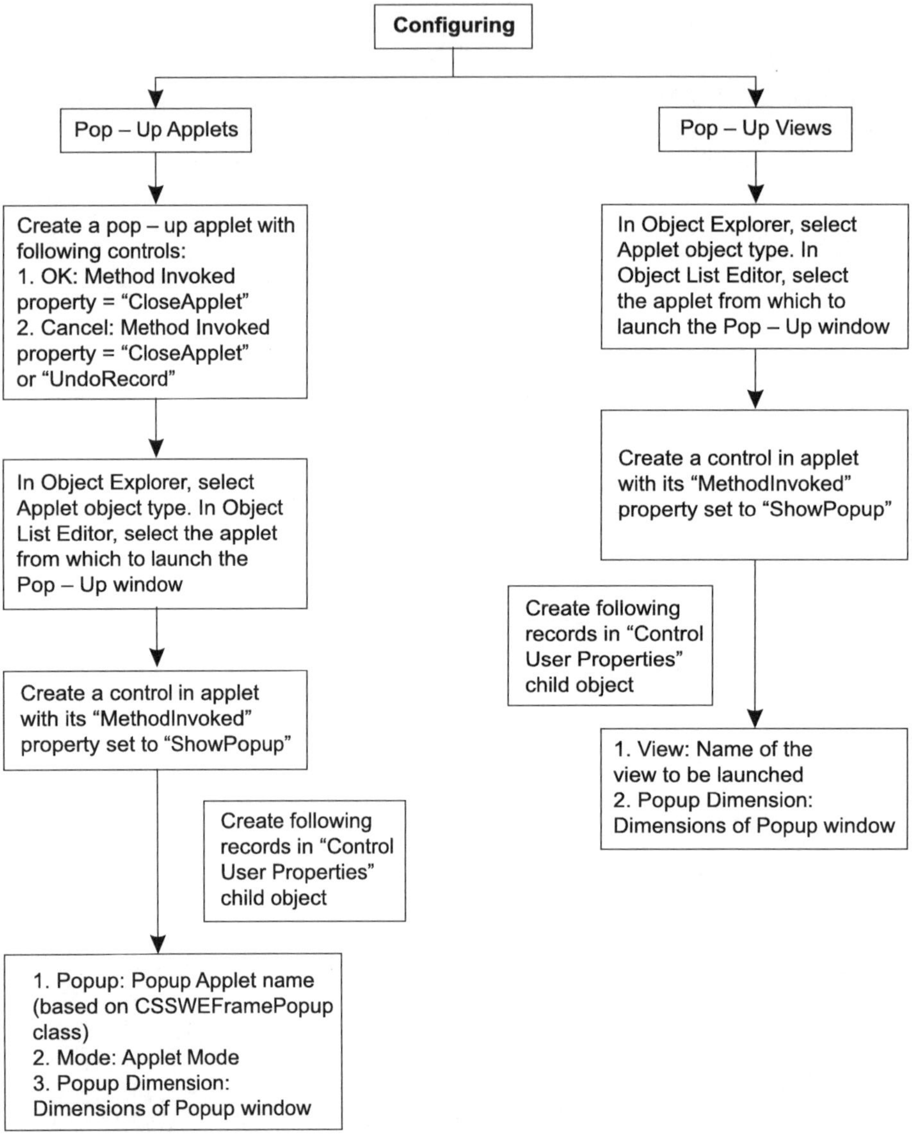

Fig. 10.5 *Pop-up applet and pop-up view configuration*

10.9 CHART APPLETS

Chart applets are used where it is required to display data graphically. These applets facilitate users with the data represented in the form of a chart, making the comparative analysis easy and systematic. Chart applets can display data in anyone of the following styles shown in Fig. 10.6[Ref. 2]:

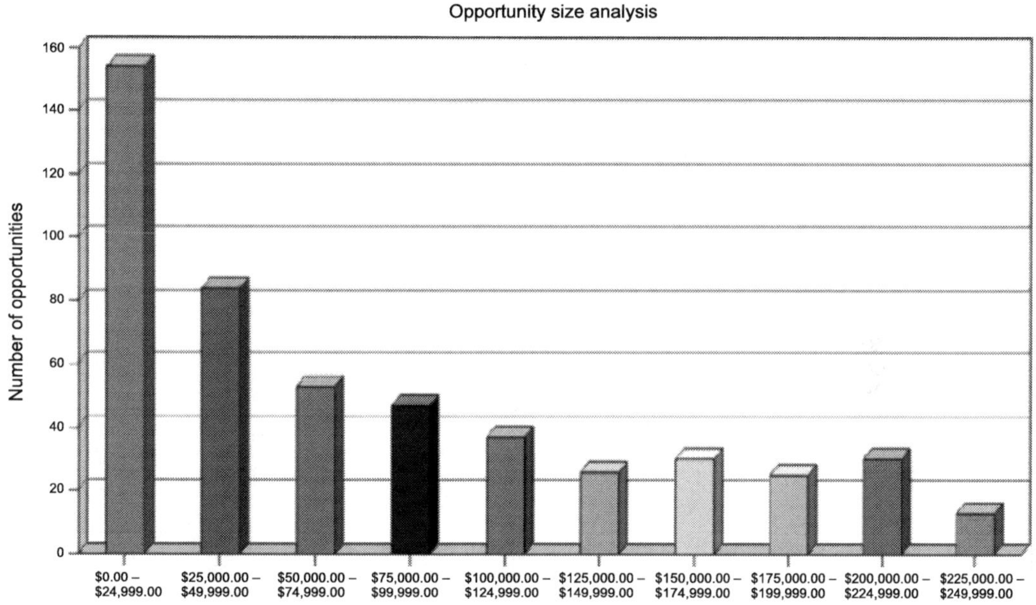

a. Bar chart

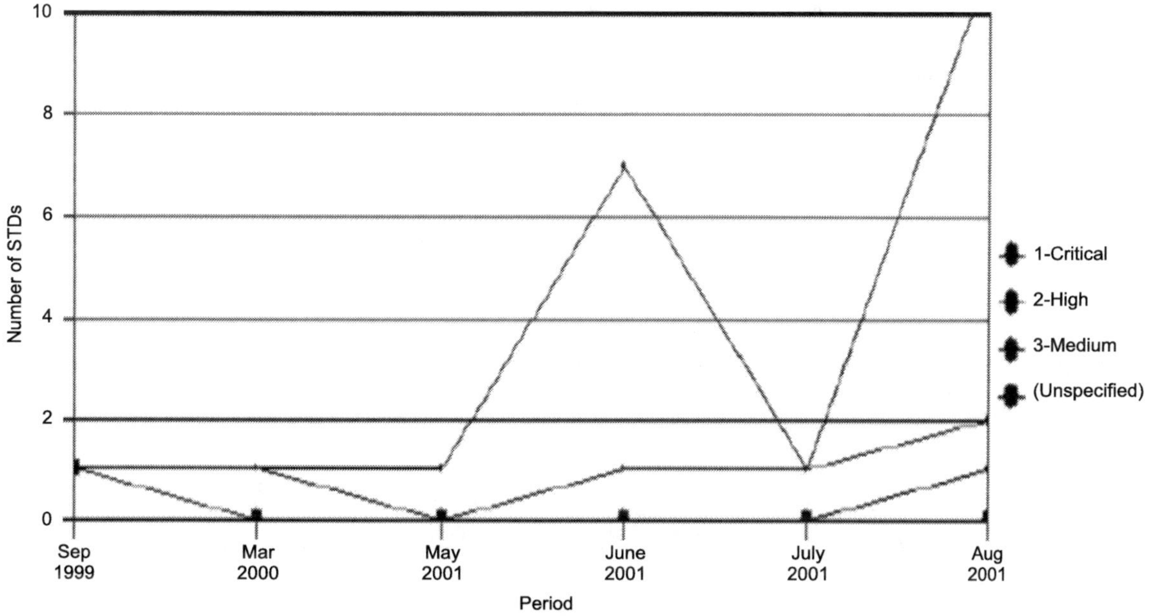

b. Line chart

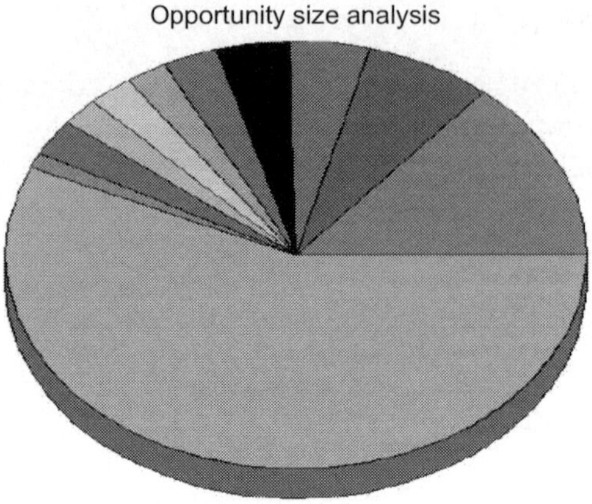

c. Pie chart

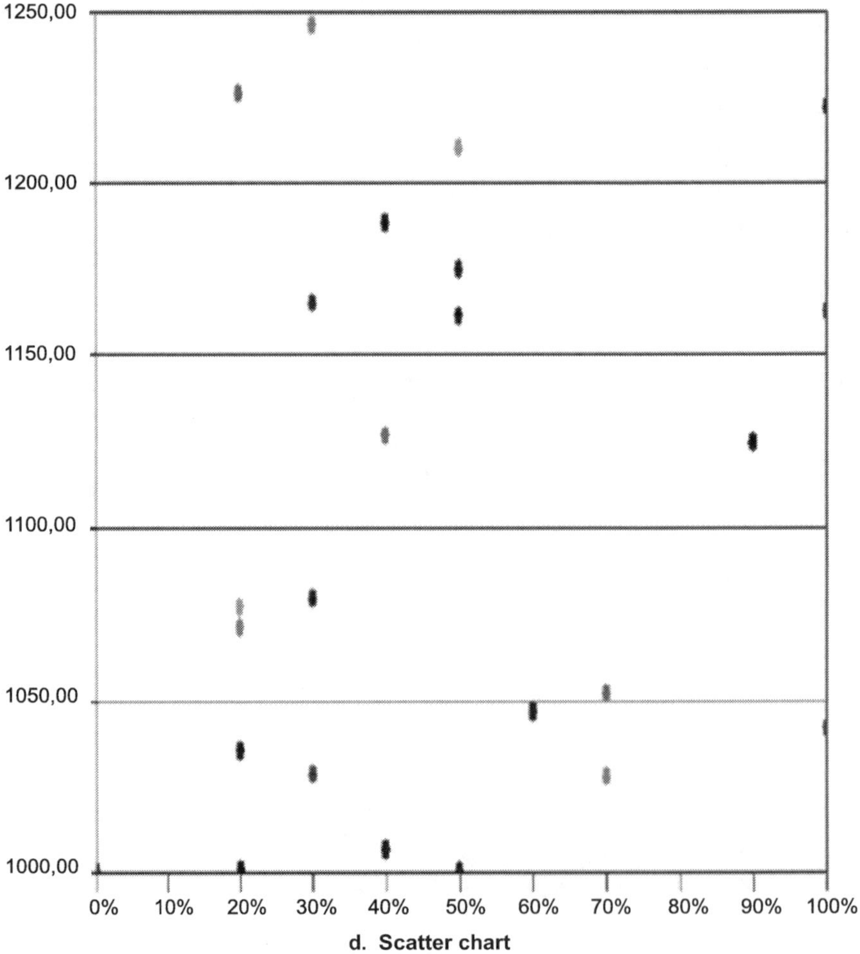

d. Scatter chart

Fig. 10.6 *Chart applet types (Source: Siebel Bookshelf)*

10.9.1 Configuring Chart Applets

In this section, we will discuss about configuring chart applets. The flow diagram shown in Fig. 10.7 shows the steps to configure a chart applet:

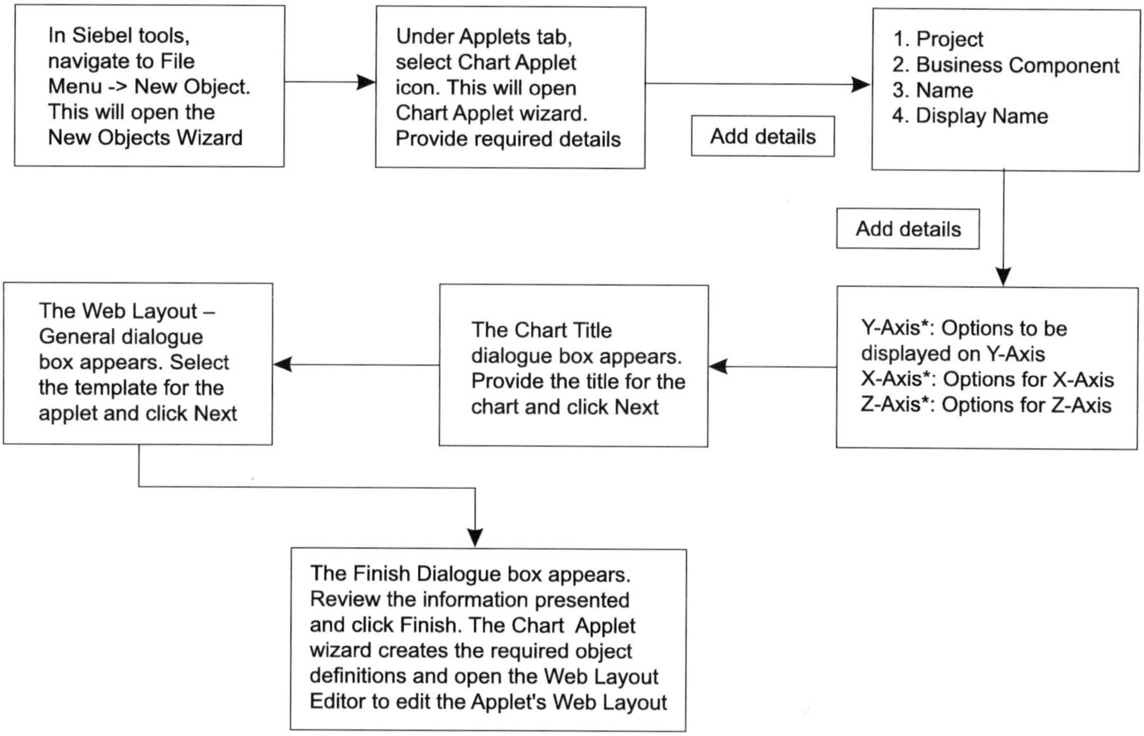

Fig. 10.7 *Steps to configure chart applets*

* In chart applets, we use three axes to represent the data in three dimensions. These are X-Axis, Y-Axis, and Z-Axis. The meaning of these axes changes according to the type of a chart applet. Also, these axes have their specific categories. The following points show the meaning of these axes for various types of chart applets:

X-Axis: This axis is used to display the category of data presented in chart. For bar charts and line charts, these axes mean the horizontal axis. For pie charts, it means the set of labels for pie slices.

Y-Axis: This axis is used to display the data values for the data presented in a chart. For bar charts and line charts, this axis means the vertical axis, whereas for pie charts, it means the portion or percentage of each slice occupied in circle, along with its numeric value.

Z-Axis: This axis is used to display the series for the data presented in a chart. This axis is not used with pie charts. For bar charts and line charts, this axis presents a set of labels in legend.

10.10 SUMMARY

Applets work as the point of contact between end user and underlying database. They provide a user-friendly way to view and modify the data. Various applets discussed in this chapter are used in Siebel applications based on the requirement. Configuration of applets is a very crucial and most widely used task for a developer. Moving ahead, we will discuss configuration of other important objects. As I mentioned earlier, the study is incomplete without practicing. Hence, readers should ensure proper practicing while reading.

REFERENCES

1. Siebel Bookshelf V8.1, Nov., 2008. Available from www.oracle.com
   PDF name: Configuring Siebel Business Applications
   Page 275.
2. Siebel Bookshelf V8.1, Nov., 2008. Available from www.oracle.com
   PDF name: Configuring Siebel Business Applications
   Page 436, Figure 98; page 438, Figure 101; page 441, Figure 106 and page 443, Figure 108.

Chapter 11

JOINS

This chapter focuses on configuring Joins. Typically, joins are used to join two tables. They facilitate users to relate and access the data from two different tables. In Siebel, joins are used to join a base table with a business component. They allow a business component to access the data from a base table other than its underlying base table.

Major topics covered in this chapter are:

- Introduction to Joins
- Implicit Joins
- Creating Joins
- Objects required to create joins
- Configuring joins
- Good practices while creating joins

11.1 JOINS

A join object defines a relationship between a business component and a table (other than business component's base table), allowing the columns of the joined table to be used by business component on a one-to-one basis by using a field from business component as a foreign key. This does not compulsorily require a one-to-one relationship between the business component's base table and the joined table.

Joins are used to implement master–detail relationship between tables. Detail table contains multiple records corresponding to one row in master table. This relationship is established by using foreign key. Multiple rows in detail table have same foreign key value, which points back to the corresponding row in base table.

For those who are not aware of foreign key concept, foreign key is used to implement master–detail relationship between tables. Foreign key column is present in detail table, and it is populated with the key value of the row to which detail records are mapped. Refer to following scenario:

A school has multiple standards {1st, 2nd, etc.} and each standard has multiple students. Now suppose 1st standard has three students {"Espider Man," "Pokkuman," and "Krussh"} and 2nd standard has two students {"Debat Man" and "Sooper Man"}. It is clear that "Standard" table and "Student" table will have 1:M relationship (or master–detail relationship). It can be implemented as shown below:

Standard Table

ROW_ID	*Standard*
Std_1	1st Standard
Std_2	2nd Standard

Student Table

ROW_ID	*Student_Name*	*Foreign Key*
Stud_1	Espider Man	Std_1
Stud_2	Pokkuman	Std_1
Stud_3	Krussh	Std_1
Stud_4	Debat Man	Std_2
Stud_5	Sooper Man	Std_2

The foreign key field in detail table (student) is mapped to corresponding key in parent table (standard). All the students having a foreign key value as "Std_1" belong to 1st standard, and those having foreign key value as "Std_2" belong to 2nd standard.

Let us just have a first look on joins by using Fig. 11.1. The following points cover the first look and feel of joins:

1. Join is a child object of business component object. In the figure below, when we expanded the business component object for "A Portfolio Account" business component and selected Join object, we can see the joins configured for this business component.
2. Referring to figure below, "A Portfolio Account" business component has join with two tables: "S_ORG_EXT" table and "S_PRTFL_CTGRY" table.

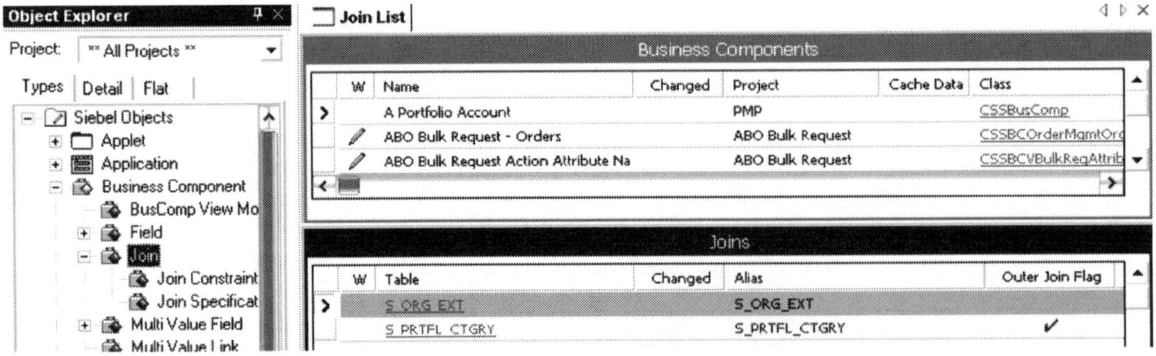

Fig. 11.1 *Join object in Siebel tools*

3. There are two child objects for join objects: "Join Constraint" and "Join Specification." We will discuss about these objects later in the chapter.
4. Also note that one of the join's property "Outer Join Flag" is checked for the join with "S_PRTFL_CTGRY" table, while it is blank for the join with "S_ORG_EXT" table. We will discuss about this property later in the chapter.

11.2 IMPLICIT JOINS

Implicit joins are the predefined joins existing as a part of Siebel Object Architecture. Implicit joins typically use the table name as the Join Alias. Implicit joins exist for the following relationships:

- All 1:1 (_X) extension tables and all relevant intersection tables.
- Extension tables of S_PARTY, such as S_ORG_EXT, S_CONTACT, S_POSTN, and S_USER. These implicit joins are used to map data to party business components.

11.3 CREATING JOINS

While creating a join, there are certain key terms that play a major role. A join construction can be summarized in the following paragraph.

In a join creation, there are three major role players: a business component, a base (detail) table and a joined (master) table. Join has a child called "Join Specification," which is responsible for defining various Join properties, such as Source Filed Property (maps to the field, acting as a foreign key in business component) and destination column property (maps to the field acting as a primary key in joined table). The name of the joined table, alias name for the join, and the outer join flag properties are present in the join object's definition.

Note: Set the outer join flag to TRUE if you want to retrieve all the records in the business component even when the joined fields are empty.

The next section elaborates our discussion about important objects in the join implementation.

11.3.1 Objects Required for Join Implementation

1. **Business component:** Business component is the parent of the join object. Business components are used to display the records from the base tables. Joins are used by business components to display the data from base tables, other than the underlying base table. In Fig. 11.1, the business component is "A Portfolio Account."
2. **Join object:** Join object contains the details about the join implemented between its parent business component and a base table (other than the business component's underlying base table). Join object has the following important properties (Table 11.1):

Table 11.1 Properties of Join object

Serial number	*Property*	*Description*
1.	Table	Name of the table that is joined with join's parent business component
2.	Alias	Name of the join used while using this join for populating joined fields
3.	Outer Join Flag	If checked, the join retrieves all the records in the business component even if the joined field is empty

Join object has two child objects: join specification and join constraint, as shown in Fig. 11.1.

3. **Join specification:** Join specification identifies the foreign key from parent business component and primary key from the joined table. In Fig. 11.2, join specification has the following important properties (Table 11.2):

Table 11.2 Properties of Join Specification object

Serial number	*Property*	*Description*
1.	Destination Column	Identifies the primary key from the joined table. This key uniquely identifies the records in joined table. In Fig. 11.2, PAR_ROW_ID field from S_ORG_EXT table (joined table) acts is the primary key for this table
2.	Source Field	Identifies the foreign key field from join's parent business component. In Fig. 11.3, Account Id field from "A Portfolio Account" is the foreign key field

In certain cases, there may be multiple join specifications defined for one join object. In such a case, the source fields of all the join specification child objects should be from the same table.

4. **Join constraint:** As is clear from the name, join constraint puts a constraint on the join. It is a constant-valued search specification imposed on a column during a join.

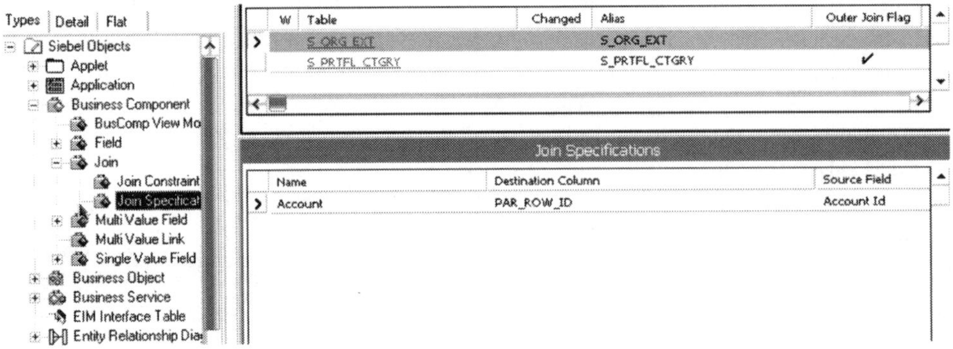

Fig. 11.2 *Join specification properties*

11.4 CONFIGURING JOINS

Implementing join relationship between a business component and a base table starts with creating a Join object and defining the Join Specification to map business component foreign key field with base table's primary key. Optionally, we can also add a Join Constraint if required. After this, we can add the joined field to business component, which will display data from the joined table.

The flow diagram in Fig. 11.3 shows the steps to configure a Join object. The next flow diagram in Fig. 11.4 shows the steps to add joined field to join's parent business component.

11.4.1 Configuring Join Object and Its Child Objects

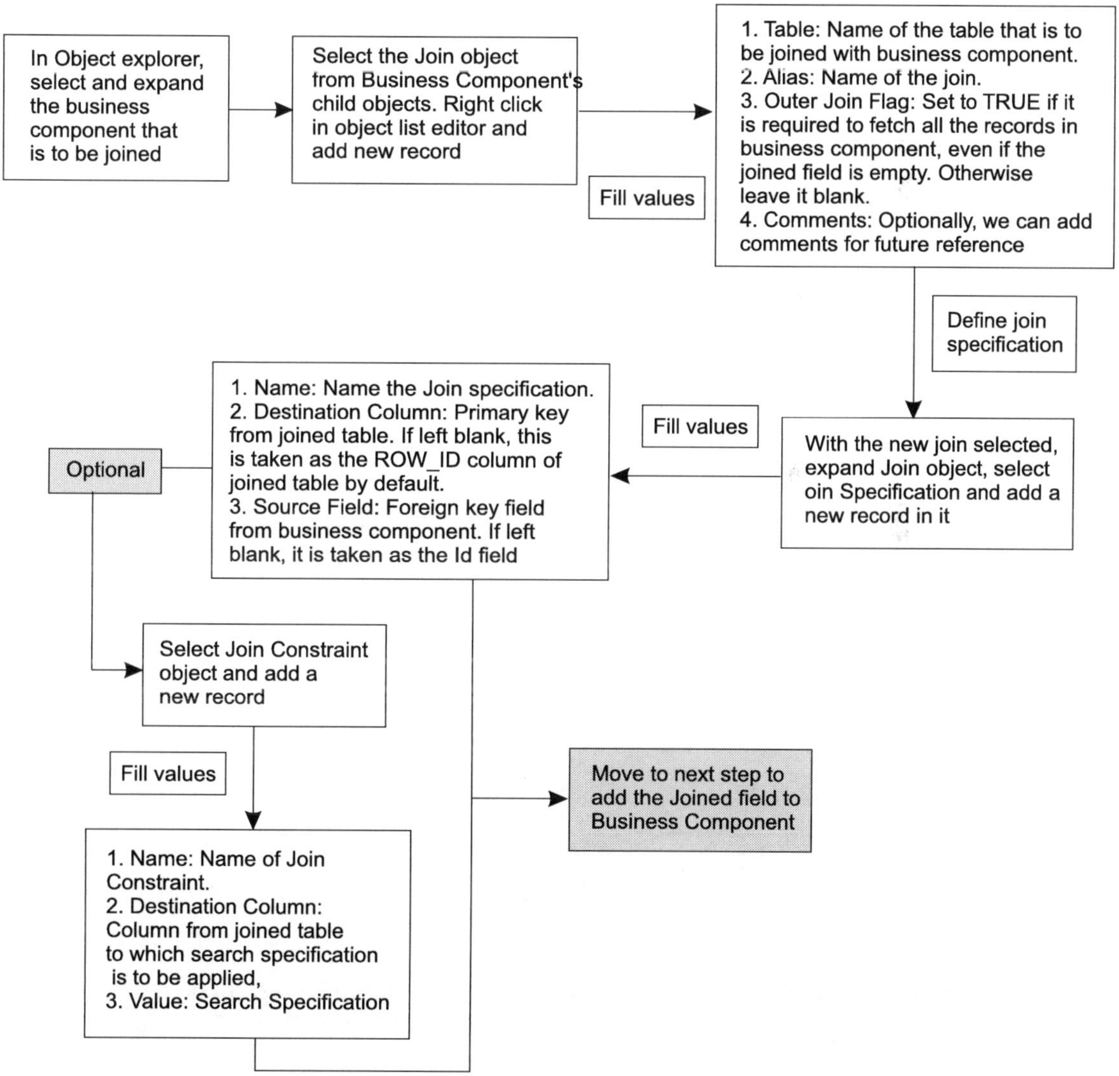

Fig. 11.3 *Steps to create join relationship*

11.4.2 Adding Joined Field to Business Component

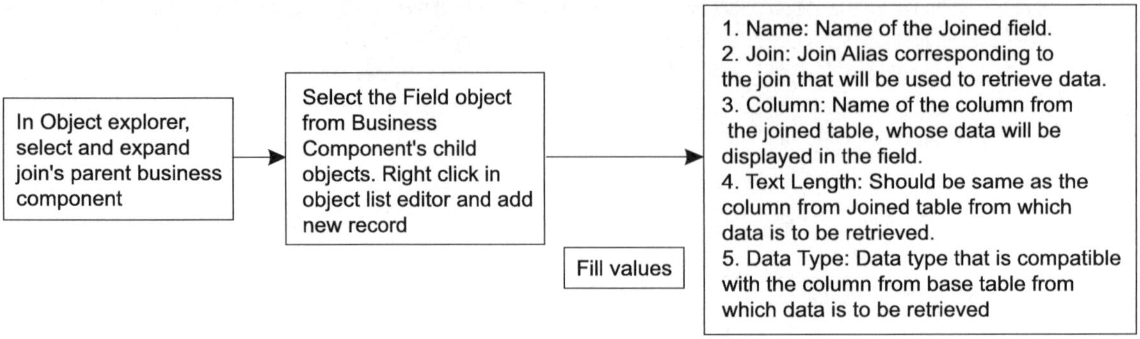

Fig. 11.4 *Adding joined fields to business component*

11.5 GOOD PRACTICES WHILE IMPLEMENTING JOIN RELATIONSHIP

There are certain good practices that should be followed while implementing the Join relationship:

- A business component may have two different joins with same base table. Referring to Fig. 11.5, the business component "ABO Bulk Request Action Set - Simple" has two different joins with S_ORG_EXT table, one for customer account information, and other for service account information. In this case, the joins are differentiated by aliases. The join aliases are "Customer Account" and "Service Account." It is always recommended that alias names should be unique for all the joins.

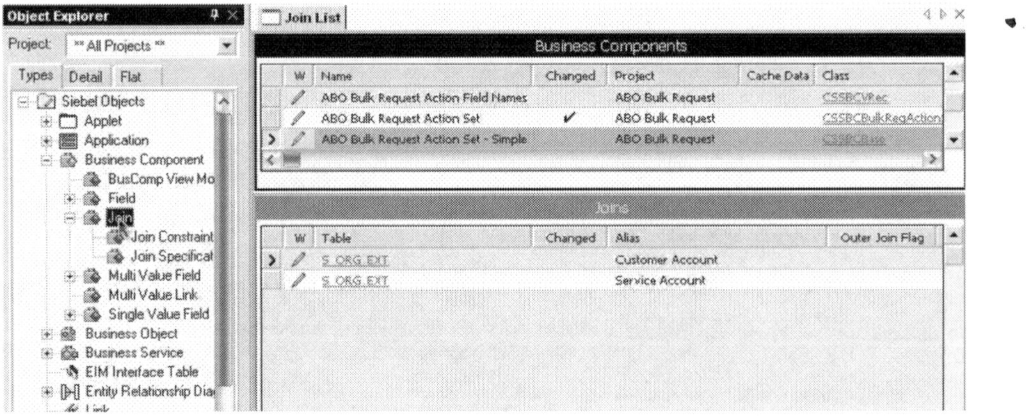

Fig. 11.5 *Business component with multiple joins to same table*

- Avoid using table names as the alias names for joins. The join name should be a unique custom name. This is because implicit joins use table names as the alias names to make sure that explicit join name is not used instead. If we use table names as explicit join's alias name, it may create conflicts in future.

- For creating join with tables that are extension tables of S_PARTY table (S_ACCOUNT, S_CONTACT, etc.), the foreign key value should be exposed as source Field, whereas the destination column must refer to the PAR_ROW_ID column in joined table.

SUMMARY

Joins play a major role in design optimization while configuring Siebel applications. Without joins, it would be hard to imagine applications in their current form. They also make combining the data from two tables simple and systematic to understand for developers and designers. Moving ahead, we will see Link object, which is used to connect two business components. Understanding joins and links is crucial for every developer before planning the strategies for developing Siebel applications.

Chapter 12

LINKS

In this chapter, we will discuss about Link object. Unlike a Join object, which is used to join a business component to a base table, Link object is used to connect two business components. It is used in the scenarios where it is required for one business component to access the data from other business component. In the "link" relationship between two business components, one acts as master business component, whereas the other one as detail business component. Link object definition is required to implement 1:M and M:M relationship between two business components.

Some of the major topics covered in this chapter are:

- Introduction to links
- Important objects in creating link
- Important properties of link object
- Configuring links
- Multi Value links
- Important objects for creating Multi Value links

12.1 LINKS

In certain cases, it is required to relate two business components where one record in one business component is associated with multiple records in another business component. Consider an example where we need to store the data of various schools in a city along with the students in them. Here, we will need two business components, one to store a list of schools and another to store students list for each school. Corresponding to one record in "School" business component, there will be multiple records in "Students" business component. This relationship is called master-detail relationship, where "School" business component is the master business component and "Student" is detail business component.

Links are used to implement such a master-detail relationship. For associating two business components in master-detail relationship, we need to create a link between them and include the link and business components in business object.

While creating multi-value group applets, we need a link between the corresponding business components. We will discuss about MVG applets in detail in Chapter 16.

There are certain objects involved in creating a link between two business components. Before moving ahead with the configuration of links, let us first have a look on these object definitions, and their significance in master–detail relationship.

12.2 IMPORTANT OBJECT DEFINITIONS FOR CREATING LINKS

1. **Master business component:** Master business component plays the role of "Master" in master–detail relationship. Corresponding to one record in master business component, there are multiple records in detail business component. In the example of Schools and Students discussed in previous section, "School" business component will play the role of master business component.
2. **Detail business component:** Detail business component is the one that stores the detail records corresponding to the records in master business component.
3. **Source field:** Source key field is basically the primary key of master business component. This field uniquely identifies the records in detail business component. Typically, it maps to the ROW_ID field in the base table of parent business component.
4. **Destination field:** Destination field is the foreign key field present in detail business component that points back to master business component's master record. In the School–Student relationship discussed in previous section, each record in Student business component corresponding to a particular School record has foreign key value pointing back to that school record in School record in School business component. Primary Key–Foreign key relation is discussed in detail in Chapter 11.
5. **Link:** Link object definition identifies the master–detail relationship between two business components. The important properties of link object are "Parent Business Component" (identifying the parent business component), "Child Business Component" (identifying the child business component), "Source Field" (identifying the primary key field from parent business component), and "Destination Field" (identifying the foreign key field from child business component).

After creating the link, we need to incorporate it into business object. The reason behind this is that a view is based on the business object, specified in its business object property. To make a view work as master–detail view, we need to incorporate the link in underlying business object. It does not require any additional configuration in view. A link object is added in business object by the means of business object component object definition. Once added, this master–detail relationship is applicable to any use of the two business components together within the context of business object.

12.3 IMPORTANT PROPERTIES OF LINK OBJECT

Along with the important objects involved in implementing a link relationship, there are certain important properties of link. They are as follows:

1. **Search specification:** Search specification is applied in child business component. It is used to filter the records that can be fetched from it. All the records that satisfy

the search specification condition will be fetched from child business component. Along with the child business component, we can apply search specification at applet level also to filter the data to be displayed. If both applet and business component have search specification defined, applet's search specification gets added to business component's search specification by AND operator.

2. **Cascade delete property:** Cascade delete property determines the actions done on the child record and foreign key column in child business component, when a parent record is deleted. It is up to the developers, whether they choose to delete all the child records, delete only the foreign key values, or keep everything intact. Based on the choice, we can provide the following values in this property (Table 12.1):

Table 12.1 Values for Cascade Delete Property

Serial number	*Value*	*Description*
1.	Delete	All the detail or child records are deleted when we delete the master record. It should be kept in mind that this option should not be used when the child business component works as child business component for any other master business component as well. This option is mostly preferred for _XM tables, as they contain only the records associated with parent record
2.	Clear	This option is preferred in the scenario where the same child records are shared between two or more master business components. If we select "Clear," it removes the foreign key reference from child business component, keeping child records intact
3.	None	This is the default value. It neither deletes the child records, nor the foreign key reference from child business component

For M:M (many-to-many) links, cascade delete property is not available. Whenever a record is deleted, Siebel applications automatically delete the intersection record corresponding to deleted record, leaving child record intact.

M:M relationship: M:M relationship between two tables is the relationship where one record in first table is associated with multiple record in second table, and vice versa. For example, let us consider the relationship between School and City. One City can have multiple schools, and one School can be present in multiple cities (in form or branches). Hence, the relationship between School and City is M:M. This type of relationship is implemented by using Intersection table, which contains the primary keys from each table.

3. **Visibility rule property:** This property determines whether visibility will be applied in the link. We can provide the following values in this property (Table 12.2):

Table 12.2 Values for Visibility Rule property

Serial number	*Value*	*Description*
1.	Always	Visibility rules will be applied in the detail records whenever the currently active master–detail view is based on this link, even though the view does not have the active visibility settings in the visibility applet and visibility applet type properties
2.	Never	Visibility rules would not be allowed in the detail records whenever the currently active master–detail view is based on this link

Links can be used to implement 1:M and M:M relationship. Often people who are new in the field get confused where to use join and where to use link. Here is one thumb rule to remember this. Joins are used to implement 1:1 and M:1 relationships (1 at second positions), whereas Links are used to implement 1:M and M:M relationships (M at second positions).

To implement 1:M relationship by using links, we need to define parent business component, child business component, source field, and destination field. The default value of source field is parent business component's ID field. If no value is provided for this property, it gets set to default value.

To implement M:M relationship using links, we need to define two links, with Opposite master–detail settings. This relationship requires an intersection table. To establish a connection between two links and intersection table, we need to provide the corresponding values to Inter Table, Inter Parent Column, and Inter Child Column Properties of two link object definitions. Let us understand this with School/City relationship discussed above. Suppose the name of intersection table for associating these two tables is SCHOOL_CITY. The Inter Table property will have value "SCHOOL_CITY," the Inter Child Column will be "School_Id" (primary key for school table), and Inter Parent Column will be "City_Id" (primary key for city table).

12.4 CONFIGURING LINKS

There are three simple steps to configure a link. They are as follows:

1. In Object Explorer, select the link object type. This will populate the Object List Editor with all the available links.
2. Create a new record in Object List Editor, and provide the required values for the properties.
3. Step-off the record in order to save it.

12.5 MULTI-VALUE LINKS

In some scenarios, it is required to attach a set of records with a control or list column in an applet. For example, a School can have multiple addresses in a city. While entering or searching data about school, user should be able to select the address from the list of available addresses. These types of requirements are fulfilled by using multi-value group

(MVG). An MVG can be considered as a list of records attached to a control or list column in an applet. (MVG is discussed in detail in Chapter 16).

A multi-value link is used to implement MVGs. It is the child object of business component object type. A MVG is used where one control or list column has multiple records associated with it, which is basically a master–detail relationship. A parent–child relationship can be implemented by using a link object definition. A multi-value link is required to use MVG applets. MVG applets contain the fields that are related to the field that invokes MVG (originating field). Figure 12.1 shows an MVG applet, along with its originating field.

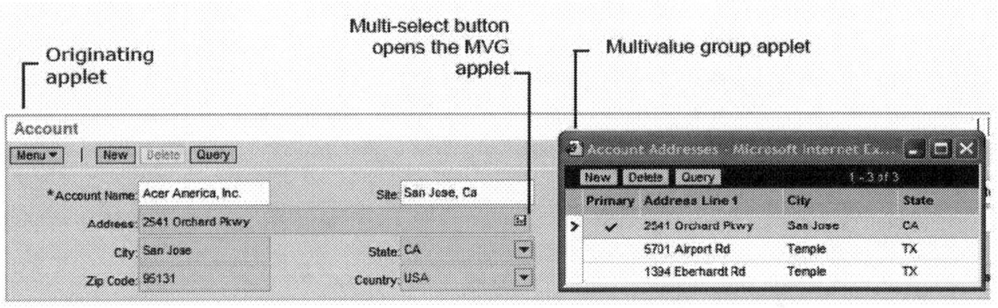

Fig. 12.1 *Multi-value group (Ref. [1])*

The above applet shows the scenario where one account can have multiple addresses, and user can select any address by using the MVG applet. As we can see in MVG applet, the fields present are "Address Line 1," "City," and "State." Whenever we select any record, the other fields also get populated automatically in the respective field in originating applet. As an illustration, when we select "2541 Orchard Pkwy," other values { "San Jose," "CA"} automatically get populated in respective fields in account applet. These fields are known as multi-value fields. Multi-value fields get populated by using underlying multi-value link between originating business component and MVG business component. The record having "Primary" field checked in MVG applet is primary record. We can change the primary record in MVG applet based on the requirement.

Originating business component, MVG business component, MVG, and MVG applets are discussed in detail in Chapter 16.

Multi-value link is based on a link object definition, which defines the master–detail relationship between master (originating) business component and detail (MVG) business component. Multi-value link object definition allows master business component's fields to access fled values corresponding to a primary record, along with embedding detail data with master business component.

12.6 IMPORTANT OBJECT FOR CREATING MULTI-VALUE LINKS

There are certain objects that play a major role in creating multi-value links. For configuring multi-value links, all we need to do is to select the multi-value link object in Object Explorer, create a new record in Object List Editor, provide values to the properties discussed below, and step off the record. Following section discusses about the objects that should be populated in various properties of multi-value link object:

1. **Master business component:** Master business component is the business component corresponding to an originating applet. This business component contains the field that invokes MVG in applet, along with the multi-value fields that get populated by using multi-value link object definition.
2. **Detail business component:** Detail business component is "Detail" in master–detail relationship. It provides the detail records corresponding to the master record.
3. **Link:** Link object forms the link between master and detail business component. Multi-value link object uses the link in its destination link property to specify the relationship between two business components.
4. **Multi-value fields:** Multi-value fields are the fields from master business component that use multi-value link and link object definitions to get values from detail business component. In the context of configuration, these fields are different from other fields in following three ways:
    - They have Multi – Value property set to TRUE.
    - They have the name of multi-value link object in their multi-value link property.
    - They have "Column" property left blank, as they obtain their value from detail business component, not from base table's column.
5. **Primary Id field:** Field from master business component that holds the ROW_ID corresponding to the record in detail business component working as "Primary Record" for each MVG. The "Primary Id" field of multi-value link object holds the value of this field.
6. **Foreign key field:** Field in detail business component that points back to the ROW_ID of the master record in master business component for each record in detail business component.
7. **Multi-value link object:** This object identifies the relationship between multi-value fields in master business component and the link object. It has the following three important properties:
    - Destination link: This property identifies the link object used to create the relationship between master and detail business component.
    - Destination business component: This property identifies the detail business component used in master–detail relationship.
    - Primary Id field: This property identifies the primary Id field.

12.7 SUMMARY

Link object plays a crucial role in making a better user interface that is more user-friendly. By using links, developers can connect two business components, allowing master business component to access the data from child business component. Moving ahead, we will discuss about some complex objects in Siebel, which include pick lists and MVGs. These objects are a bit more complex to understand and develop as compared to the objects discussed till now. Hence, I would suggest a proper practice to all the readers in order to get familiar with these objects.

REFERENCE

1. Siebel Bookshelf V8.1, Nov., 2008. Available from: www.oracle.com.
   PDF name: Configuring Siebel Business Applications
   Page 408, Figure 80

Chapter 13

VIEWS

In this section, we will discuss about Siebel views. At user interface level, views can be called as a collection of related applets, which display the data for a particular context. Applets always require a view to get displayed at user interface. At tools level, the objects playing a major role in displaying data at user interface are applets, business components, business objects, and views. Although a view is a collection of related applets at user interface level, it does not have any direct relationship with applets. Applets get mapped to view through the relationship between business component and business object. An applet is based on a business component, whereas a view is based on a business object. To map an applet to a view, we will need to map the business component of that applet to the business object of view. Throughout our discussion in this chapter, we will elaborate this point while discussing the configuration of views.

Major topics covered in this chapter are:

- Introduction to Views
- UI based classification of Views
- Creating Views
- Child Objects of View object
- Editing View Layout
- Adding View to a screen
- Registering Views
- Things to remember while configuring views

13.1 VIEWS

Siebel view is basically a collection of related applets. Views are used to expose applets and their controls on user interface. As discussed in Part 2, a view is a group of related applets, and a screen is a collection of related views. We navigate between screens and views by using tabs, drop-down menus or links. These can be classified in four levels at UI.

1. **First level (screen tabs):** This level contains the screen tabs, which allow us to navigate between screens. As displayed in Fig. 13.1, screen tabs are the topmost tabs in application. We can also navigate to screens by using site map.
2. **Second level (link bar and view drop-down list):** Second level comprises of link bar and view drop-down list. Link bar contains links right below Screen tabs that will

take us to the desired views in current screen. It is shown in Fig. 13.1. View drop-down list appears at the header of applets, mostly at the upper left corner of applet. It is basically a drop-down list that contains view names. Typically, views present in this list filter data based on the visibility rules. For example, "My Accounts," "My Team's Accounts," "All Accounts," and "All Accounts from Organization" shown in Fig. 13.1.

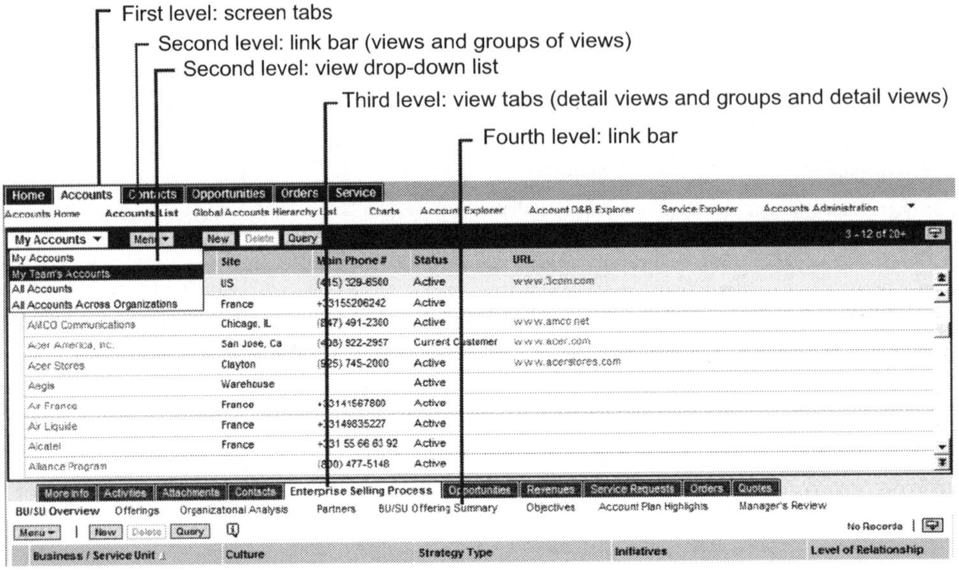

Fig. 13.1 *Four levels of View navigation (Ref. [1])*

3. **Third level (view tabs):** This level comprises of view tabs. These tabs are typically present in the child applet of the primary applet, and are used to navigate to group of detail views. Detail views are used to display the details about the record selected in primary applet.
4. **Fourth level:** The composition of this level depends on the templates selected while configuration. Based on the template, it may contain links in the form of drop-down list, link bar right below the view tabs or a grandchild applet having view tabs. Figure 13.1 shows this level in the form of link bar.

13.2 UI BASED CLASSIFICATION OF VIEWS

View is a collection of various types of applets. It may contain list applets, form applets, or various other special purposes of applets. In most of the scenarios, views are configured with "List–Form" or "Master–Detail" combination. This section covers discussion on both of these types.

1. **List–Form view:** As clear from the name, a list–form view contains a list applet and a form applet. The list applet contains a list of records, and form applet shows the details about the record selected in the list applet. Both of these applets contain the records from same business component. The record that we select in list applet gets highlighted

with a different color, and detailed information about that record gets populated in form applet, which (typically) lies below the list applet. Along with viewing the records, we can also add new records in this view. Figure 13.2 shows a list–form view.

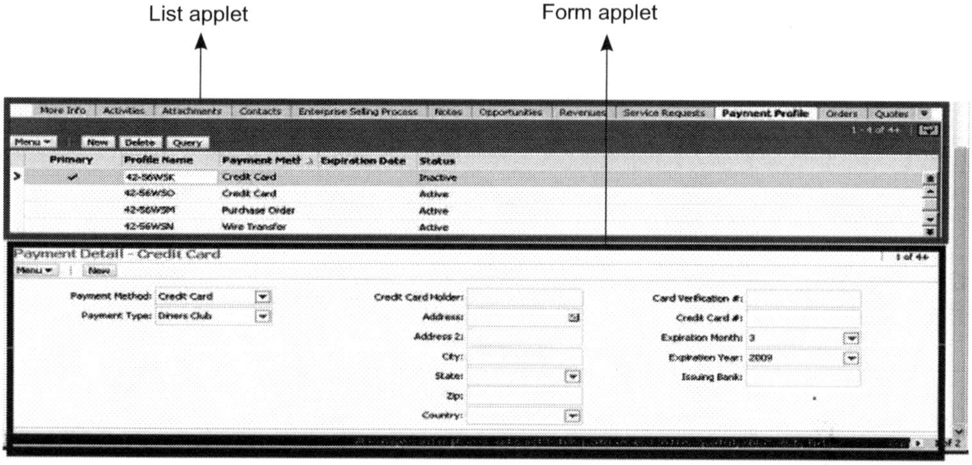

Fig. 13.2 *List–form view (Ref. [2])*

We can see here that the record that is selected in list is highlighted with yellow shade, and its details are present in below form applet. We can perform operations, such as creating new record, deleting existing record, and querying for the records using "New," "Delete," and "Query" buttons present in the list applet.

2. **Master–detail view:** Master–detail view is typically configured in opposite manner than that of list–form view. In this view, form applet lies above the list applet. Form applet contains the details of "Master" record, whereas a list applet contains all the child records associated with the "Master" record (Fig. 13.3).

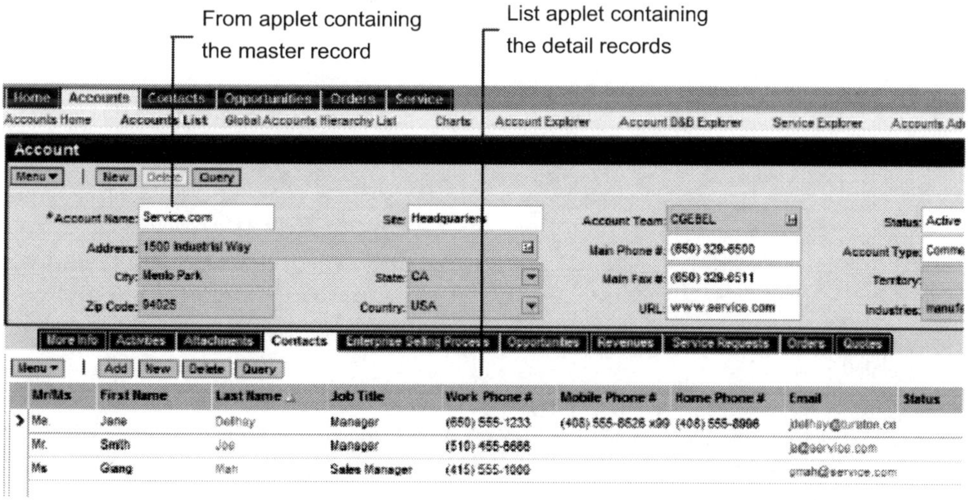

Fig. 13.3 *Master–detail view (Ref. [3])*

One basic difference between the two views is that the applet present in master–detail view display data from different business components. As discussed in Chapter 12, a master–detail relationship between two business components is implemented by using a link between them. For implementing a master–detail view, we need to configure a link between master and detail business components.

Along with the format shown above, a master–detail view can also contain two list applets, with the top list applet showing the list of parent records, and that at bottom showing the child records associated with currently selected master record in top list applet.

13.3 CREATING VIEWS

Views can be created either by using New Object Wizard, or from Object List Editor. In this section, we will discuss about the both the approaches.

13.3.1 Creating Views by Using New Object Wizard

Figure 13.4 shows the steps involved in creating new view by using New Object Wizard. After creating a view, the next steps are associating it with a screen and registering it at application level.

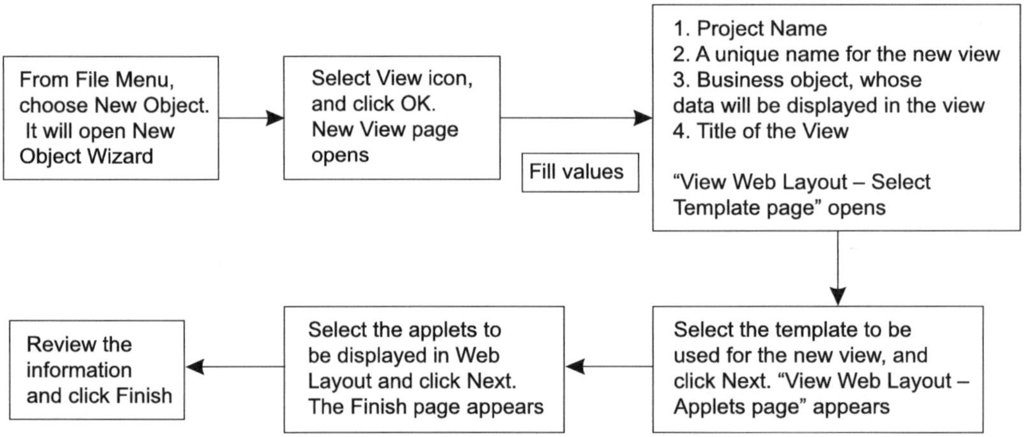

Fig. 13.4 *Steps to create view by using New Object Wizard*

After clicking Finish in Finish page, the View Layout Editor appears. We can edit the View Layout here, if required. The editor also allows us to preview our view with the current layout. To preview the view, we have to right-click on layout editor, and select "Preview" option. To come back again to editor mode, right-click again and uncheck "Preview" option.

View Layout Editor also allows us to open the applet layout editor for the applets present in the view's current layout. To do this, select the applet in editor mode, and double-click on it. This will open the applet layout editor for that applet, allowing us to edit the layout of applet.

We will discuss about editing view layout in detail in the next section.

13.3.2 Creating Views by Using Object List Editor

Like other objects, a view object can also be created directly at Object List Editor. The obvious advantage of using New Object Wizard approach over Object List Editor approach is that New Object Wizard creates the objects after taking all the necessary details from user. Figure 13.5 shows the steps required to configure a view from Object List Editor.

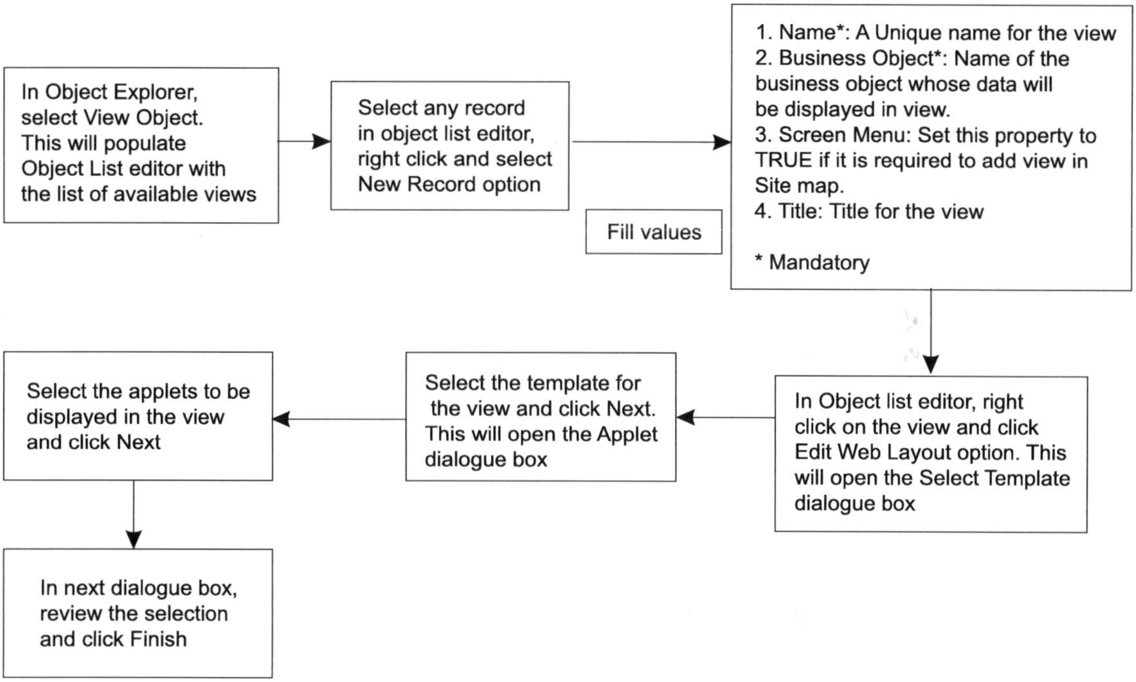

Fig. 13.5 *Creating views by using Object List Editor*

13.4 CHILD OBJECTS OF VIEW OBJECT

Before moving ahead with the discussion on view, let us have a brief look on the child and grandchild objects of view object. View has the following child objects:

1. View Locale
2. View Report (with one child object View Report Locale)
3. View Task Group (with one child object Task Group Locale)
4. View User Prop
5. View Web Template (with one child object View Web Template Item)

Out of these objects, most commonly used objects (based on my experience□) are View Web Template and View Web Template Item.

13.4.1 View Web Template

View Web Template object definition specifies various modes of view (e.g., Base mode, Edit mode, etc.), along with the template used for the mode. For each mode, there are certain applets defined, that are visible only in the specific mode. These applets are defined in "View Web Template Item" object.

To add a new mode for the view, we need to add a new "View Web Template" record in Object List Editor and provide the following mandatory values:

- Name: Name of the mode (e.g., Base, Edit, etc.)
- Web Template: Template to be used for this mode.
- Upgrade Behavior: Typically "Preserve."

13.4.2 View Web Template Item

View Web Template Item is the child object of View Web Template object. It contains the applets corresponding to the Web template. The applets added here are available to be displayed in the mode for which these applets are added. For instance, the applets added in Base mode of view will be available only in Base mode. We can add applets in View Web Template Item by using the following steps:

- Select the View Web Template record for which applets have to be added.
- Select the View Web Template Item child object for this View Web Template record.
- This will populate the below object list editor with the list of applets present for this View Web Template record. Right-click in below object list editor and select New Record.
- Provide the following mandatory values:
  - (a) Name: Name of the view Web template item.
  - (b) Item Identifier: Item Identifiers decide the position of Web template item in template. These can be considered as the identifiers of the placeholders present in the template. We can simply drag and drop the items to the desired placeholder instead of providing item identifier here.
  - (c) Applet: Identifies the applet that is mapped to this Web template item.
  - (d) Applet Mode: Mode of the applet (Base/Edit/Edit List/New/Query) to be displayed in view.
  - (e) Upgrade Behavior: Typically "Preserve."

After creating views, the next step is to edit and finalize the Web layout of the view, that is, deciding the look and feel of view in user interface. This includes placing the applets at desired position in view. After this, we will add the view in screen, followed by registering the view in application and adding responsibilities to it.

13.5 EDITING VIEW LAYOUT

We use Web Layout Editor to edit view Web layout. Editing layout is basically a process of placing/replacing applets to the desired placeholders in view Web template. (This can be done by using "View Web Template Item" child object's "Item Identifier" property.) In

Web layout, we can drag and drop the applets mapped to the view to the desired location in template. To open the Web Layout Editor, right-click on the view name in Object List Editor and select "Edit Web Layout" option. This will open the Web Layout Editor. We can perform the following operations:

- **Add an applet in Web layout:** Applets can be added by dragging them from Applets window and dropping them at the desired position in Web layout. A view is based on business object, and business object is a group of related business components. All the applets that are based on business components present in view's business object can be added in view. A list of all these applets is shown in "Applets Window," present in Web Layout Editor.
- **Deleting the applet from layout:** We can delete an applet from View Web Layout by selecting the applet and pressing Delete. This will remove the applet from Web Layout. This applet will be available in applets window and we can place it again in future at desired placeholder.
- **Editing the applet's layout:** We can also edit the applet's layout. For editing the applet's layout, we have to double-click on that applet in View Web Layout Editor. This will open another window of Web Layout Editor to edit the applet's layout. We can add or remove the controls in applet or change their position in applet's Web layout. On saving, the changes made in applet's layout are reflected in it while adding it to view Web layout.
- **Preview the Web layout:** Web Layout Editor also provides the facility to preview the design before finalizing it. In preview, all the unmapped placeholders are removed and only the mapped ones are visible. It provides a rough estimate of how the view will look like in user interface. It is not intended to provide the exact representation of the user interface output. To preview the design, right-click on Web layout editor window and select "Preview."
- **Export preview to HTML file:** For exporting preview to HTML file, select File menu -> Export option, browse to the path where file should be saved, provide the name to the file and click Save.
- **Change Web template:** We can also change the underlying Web template used for the view. To do this, click on "Change Template" button present next to the template text box in Web Controls toolbox.

Before leaving Web Layout Editor, make sure changes have been saved. To save the changes, we can either select "Save" from File menu, or press CTRL + S, or click on Save button present at second position in the buttons present just below the application-level menu.

Till now, we have created our view, added applets in it, and edited and finalized its Web layout. The next step is to add the view to the desired screen and associate responsibilities with it.

13.6 ADDING VIEW TO SCREEN

The next step after creating a view is to associate this view with a screen. The following steps are involved in adding the view to the screen:

1. Select the Screen object and search for the Screen to which this view is to be associated.
2. Expand the Screen object in Object Explorer and select "Screen Views" child object. This will display the list of views associated to the currently selected screen.
3. Create a new record in this list with the details of our new view and save the record.

13.7 REGISTERING VIEWS

Registering view is a two-step process. It includes registering view in application and assigning responsibilities to it. Registering the view adds a new record for the view in Siebel database. Assigning responsibility to the view decides who can see this view and access the information in it. If we do not assign any responsibility to our view, it would not be visible in Web client. Following are the steps to register the view at application level:

1. Login to Siebel Application: Go to Administration -> Site map -> Administration Application screen.
   To register the view, we should login to the application as a user with administrative responsibilities. This is basically an administration task.
2. Navigate to "Views" view in this screen: This will show the list of all views currently registered in application.
3. Select the drop down arrow in View Name field. Select the view from the pick list and click OK.
4. For adding responsibilities to the view, navigate to Administration–Application screen, Responsibilities view.
5. This will open all the available responsibilities. Select the responsibility that is to be added to the view.
6. In views list, enter a new record for the view to which this responsibility is to be added and save the record.

13.8 THINGS TO REMEMBER WHILE CONFIGURING VIEWS

1. Views "Administration - Server Configuration" and "Administration - Server Management" should not be modified. The information present in these files are read by the siebens.dat file and displayed on user interface by server manager. Any configuration change in these views should also be reflected in the siebens.dat file. As the product is not configured to make these changes, we should not make any change in these two views.
2. We should never associate a view with more than one screen. This will make thread manager to work abnormally. Whenever a thread is stored in session file, it contains the name of a view, but not the name of screen to which the view is associated. When a user wants to navigate to the duplicated view, he will be taken to the same screen every time. Also, if the same view is defined as the default view for both the screens, we will see only one screen tab as an active tab, when either of them is selected, that is, the screen tab having duplicate view as default view never appears to be active.

3. Always name the view by using the following rules:
   - Name should be in Initial Caps form, that is, Initial Capital form. Instead of "My team details view," it should be "My Team Details View."
   - Like other objects, the name of view should be meaningful.
   - Name should start with company's name as prefix. If the view is for some organization called "cartoon-sons pvt. Ltd," the view name should be in form "Cartoon-Sons <Some descriptive name in Init-Caps form>."
   - Special characters should never be used while naming the views.

Apart from the rules mentioned above, we should refer to the following tables while naming the views. The first Table 13.1 classifies the views based on the type of view, while the second Table 13.2 classifies the view based on View's visibility type.

Table 13.1 Naming Conventions for Views

Serial number	*View type*	*Naming convention*	*Example*
1.	Master–detail view	<Business Component1> Detail - <Business Component2> View	Contact Detail – Account View
2.	List–form view	<Business Component> List View	Opportunity List View
3.	Chart view	<Business Component> View - <XXX> Analysis	Opportunity Chart View – Area Analysis
4.	Explorer view	<Business Component> Explorer View	Contact Explorer View

Table 13.2 Naming Conventions for View's Visibility Types

Serial number	*Visibility type*	*Naming convention*
1.	Administration mode	Opportunities Administration
2.	Organization	All Opportunities
3.	Sub-organizations	All Opportunities Across My Organizations
4.	All	All Opportunities Across Organizations
5.	Personal	My Personal Opportunities
6.	Manager	My Team's Opportunities
7.	Sales Rep	My Opportunities

13.9 SUMMARY

Views facilitate applets to display the data from business components at user interface in user-friendly manner. They allow users to access and modify the data. Different types of views display data in various formats based on the requirements and ease of understanding for user. Views always need screens to get displayed. In Chapter 14, we will discuss about configuring screens, and adding views to it.

REFERENCES

1. Siebel Bookshelf V8.1, Nov., 2008. Available from: www.oracle.com.
   PDF name: Configuring Siebel Business Applications.
   Page 293, Figure 59.
2. Siebel Bookshelf V8.1, Nov. 2008. Available from: www.oracle.com
   PDF name: Configuring Siebel Business Applications.
   Page: 294 Fig. 60
3. Siebel Bookshelf V8.1 (Nov. 2008). Available from: www.oracle.com
   PDF name: Configuring Siebel Business Applications.
   Page: 295 Fig. 61

Chapter 14

SCREENS

Screen is a collection of related views. It represents a particular entity of organization. A screen representing a specific entity contains all the views relevant to it. It is the first level of application navigation for users. Navigating among screens by using a site map and screen tabs is discussed in part – 2. In this chapter, we will discuss about the steps to configure a screen and adding views to it.

Major topics covered in this chapter are:

- Introduction to Screens
- Types of screen views
    - Aggregate Category
    - Aggregate View
    - Detail Category
    - Detail View
- Configuring Screens
- Defining the display order of views in a screen
- Things to remember

14.1 SCREENS

Screen is basically a collection of related views. It represents a specific business entity, such as account, contacts, and opportunities, and so on. All the views present in a screen implement a part of business function, which is represented by screen. Typically, all the views present in a screen map to a single business object. Figure 14.1 shows accounts screen.

Screens are accessible through screen tabs or site map. Screen tabs are enclosed in yellow box in Fig. 14.1.

Most of the aspects about screen-level navigation are already discussed in Part 2 of book. In this section, we will focus more on configuration aspects of Siebel screens. Hence, we will shift our attention from the screen visible at UI level to "Screen Object" in Siebel tools. On selecting screen object in Siebel tools' Object Explorer, all the available screens will get populated in Object List Editor. If we expand it, we will see the only one child object of screen object, that is, "Screen View." Screen view object contains all the views present in its parent screen. Screen view object decides how views should appear in the screen. There are four types of screen views:

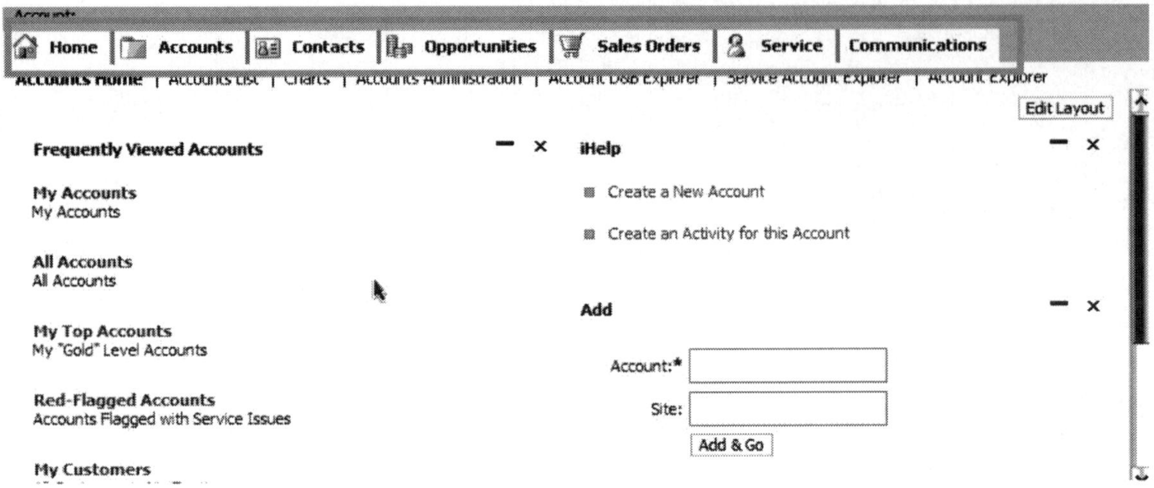

Fig. 14.1 *Accounts screen*

1. **Aggregate category:** In this type, the views are visible in the form of link in the link bar below the screen tabs. (Screen tabs and link bar are discussed in Chapter 12.) We can access the views by clicking on the link corresponding to that view. On clicking a particular link, the color of that link changes, which differentiates an active link from other links in link bar.
2. **Detail category:** In this type, views appear in the form of tabs in view tab bar. While implementing master–detail relationship by using views, detail category is used to group detail views. On clicking a particular tab, its color changes, differentiating it from other tabs in view tab bar. (View tabs are discussed in Chapter 12).
3. **Aggregate view:** In this type, the view appears in the form of a link in view drop-down list present at applet header. All the views present in this drop down are typically used to filter data presented by them. (View drop-down is discussed in Chapter 12.) This requires the parent category property to be set to a valid aggregate category. If parent category property is blank, the view appears as a link in the link bar below the screen tabs.
4. **Detail view:** In this type, the view appears in view tab when the parent category property is set to a valid aggregate category. If the parent category property is set to a valid detail category, the view appears as a link in the link bar below the view tab, or at other locations depending on underlying Web template.

14.2 CONFIGURING SCREENS

In this section, we will discuss about configuring screens and adding views in screen view child object. The first flow diagram shown in Fig. 14.2 shows the steps to configure a screen by using Object List Editor, whereas that shown in Fig. 14.3 represent the steps to add views to a screen.

14.2.1 Configuring Screens from Object List Editor

Figure 14.2 presents the steps for configuring screens.

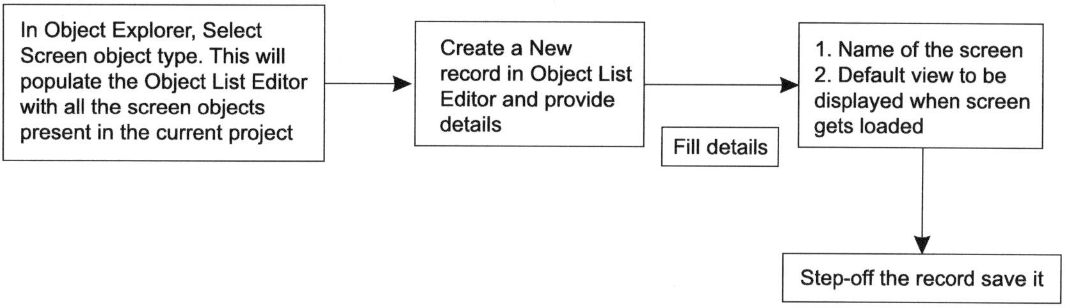

Fig. 14.2 *Configuring screens by using Object List Editor*

14.2.2 Adding Views to Screen

The next step after configuring the screen object is to add views in it. As we discussed earlier, all the views that we want to display in our screen should be added to screen views child object. Figure 14.3 presents the steps to add views in screen views child object.

* For aggregate view or detail view, these properties are read-only.

This property is left blank for aggregate category, as there is no parent for it. Also, for an aggregate view, this property may or may not be blank.

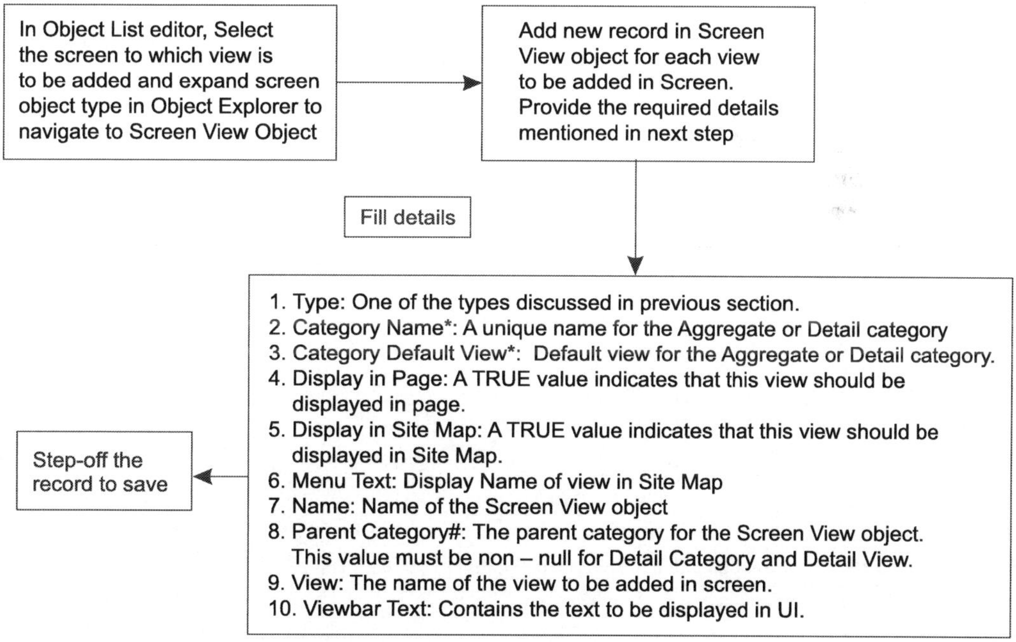

Fig. 14.3 *Steps to add views to a screen*

14.3 DEFINING THE DISPLAY ORDER FOR VIEWS IN SCREEN

It is always recommended to determine the sequence of views by using Screen View Sequence Editor. We should not manually edit the sequence property of screen view. Screen View Sequence Editor is a design tool that visually shows the hierarchy of screen views in the form of a tree structure and allows us to move screen views to a desired position. Once we make the required changes in screen view positions and save them, the sequence property automatically gets updated with a numeric value showing the screen view's position in hierarchy.

Following are the steps to define the display order of screen views in screen (Fig. 14.4):

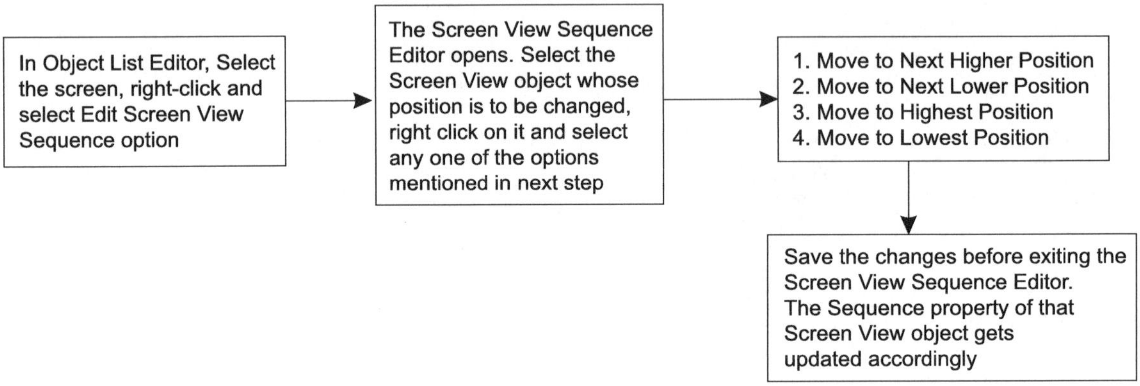

Fig. 14.4 *Editing view sequence in screen*

Things to remember

1. Editing the sequence of screen view objects by using Screen View Sequence Editor does not affect its position in site map. In site map, views are displayed in an alphabetical order.
2. If sequence is not defined, Siebel Web engine orders the views in alphabetical order.
3. A view having null value in its sequence property is ordered at last in sequence.

14.4 SUMMARY

Screens form the first layer of navigation for the users. They represent a particular entity of organization, and encapsulate all the views related to that entity. They provide a systematic approach for the users to navigate through the application and do specific tasks. Till now, we have discussed about the simple and most basic objects for configuring Siebel applications. Moving ahead, we will discuss about more complex objects. These objects are not mandatory, but they are used to make navigation and data modification easy for users.

Chapter 15

PICK LIST

In this chapter, we will discuss about Pick Lists. A Pick List is basically a list, which allows users to pick a value from various available values. Pick list makes data entry easy for users, as they do not need to type it. They can simply select a value from various available values. As users do not need to type values, using pick lists provides some benefits to developers as well, as they do not need to add validations on those values that are present in pick list.

Major topics covered in this chapter are:

- Introduction to Pick List
- Types of Pick List
- Static Pick List
  - Important objects in creating static pick list
  - Creating static pick list
- Dynamic Pick List
  - Important objects in creating dynamic pick list
  - Creating pick Applet
  - Creating dynamic pick list
- Hierarchical Pick List
- Configuring Hierarchical Pick List

15.1 PICK LIST

Pick list allows picking the values from a list. It enables the user to select a value from a list, rather than typing it. As user does not have to type the values, it reduces a lot of validation efforts at developer's side. Also, it is easy and comfortable approach to allow users to select values, instead of asking them to type it manually. Figure 15.1 below demonstrates a pick list.

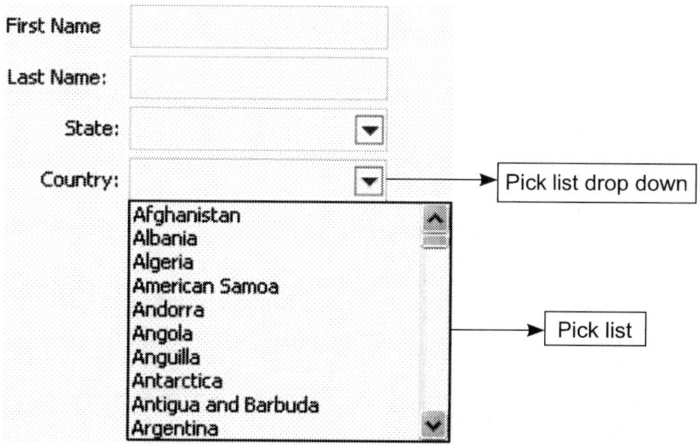

Fig. 15.1 *Pick list*

15.2 TYPES OF PICK LISTS

Pick lists are of two types, static and dynamic.

1. **Static Pick List:** As clear from name, the data in static pick list is fairly static, which does not change frequently. Static pick list gets the data from Siebel list of values table, which is maintained by an administrator. It is basically a list of predefined values that the user invokes from a field in an applet. This field has a drop-down arrow on right side, which on clicking shows a single column pick list, from which a user can select one value.
2. **Dynamic Pick List:** Unlike static pick lists, the values in dynamic pick list are not fixed. The values in these pick lists come from user-maintained tables, such as S_ORG_EXT or S_CONTACT.

There are certain key terms about pick lists, which are common for both static as well as dynamic pick lists. Pick lists may be ***bounded or unbounded***. Bounded pick lists allow a user to select the value from the list only, whereas ***unbounded pick lists*** allow a user to enter their own values, apart from those that are present in the list. The applet that contains the control or list column that invokes the pick list is called ***originating applet***, and these controls or list columns are called ***originating control or originating list column***. The underlying business component is called ***originating business component*** and the corresponding field is called ***originating field***. Originating field is associated to the value field in pick list generic business component via ***pick map object definition***. The selection of value from pick list updates the corresponding field of current record in this business component. The sequence for updating fields with information from pick business component record is defined by ***sequence property***. If this property is not specified, the fields are updated in the order in which they were created. Also, in case the originating field is custom field, we will need to ensure that it can accommodate values from LOV table. If our field is shorter than LOV table value, it will result in truncation of data while displaying, or storing in database.

The special-purpose business component for the list of value lists that are used in static pick lists is called ***pick list generic business component***. The administration of this business component is done through Administration -> Data Screen, List of Values view.

The field in Originating Business Component references the ***pick list object*** definition, which identifies the Pick Applet's Business Component. Pick Applet's Business Component is always Pick List Generic.

In the next section, we will concentrate on Static Pick List's Originating Applet and Business Component's properties, followed by configuring static pick lists. After that, we will move toward dynamic pick lists.

15.3 STATIC PICK LISTS

In this section, we will discuss about creating static pick lists. Before discussing the steps to create them, we will first discuss about important objects involved in creating static pick lists. The next section discusses about some important objects involved in creating static pick lists. After this, we will discuss about steps involved in creating static pick lists.

15.3.1 Important Objects for Creating Static Pick List

15.3.1.1 *Originating business component*

As discussed earlier, an originating business component is the business component of originating applet. The two most important object definitions for originating business component are field (child object), which identifies the pick list object definition, and pick map (grandchild object). Pick map is child object of originating field. It has following two properties:

- **Field:** Identifies the name of originating field.
- **Pick list field:** In this property, we will need to enter "Value." This setting references the value field in the Pick List Generic business component.

15.3.1.2 *Originating applet of static pick list*

Some of the important properties of originating applet of static pick list are mentioned in Table 15.1. The properties marked * belong to originating control (control object type) or list column (list column object type):

Table 15.1 Properties of Originating Applet

Property name	*Description*
Business component	Identifies the originating business component
Field*	As clear from name, it identifies the originating field from originating business component
Pick list	Identifies the pick applet. In case of static pick list, this property should be kept blank
Runtime	A static pick list is activated in response to the user click at runtime only when this property is set to TRUE

* In static pick list, generally there is exactly one pick map object definition. Multiple pick maps are used only when we need to use a multiple column selection list.

15.3.1.3 *Pick list generic business component*

This business component is reserved for a list of values for static pick lists. For the definition and grouping of a list of values, the generic business component uses its two fields: Type and Value.

Type specifies the type of list of values. For example, PERSON_TITLE specifies the person title list of values (Mr., Mrs., Etc.) and ACCOUNT_TYPE specifies account type list of values (Customer, Partner, etc.). Type is used for the grouping of all records that are in one list of values.

Value is that portion of record that is displayed in static pick list. For example, PERSON_TITLE values may be Mr., Ms., Dr., and so on.

15.3.2 Creating a Static Pick List

A pick list is created by using Pick List Wizard. Follow the steps below to create a static pick list:

1. Go to File Menu, and select New Object. The New Object Wizard appears.
2. From this wizard, select pick list icon and click OK. The pick list dialogue box appears next.
3. You will be required to enter the following values in this dialogue box:

Project	Select the project for your pick list. Only locked projects appear in this list.
Business component	Here the name of originating business component is to be filled
Field	The name of the field

4. In next step, pick list type dialogue box appears. Select "Static" here and click Next. The pick list definition dialogue box appears.
5. Here you will have two options. Either you can create a new pick list, or use an existing one.
   - To create a new pick list, select "Create New Pick list" option button and click next. This will take you to pick list definition dialogue box. Now, perform any one step from the following table:

Create new LOV	Do the following: • Enter unique pick list name, select "Create New Pick List" button and click Next. • In next box, enter a unique name for a list of values and corresponding values and click Next.
Create New Pick List by using existing LOV	Do the following: • Enter unique pick list name and select radio button "Use predetermined List Of Values." • Select a list of values type and click Next. • In next box, provide a search specification. Also, select whether you want the pick list to be bounded and click Next.

   Any one of the above-mentioned approaches will take you to finish the dialogue box.
   - To use an existing pick list, select the pick list and associated LOV to be used, and click Next. This will take you to the Finish dialogue box.
6. In Finish dialogue box, review the information present and click Finish.

Static pick lists should be used where the data to be displayed is fairly static, that is, it does not change frequently. For displaying frequently changing data (e.g., Names of all the members in a particular Account), we use dynamic pick lists.

With this, we will turn our discussion toward discussing dynamic pick lists and pick applets. Dynamic pick lists are typically implemented by using pick applets. In next section, we will discuss about dynamic pick list and the use of pick applet, followed by the steps to configure them.

15.4 DYNAMIC PICK LIST

Like static pick lists, dynamic pick lists also help users to provide values to the fields by selecting values from the list. The main difference between static and dynamic pick list is that in dynamic pick list, data is not static. Static pick lists draw their data from predefined list of values maintained by administrator. On the other hand, dynamic pick lists draw their data from user maintained business components. Fields that implement a dynamic pick list are typically joined fields with the data from the table other than underlying business component's base table. Using a dynamic pick list, we can update the data of the joined field.

Dynamic pick lists are typically implemented by using a pick applet. Pick applets are basically applets based on a business component, which is called "Pick Business Component." Data present in pick applets come from Pick Business Component. From the pick applet, user can select any one row. On selection, the data from that row of pick applet gets populated in the corresponding fields of originating applet. Figure 15.2 shows a dynamic pick list.

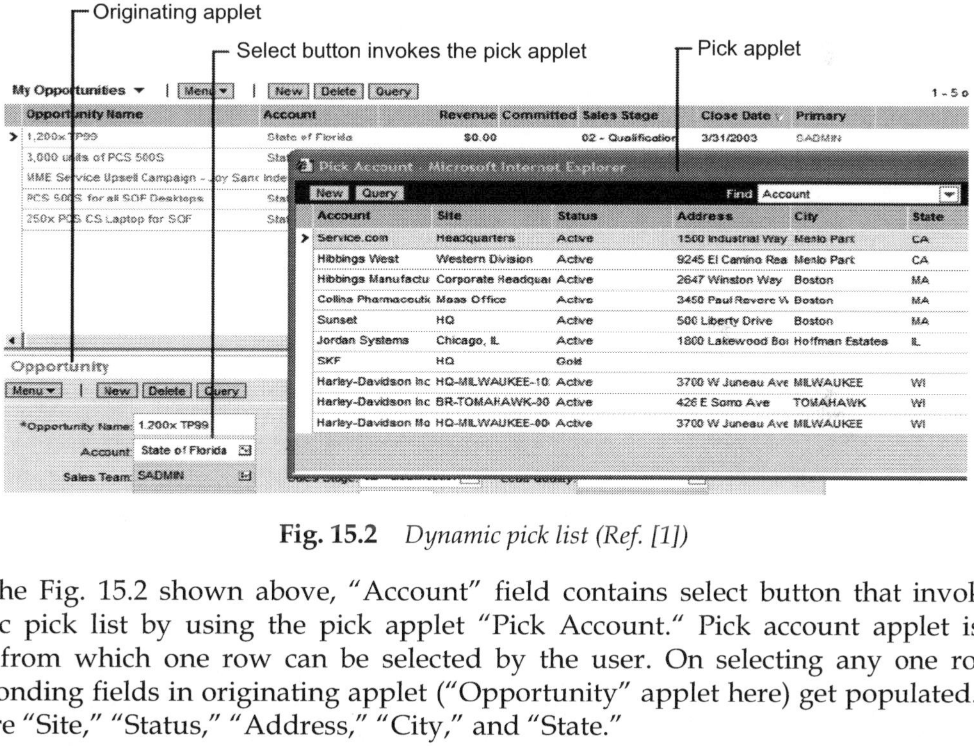

Fig. 15.2 *Dynamic pick list (Ref. [1])*

In the Fig. 15.2 shown above, "Account" field contains select button that invokes the dynamic pick list by using the pick applet "Pick Account." Pick account applet is a list applet, from which one row can be selected by the user. On selecting any one row, the corresponding fields in originating applet ("Opportunity" applet here) get populated. These fields are "Site," "Status," "Address," "City," and "State."

The example shown above uses a join between account and opportunity business components. In opportunity business component, there is a foreign key that identifies an account for each opportunity. When the user selects any account from the pick applet "Pick Account," the foreign key gets populated and the selected account gets associated with this opportunity.

Before moving ahead with configuring dynamic pick lists and pick applets, let us first discuss various object definitions and their properties specific to dynamic pick lists.

15.5 OBJECTS DEFINITIONS REQUIRED FOR DYNAMIC PICK LISTS

1. **Originating Applet:** Originating applet is the applet that contains the control or list column that invokes the pick list. In the example shown above, the form applet "Opportunity" is the originating applet. The Business Component property of an originating applet contains the name of originating business component. Some of the important child object definitions for originating applet are mentioned in Table 15.2.

Table 15.2 Child objects for Originating Applet

Serial number	*Child object*	*Description*
1.	Originating control	The control in the originating applet that invokes the pick applet. A special property of originating control is its pick applet property, which contains the name of the pick applet. This control maps to the originating field in originating business component. More on originating business component and originating field is discussed in next topic
2.	Related controls	These controls get automatically populated when user selects a value for originating control from pick applet. These controls are mapped to the fields that are present in the "Pick Map" property of originating field in originating business component
3.	Unrelated controls	Other controls apart from the related controls in the applet

2. **Originating Business Component:** Originating business component is the business component that contains the originating field. An originating applet is always based on originating business component. It has no special properties for dynamic pick lists, but some of its child object definitions mentioned in Table 15.3 are specific to pick list.

Table 15.3 Child objects of Originating Business Component

Serial number	*Child object*	*Description*
1.	Originating field	Field that is mapped with originating control in originating applet. This field has a pick map child object defined. Pick map is used to associate pick list fields with the corresponding fields in business component. Also, the pick list property of this field contains the name of the pick list being used

Serial number	*Child object*	*Description*
2.	Pick map	Child of originating field. Pick map is basically a map between fields in pick business component and originating business component. Pick maps are defined as child objects of originating field, rather than originating business component. This makes it possible for multiple fields in originating business component to have pick applets defined for them. The pick map definition is responsible to populate the "Related Controls" in originating applet when a value is picked for originating control. All the related controls are mapped to the fields present in pick map. On selecting the pick map object, we will find two important properties: Field and Pick List field. Field property contains the name of originating business component's field, and pick list field property contains the name of fields in pick business component
3.	Joins	Joins are used to implement the relationship between originating business component and pick business component. It is a join between base tables of both the business components. This join is responsible to populate all those fields in the originating business component that have this join's name in their "Join" property
4.	Join field	Join field plays the role of a foreign key in Join relationship used by pick applet. If we open "Join Specification" child object of Join object, we can find the join field in the "Source Field" property. This field gets updated when a user selects a record in pick applet, and based on the value of join field, all the related fields in the pick map get updated
5.	Related fields	Related fields are the fields mapped to related controls in the originating applet. These fields are mapped to pick business component fields in the pick map child object definition of originating field. One important thing to note here is that all these fields use the same join name in their "Join" property, which is used by the originating field. This join is responsible to set the value of these fields in database, when user makes a selection in pick applet

Now, as we are aware of the concept of dynamic pick list and important objects associated to it, let us now have a look on configuring dynamic pick lists. But, before configuring the pick list, let us first configure a pick applet that we will use to display our pick list in UI.

15.6 CONFIGURING PICK APPLET

Figure 15.3 shows the steps to configure a pick applet. The points to note here are as follows:

- Pick applet is based on pick business component.
- As it is a list applet, we should define both base and edit list mode for the applet.

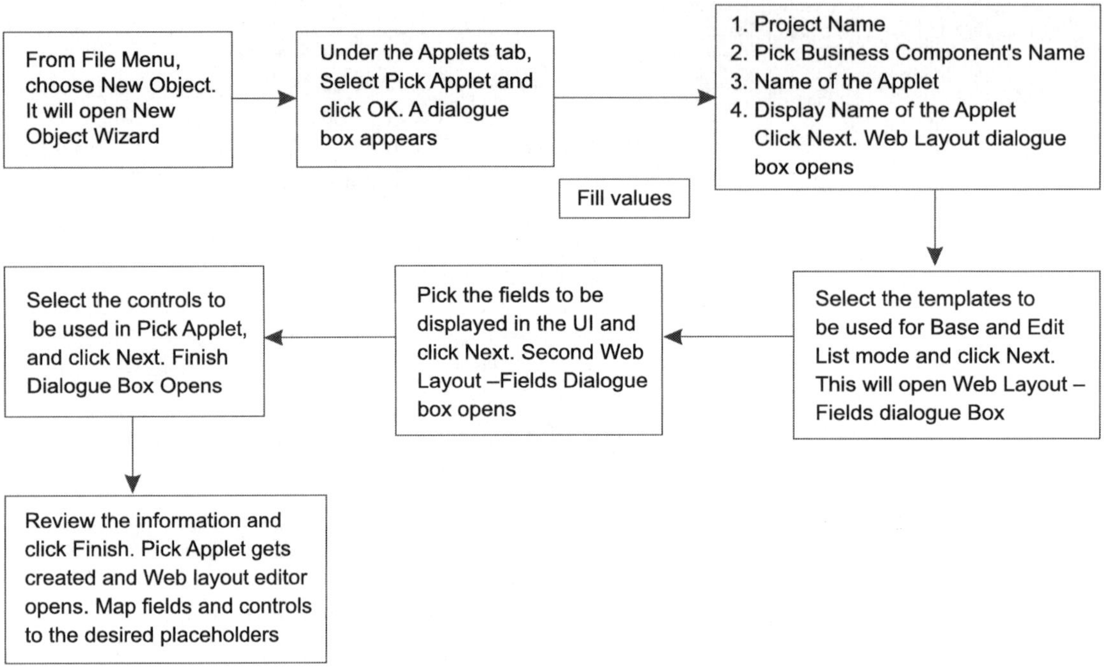

Fig. 15.3 *Creating pick applet*

After creating the pick applet, we are now ready to proceed with configuring the dynamic pick list.

15.7 CONFIGURING DYNAMIC PICK LISTS

Figure 15.4 shows the steps to configure a dynamic pick list by using a pick list wizard. Along with creating the pick list, the pick list wizard also creates related objects that include pick maps and pick applets. As discussed while configuring static pick lists, we should always create the pick list with the name in format ABC Pick List <Entity>, where Entity is the object on which pick list is based.

Moving ahead, we will discuss about one more type of pick list, that is, hierarchical pick list. Hierarchical pick lists are used in the scenarios where the data in one pick list is populated based on the value selected in some other pick list. In next section, we will discuss about the significance of hierarchical pick lists, along with the steps to configure them.

15.8 HIERARCHICAL PICK LISTS

Hierarchical pick list is basically used to implement relationship between two pick lists, where data in one pick list depends on the data selected in another pick list. Let us understand this with an example of school. Suppose, we have two pick lists: one that displays the standards in school (e.g., 1st standard, 2nd standard, etc.) and second one displays the list of students based on standard. Our requirement says that when we select

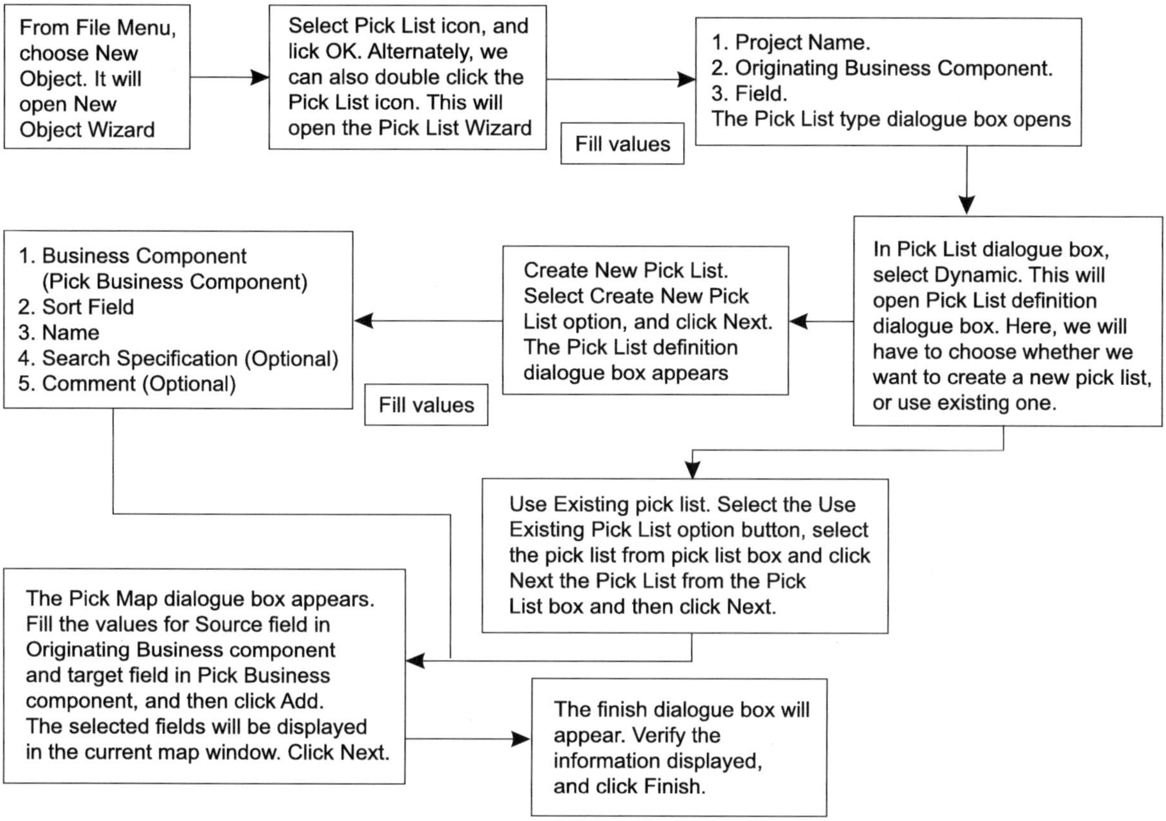

Fig. 15.4 *Creating dynamic pick lists*

1st standard, the second pick list should be populated with the list of students from 1st standard, when we select 2nd standard, the second pick list should be populated with the list of students in 2nd standard, and so on.

This can be done by using hierarchical pick list, in which the data in second pick list should be populated based on that selected in first one. This relationship is developed in List of Values table. One thing to be kept in mind here is that the values used in both the pick lists should have same LOV type. Table 15.4 illustrates a possible implementation of the example of school discussed above:

Table 15.4 Example scenario for Hierarchical Pick List implementation

Type	*Display value*	*Language independent code*	*Parent LIC*
STD_LOV	1	1	None
STD_LOV	Krushh	Krushh	1
STD_LOV	Espider Man	Espider Man	1

Type	*Display value*	*Language independent code*	*Parent LIC*
STD_LOV	Sooper Man	Sooper Man	1
STD_LOV	2	2	None
STD_LOV	Debat Man	Debat Man	2
STD_LOV	Harry Kotar	Harry Kotar	2
STD_LOV	Pokkuman	Pokkuman	2

How the relation works: In the table mentioned above, we can see four columns, Type, Display Value, Language Independent Code, and Parent LIC. Here, first thing to notice is that Type column has same value in all the rows. In display value, we have values {1, 2} along with some names. In Parent LIC column, we have provided the name of parents for the corresponding items.

Now, we can create two pick lists, one parent pick list showing "Standards" as "1" and "2," and second child pick list "Student" to show the names "Krushh," "Espider Man," "Sooper Man," "Debat Man," "Harry Kotar," and "Pokkuman." Configuring hierarchical pick lists is discussed in next section.

Now, when we select "1" in "Standards" pick list, all the names having "1" in the "Parent LIC" column in List of Values, that is {"Krushh," "Espider Man," and "Sooper Man,"} will be populated in "Student" pick list. Similarly, when we select "2" in "Standards" pick list, the corresponding student names, that is, {"Debat Man," "Harry Kotar," and "Pokkuman"} will be populated in "Student" pick list.

Let us now have a look on steps to configure a hierarchical pick list, with which we will wind up our discussion on pick lists.

15.9 CONFIGURING HIERARCHICAL PICK LIST

Following are the steps to configure a hierarchical pick list:

1. **Configure parent and child pick lists:** The only thing to note here is the name of business components for parent and child pick list. We have to set the following values:

Parent Pick List's Business Component = "Pick List Hierarchical"

Child Pick List's Business Component = "Pick List Hierarchical Sub-Area"

Note: Apart from typing Business Component's name, we can also select these names from the available drop-down list.

2. Next step is to make required changes in the fields for which we are creating pick lists. For this, we have to go to business component in which these fields are present and make the following changes:
   - Choose the field that will be associated with parent pick list, and set the "Pick List" property of this field to the name of parent pick list.

- Set the "Immediate Post Changes" property of this field to TRUE.
- Similar to the first step, set the "Pick List" property of child field to the name of child pick list.
- Configure the pick map child object of child field as mentioned in Table 15.5 below:

Table 15.5 Pick Map example for Hierarchical Pick List

Field	*Pick list field*	*Constrain*
[Parent Field]	Parent	TRUE
[Child Field]	Value	Leave blank

3. Compile the changes.
4. Add values in LOV. (Refer the sample values shown at previous page to put values in LOV. Use Parent LIC column to assign parent values to corresponding child values.)
5. Open the client to check and verify the hierarchical pick list.

15.10 SUMMARY

Pick lists are the lists that allow users to pick values. They make using the application easy for users. Also, they reduce some burden, both for users as well as developers. For users, they make it easy to enter the data by prohibiting the manual typing of values, whereas for developers, they make it easy by freeing them from the burden of putting validations on the values entered by users. Moving ahead, we will discuss about one more complex object, that is, multi-value group (MVG).

REFERENCE

1. Siebel Bookshelf V8.0 (Nov., 2008). Available from: www.oracle.com.
   PDF name: Configuring Siebel Business Applications.
   Page: 359 Figure 7

Chapter 16

MULTI-VALUE GROUP

Multi-value groups are used with the fields having multiple values. Multi-value groups, popularly known as MVG, are typically used where the data from one business component is required to be displayed and modified in other business component. The business component on which MVG applet is based is called as MVG business component, whereas the business component corresponding to the field that displays data from MVG business component is known as originating business component. MVG is implemented by using a link between the two business components, where originating business component works as master, and MVG business component works as detail business component.

Major topics covered in this chapter are:

- Introduction to Multi Value Groups
- Important objects involved in creating MVG
- Configuring MVG
- Configuring MVG Applet

16.1 MULTI-VALUE GROUP

In some scenarios, it is required by one business component to display and maintain a set of records from another business component. In the example shown in Fig. 16.1 below, the "Address" field in "Account" applet needs to display address-related data. It has a "multi-select" button, which opens another applet "Account Addresses," which includes multiple fields, such as "Address Line 1," "City," and "State." If you see the diagram properly, the row selected in "Account Addresses" applet has values "Address Line 1 = 2541 Orchard PKWY," "City = San Jose," and "State = CA," and these values resemble the corresponding values in originating applet "Account." If we select some other record from "Account Addresses applet," the values will be populated in the corresponding fields in "Account" applet. Such relationships are called master–detail relationships, where "Account" applet plays the role of master, and "Account Addresses" plays the role of detail.

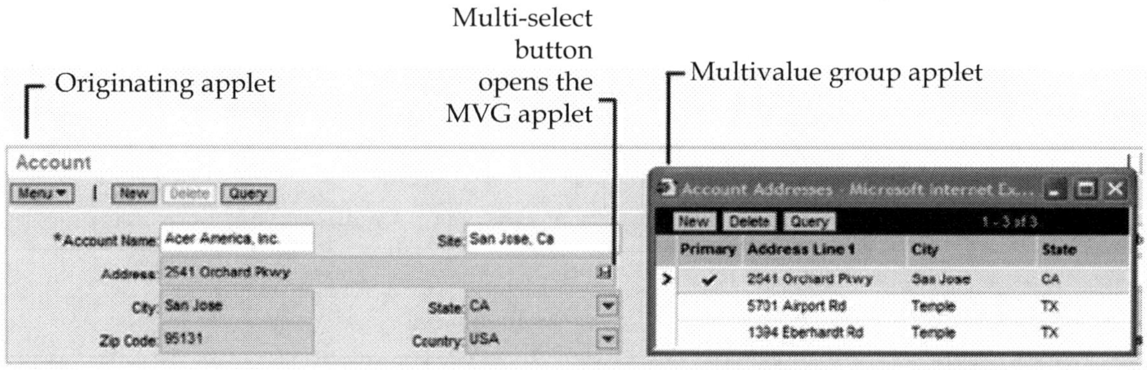

Fig. 16.1 *Multi-value group applet (Ref. [1])*

An MVG is used to implement such master–detail relationships. The applet "Account Addresses" is actually a MVG applet, based on MVG business component. Also, you can see "New" and "Delete" buttons on the top of "Account Addresses" applet. These buttons facilitate the addition of new records or deleting existing records from MVG applet itself.

16.2 IMPORTANT TERMS RELATED TO MVG

Before moving ahead toward the important properties of MVGs, let us first discuss some important terms related to it. Some of the important terms related to MVG are as follows:

1. **Originating Applet:** As is clear from the name, an originating applet is the applet that contains the control or list column used to invoke MVG applet. In the example shown in Fig. 16.1 above, "Address" field of "Account" applet invokes the MVG applet "Account Addresses." Hence, "Account" applet is the originating applet. The business component corresponding to originating applet is called as originating business component. We will discuss about originating business component later in this section.
2. **Originating Control/List column:** Originating control or list column indicates the control or list column of originating applet that is used to invoke MVG applet. Originating control or list column contains multi-select button, which invokes MVG applet when clicked. In the example shown in Fig. 16.1, "Address" field of "Account" applet is working as originating control. An originating control has two important properties, that is, Field and MVG Applet. Field identifies the originating field in originating business component, and MVG applet identifies the MVG applet that is invoked on clicking the multi-select button in originating applet.
3. **Originating Business Component:** As discussed in point 1 above, an originating business component is the business component on which originating applet is based. Similar to the relationship between other business components, applets and the data in originating applet's originating field and other multi-value fields is obtained from corresponding fields from a record in originating business component. Two most significant properties of an originating business component are field and multi-value

link. Multi-value link object definition identifies the multi-value link that provides values from MVG business component by using a link. The field object definition identifies the field in MVG business component which provides value to the field in originating business component, using multi-value link. We will discuss more on this while discussing the configuration of MVG.

4. **Pick Map object:** Whenever we select a record from MVG applet by using originating field from originating applet, there are certain related fields in originating applet that automatically get populated after the selection. If we refer to the example shown in Fig. 16.1, when we select "Address Line 1" field as "2541 Orchard PKWY," the fields "City" and "Address" automatically get values "San Jose" and "CA." This mapping is done by using a pick map object definition. A pick map object is the child object of multi-value field, which identifies the relationship between a field in origination business component with the corresponding field in MVG business component. A pick map has following two important properties, which identify this relationship:
   - Field: Field property identifies the field in originating business component that needs to be populated by using this relationship. The value from MVG business component's field is provided to this field when pick record method is invoked.
   - Pick List Field: This property identifies the field in MVG business component that provides value to the corresponding field in originating business component.
5. **MVG Business Component:** MVG business component is the business component on which MVG applet is based. It stores the detail records in master–detail relationship. In Fig. 16.1, the MVG applet "Account Addresses" is based on MVG business component. MVG business component is just a normal business component, with no special properties.
6. **Link Object:** The master–detail relationship between originating business component and MVG business component is implemented by using a link object definition. Link object definition works as a link that supplies data to the fields in originating business component from the corresponding fields in MVG business component. Link object has four important properties: parent business component (originating business component), child business component (MVG business component), source field (Unique ID field from originating business component) and destination field (field from MVG business component, foreign key pointing back to originating business component). For more details on link object, refer Chapter 12.
7. **Multi-value link object:** After defining link object between master and detail business component, multi-value link object definition is required. Multi-value link object is child object of business component. For implementing MVG, we will need to define the multi-value link object for originating business component. It identifies the link object that provides the field values from MVG business component. A multi-value link object has three important properties: Primary Id Field (identifies the foreign key field in originating or joined business component), Destination Link (identifies the link that is used to connect originating business component with MVG business component), and Destination Business Component (the child business component, here it is MVG business component).

16.3 CREATING MVG

Now as we are aware of all the important objects required for configuring MVG, let us now move our discussion toward configuring MVG. This is accomplished in two steps. First step is to configure an MVG. The second step is for configuring MVG applet. First flow chart shows the steps to configure an MVG, the second one shows configuring MVG applet.

16.3.1 Configuring MVG

Figure 16.2 shows the steps to create an MVG.

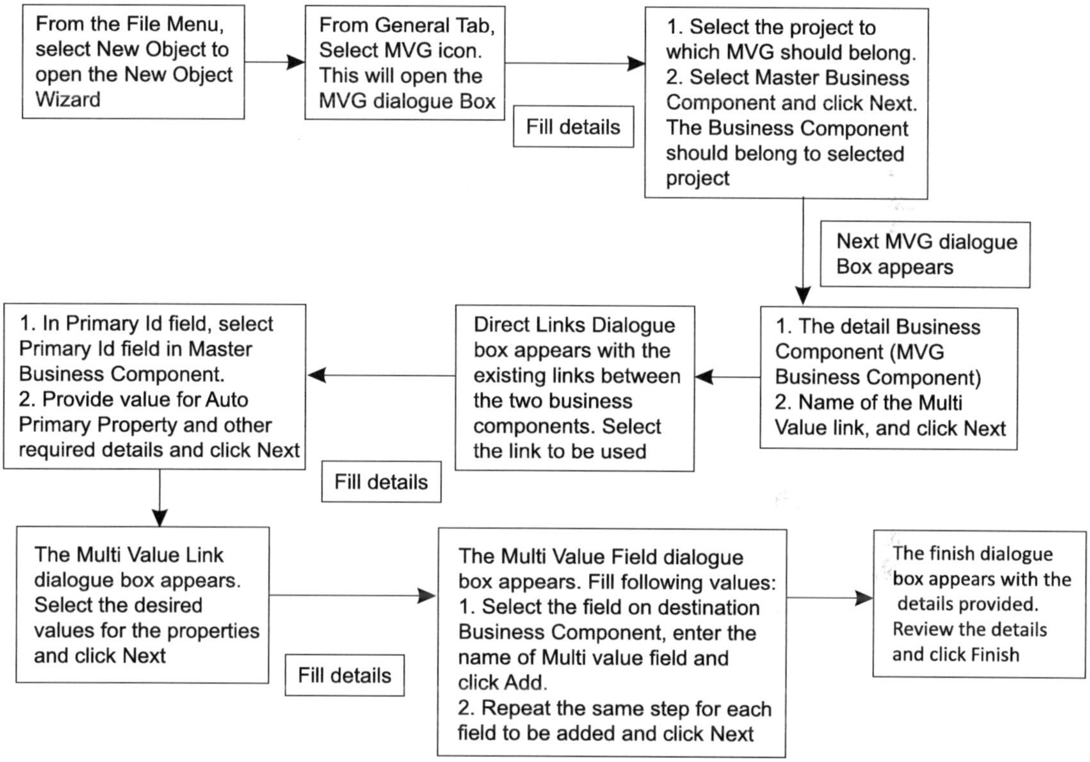

Fig. 16.2 *Steps to create MVG*

16.3.2 Creating MVG Applets

Figure 16.3 shows the steps to create MVG applets.

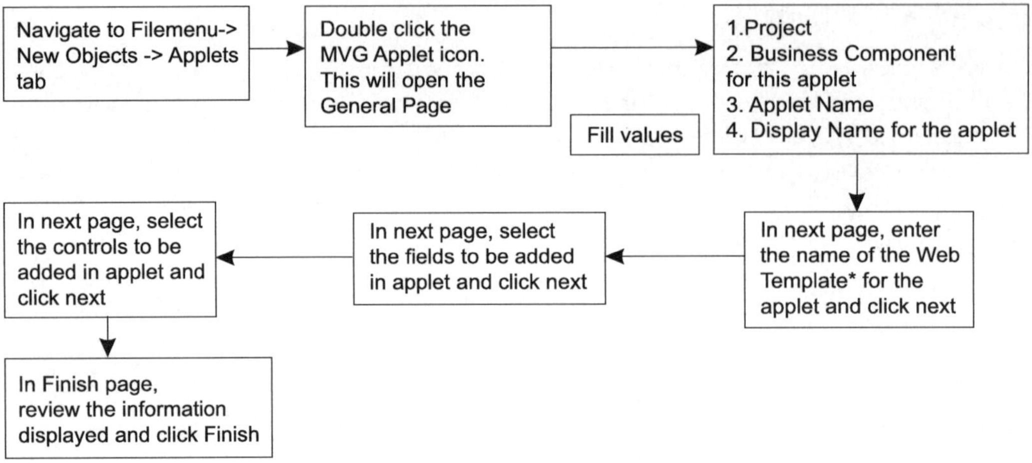

Fig. 16.3 *Creating MVG applets*

* If all the three modes (base, edit, and edit list) are defined for an MVG applet, it inherits the mode from its parent applet. However, if we define only base mode for this applet, then base mode is always used, regardless of parent applet's mode.

16.4 SUMMARY

MVGs allow users to create and maintain a set of values for a particular field. They make viewing and modifying the data corresponding to a multi-value field easy and systematic. Typically, most of the beginners get confused between an MVG and a dynamic pick list. The most basic difference between these two lies in their name itself. Dynamic pick list is used in the scenarios where it is required to select one value from a list of values available. In this case, the field contains only one value, which is selected by user. On the other hand, MVG is used where a field has multiple values, and all the values are displayed when the MVG icon attached with the field is clicked. Moving ahead, we will discuss about toolbars and menus.

REFERENCE

1. Siebel Bookshelf V8.0 (Nov., 2008). Available from: www.oracle.com.
   PDF Name: Configuring Siebel Business Applications
   Page: 408 Figure 80

Chapter 17

TOOLBARS AND MENUS

This chapter focuses on configuring toolbars and menus. While discussing navigation in Chapter 5, we discussed about various options present in application-level menu and toolbars, along with the actions performed by using those options. In this chapter, we will focus more toward configuration aspects of toolbars and menus.

Toolbars and menus are basically the collection of various actions that can be performed by user. Toolbars show these actions in the form of icons, whereas menus show them in the form of options in the list.

Major topics covered in this chapter are:

- Introduction to Toolbars and Menus
- Important objects involved in creating Toolbars and Menus
- Configuring Toolbars and Menus

17.1 TOOLBARS AND MENUS

Toolbars and menus can be considered as a bunch of various actions that can be performed by user at user interface. The basic difference between two is the way they display these actions. Let us first understand this difference between the two, after which we will move toward configuring them.

Menu: Menu can be considered as a group of various options that allow users to perform specific tasks. Just like menu in a restaurant which allows us to select from various dishes, menu in user interface presents various actions that can be taken, and allow us to select the desired actions. Figure 17.1 shows the Edit menu.

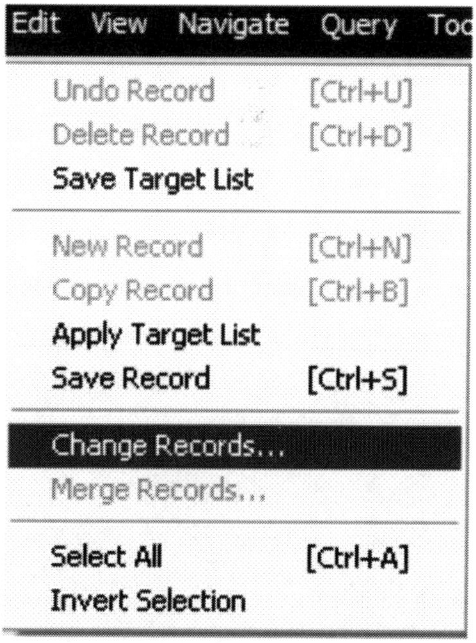

Fig. 17.1 *Edit menu*

Fig. 17.2 *Application toolbar*

Toolbar: Just like a menu, a toolbar can be considered as a group of various options. The basic difference between a toolbar and a menu is while a menu represents options in the form of list, toolbar represents options in the form of icons (Figure 17.2). To perform a desired task, we need to click on the icon.

On clicking any menu item or toolbar, an action is performed. This action is based on the method to which that menu item or toolbar icon is targeted. The method invoked may reside in a service (on server or browser) or in classes in browser application or server infrastructure. Along with the method name, toolbar icon or menu item target a method handler, which is used to automatically retarget it if the specified method is not found. Optionally, they can target a service as well.

17.2 CONFIGURING TOOLBARS AND MENUS

In this section, we will discuss about steps to configure toolbars and menus. But before discussing about configuring toolbars and menus, let us first have a quick look on various objects involved in configuring them.

17.2.1 Important Objects Involved in Configuring Toolbars and Menus

Table 17.1 shows the important objects involved in configuring toolbars and menus. The objects mentioned in points 2, 3, 4 and 5 are specific to menus, whereas the objects discussed in points 6 and 7 specific to toolbars:

Table 17.1 Objects for configuring toolbar and menu

Sl. No.	*Object type*	*Used for*	*Important properties*
1.	Command	Specifies the invoke method called when toolbar or menu item is executed. (Applet-level menus do not use command object. Only application-level menus use it)	1. **Target:** This property identifies the entity (Browser/server/ browser applet) that will handle the invoke method called by command. More about this is discussed in Section 17.2.2 2. **Business service:** This property identifies the service (browser/service) that handles the invoke method. This selection is based on the value provided in target property 3. **Method:** This property identifies the invoke method name. More about this is discussed in Section 17.2.2 4. **Method argument:** This property identifies the input argument to the invoke method. For example, if invoke method is "GotoView," the argument can be the view name 5. **Show pop-up:** This property decides whether to open a new browser window should be opened before invoking the method. If set to TRUE, a new browser window is opened, otherwise the method is invoked in current window 6. **HTML pop-up dimensions:** This property specifies the dimensions of the pop-up window

Sl. No.	*Object type*	*Used for*	*Important properties*
2.	Menu	Identifies the menu that is displayed in user interface	1. **Name:** This property specifies the name of the menu object 2. **Project:** This property specifies the project to which the menu belongs
3.	Menu item	Child object of menu object. Used to associate a command object definition with the menu item object definition. This association determines the method invoked when this menu item is selected	1. **Name:** This property specifies the name of the menu item 2. **Caption:** This property specifies the display name for the menu item 3. **Command:** This property specifies the command object definition that provides invoke method and target to menu item 4. **Position:** This property identifies the order of menu items
4.	Applet method menu item	Child object of applet object type. Identifies the menu object definition for applet-level menu	1. **Command:** This property identifies the command object definition that provides method invoked, target, and bitmap to applet method menu item 2. **Menu text:** This property specifies the display text in menu item 3. **Position:** This property specifies the sequence of the menu item
5.	Class method menu item	Child object of class object. Used to add menu item on applet-level menus for SWE applets of specified applet class along with its subclasses	1. **Target:** This property identifies the entity (Browser for handling method using JavaScript service on browser, Server for handling it by using an Object Manager Service) that handles the method specified in method property 2. **Business service:** This property identifies the business service on which method is invoked. If left blank, method is invoked on applet class 3. **Suppress menu item:** A TRUE value removes the applet-level menu items from applet-level menus of all the applets derived from this class and its subclasses 4. **Method:** This property identifies the method invoked on selecting this menu item 5. **Position:** This property identifies the sequence of menu item 6. **Menu text:** This property provides the text displayed in the menu item

Sl. No.	*Object type*	*Used for*	*Important properties*
6.	Toolbar	Provides a named toolbar to be used in Siebel applications	1. **Name:** This property identifies the name of the toolbar object 2. **Class*:** This property identifies the name of the class that implements the toolbar
7.	Toolbar item	Associates toolbar object with command object definition, which provides target, method invoked, and bitmap to toolbar	1. **Name:** This property identifies the name of the toolbar item object 2. **Command:** This property identifies the command object that provides target, bitmap, and method invoked to toolbar 3. **Position:** This property identifies the order of toolbar items 4. **HTML type:** For each toolbar item, this property specifies the type of control to be displayed. Common options are MiniButton, hyperlink, ComboBox, label, and so on

- HTML toolbar: Shows buttons as static images, which can be dimmed when they are unavailable.
- Java toolbar: This is used for implementing communication toolbars, which facilitate users with additional functionalities, such as blinking of toolbar button at a certain event.

For HTML toolbars, the class property is left blank. For Java toolbars, this property specifies the Java class that implements the toolbar.

17.2.2 Targeting Invoke Method

As we are aware, the method invoked by toolbar or menu item is specified in the command object associated with it. Every method needs an object or service to process it. For specifying the object or service to process the method, we use target property of command object. Siebel provides us seven options to target the method. These options are as follows:

- Active applet
- Application
- Browser
- Browser applet
- SI plus
- Server
- Service

Out of these seven options, only two options are available for us when we create command object by using command wizard. These options are Browser and Server.

1. **Browser:** If we select browser option in target property, the method is handled by JavaScript applet, JavaScript service, or JavaScript application on browser side. In this case, it is mandatory to provide a method name in method property. In addition,

if we specify a service name in service property, it is targeted. If we do not specify it, the method is handled based on whether the calling entity is application-level or applet-level. If the calling entity is application-level, method handling targets the specified method in JavaScript application. If the calling entity is applet-level, it targets to the specified method in the JavaScript applet.

2. **Server:** We select this option to invoke a method in a C++ class. If we specify a service in service property, at application-level, the method is handled by the business service on server (specified in business service property), whereas at applet level, the method is handled by the service on server. In both the cases, the method handler does not retarget.

If we do not specify a service in service property, at application level, the method is handled by the base functionality associated with the application object, whereas at applet level, it is handled by the applet's class. If unhandled, it is retargeted to the classes above the current class in class hierarchy. If, after reaching the highest class (CSSSWEFrame), it is unhandled, it is retargeted to applet's business component's class, and successfully to the classes at higher level in class hierarchy.

17.2.3 Creating Menu and Toolbar

In this section, we will discuss about creating new toolbars and menus. As we can see in Table 17.1 showing the important objects involved in creating toolbars and menus, we can see that the command object is the common and most important object in creating toolbars and menus. Hence, before moving ahead with creating toolbars and menus, we will first discuss about creating command object.

17.2.3.1 Creating command object

Figure 17.3 shows the steps to configure a command object.

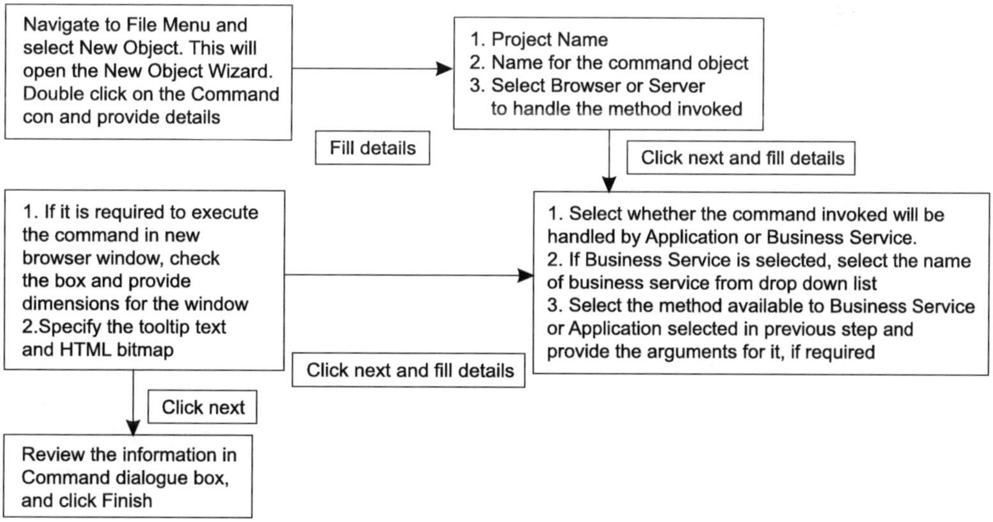

Fig. 17.3 *Steps to create a command object*

After creating the command object, let us move ahead to create toolbars and menus.

17.2.3.2 Creating applet menu

Figure 17.4 presents the steps required to create applet menu. In addition, it also provides the steps to make a menu item visible or suppress it. All the steps are shown in same flow diagram; however, the flow differs a bit if we create a new menu item. Follow the steps as required.

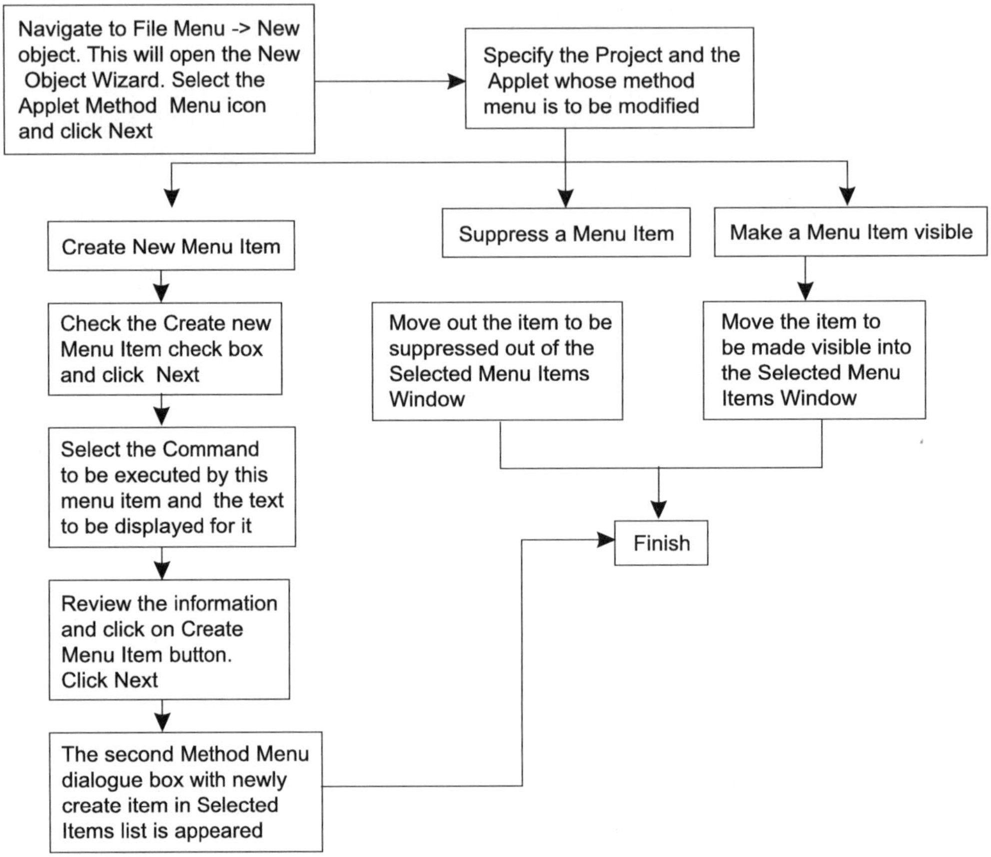

Fig. 17.4 *Steps to create applet menu*

17.2.3.3 Creating a new toolbar

In this section, we will discuss about creating new toolbars and adding a new toolbar icon to an existing toolbar. For creating a new toolbar, we just need to navigate to a toolbar object in Object Explorer, create a new record in Object List Editor and provide the name to the new toolbar. In order to expose the toolbar at UI, we will have to add the specific tab to the container page. Refer to Siebel Developer's Reference to know about templates and tags.

For adding a new toolbar icon to an existing toolbar, we need to first create a new command object to be used with this icon. For creating a new command object, refer to Section 17.2.3.1. After this, navigate to toolbar object definition, select the toolbar to which the new item is to be added, and select toolbar item object. Create a new record and provide require details including name of the toolbar item, name of the command object and position. To save the record, step-off from it.

While adding a new toolbar item to an existing toolbar, we should verify that the method we are planning to specify in command object and the bitmap image that will be used for toolbar icon currently exist. If anyone of these two does not exist, we will need to create them manually and add them.

17.3 SUMMARY

Toolbars and menus facilitate users with user-friendly way to choose and perform specific actions from available actions. They make application navigation simple and systematic for users by collecting commonly used actions at one place. Unlike other objects that focus more on displaying and modifying data, toolbars, and menus mainly deal with application-level actions. Configuration of toolbars and menus is a bit more difficult and confusing; hence, it requires more frequent practice to get handy with it.

Chapter 18

LIST OF VALUES

List of values, as clear from the name itself, is basically a list containing various values. The most common use of list of values (LOV) is to provide values to all the static pick lists in application. While our discussion on configuration of static pick lists, we saw how to associate a static pick list with LOV. The data from LOV is distributed to static pick lists by using "Type" column in LOV. In this chapter, we will discuss about creating and administering LOV.

Major topics covered in this chapter are:

- Introduction to List of Values
- Configuring List of Values
- List of Values fields
- Adding values to an existing List of Values
- Modifying records in existing LOV
- Multi – Lingual LOV

18.1 LIST OF VALUES

LOV is basically a "List," which contains some values. These values are used to populate static pick lists (static pick lists are discussed in Chapter 15). Static pick list is implemented in the form of a drop-down box at user interface, which allows user to select one value out of all the values. Typically, we display some values from LOV in a static pick list. These values are filtered based on "Type" of values. We can compare this with menu in a restaurant. The menu contains a list of all available dishes, classified based on their type, for example, "Vegetarian Dishes," "Non-Vegetarian Dishes," "Ice creams," "Juices," and so on. For selecting dishes, customers first filter them based on their "Type," and then put their order. Similar scenario happens in case of LOV, where "Menu" works as "LOV" and the list of order placed by customer works as "static pick list." Throughout this chapter, we will elaborate our discussion about "Values" and "Type" in LOV.

18.2 CONFIGURING LIST OF VALUES

In this section, we will discuss about configuring LOV. Siebel applications contain some vanilla LOV that can be used to supply values to various static pick lists across the application. Based on our requirement, we can choose from any one of following options (Fig. 18.1):

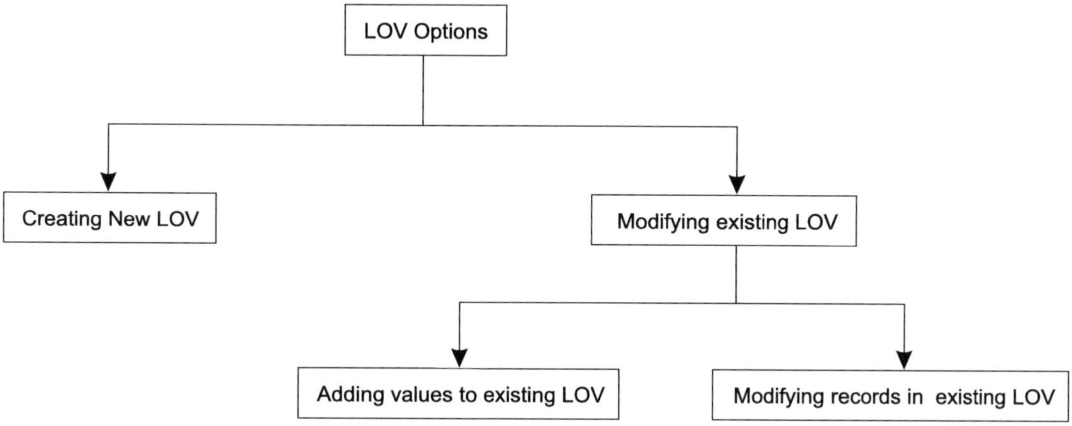

Fig. 18.1: *LOV options*

Before starting the discussion on these options, let us first have a look on various LOV fields. We will use these fields while configuring the LOVs.

18.3 LIST OF VALUES FIELDS

The data present in LOVs is stored in S_LIST_OF_VAL table in database. Table 18.1 shows some of the important fields present in LOV in UI. In UI, only some fields out of all are displayed by default. For viewing other fields, we will need to use "Columns Displayed" menu option.

Table 18.1 Fields in LOV UI

Serial number	*Field*	*Description*
1	Type	Stores and displays the "Type" of LOV
2	Display Value	Stores the values that are displayed in static pick list as drop-down options
3	Multilingual	When checked, this field indicates that LOV is a part of multilingual list of values (MLOV). MLOVs are discussed later in this chapter
4	Language Independent Code (LIC)	Typically, the value of this field is same as display value. Together, these fields uniquely identify a value for a particular LOV type. In case of MLOVs, these values are different from each other
5	Parent Language Independent Code	Used with hierarchical LOVs. In hierarchical LOVs, the values displayed in child LOV are based on the value selected in parent LOV. If we implement hierarchical LOV, this field stores the LIC for parent LOV
6	Translate	This field, when checked, indicates that internationalization is required

Serial number	Field	Description
7	Order	Specifies a numerical order for a value. The value gets displayed in static pick list in this order
8	Active	Decided whether the value is displayed to the end user. Only those values having active field checked are displayed
9	Language Name	Contains the language in which the value is displayed
10	Description	Contains description to a value

With this, let us proceed toward the various options discussed above. We will start with "Creating New LOVs," followed by various options available for modifying the existing LOVs.

18.4 CREATING NEW LIST OF VALUES

Figure 18.2 shows the steps to create new LOVs by using Siebel tools.

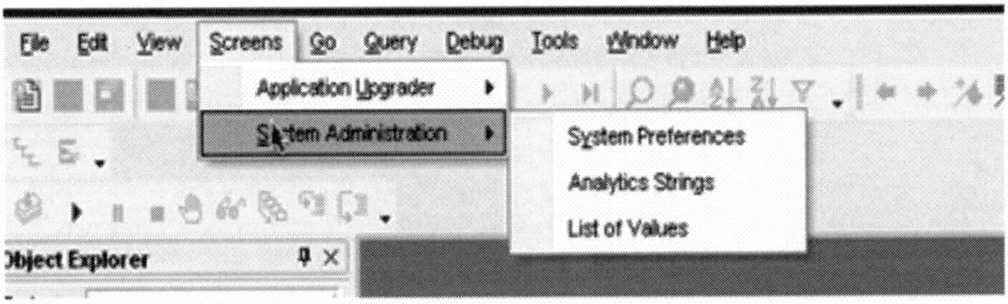

Fig. 18.2 *Screens menu -> System Administration options*

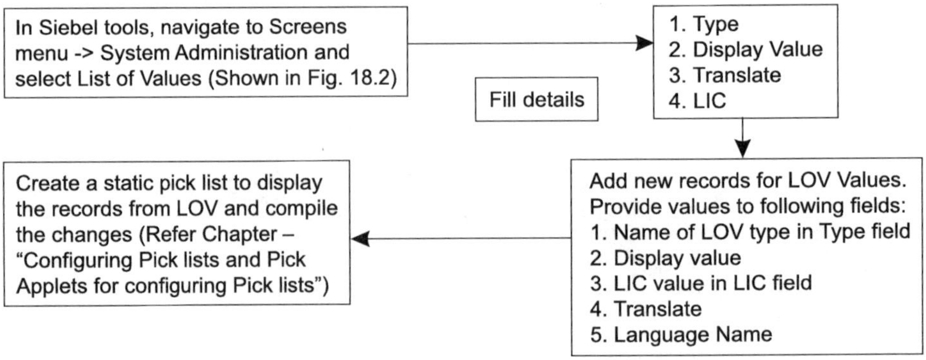

Fig. 18.3 *Steps to configure list of values*

If our requirement can be fulfilled by modifying the existing pick lists, we can select any one from the following options:

- Adding values to existing LOV
- Modifying records in existing LOV

18.5 ADDING VALUES TO EXISTING LIST OF VALUES

We can add new values to existing LOVs in order to fulfill our requirement. Figure 18.4 shows various steps to add new values in an existing LOV.

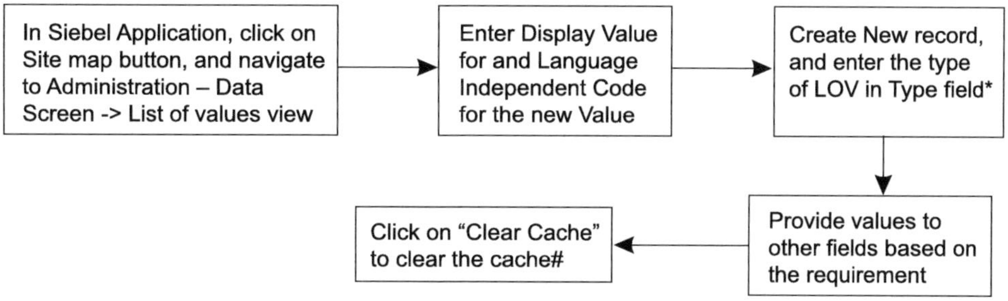

Fig. 18.4 *Steps to add values in existing LOV*

* In order to add a new value in existing LOV, the first thing we should know is the "Type," for which we want to add a value. For example, to add Butter Scotch Ice cream in restaurant menu, the first thing we should know is that the "Type" is "Ice cream." In order to get the type, follow these steps:

- In application, navigate to the screen that contains the static pick list in which the new value is to be added and make note of any one of the values in it.
- Navigate to Sitemap -> Administration Data screen -> List of Values view and query for the display value field noted in previous step.
- In the record returned as a result of query, identify the "Type" value. We will use this value while creating our new Value.

After adding new LOV, always remember to clear the cache by clicking the "Clear Cache" button to reflect the changes made in it.

18.6 MODIFYING THE RECORDS IN EXISTING LIST OF VALUES

In certain circumstances, it may be required to modify the values present in existing LOV. Figure 18.5 shows the steps to modify the existing values in LOV.

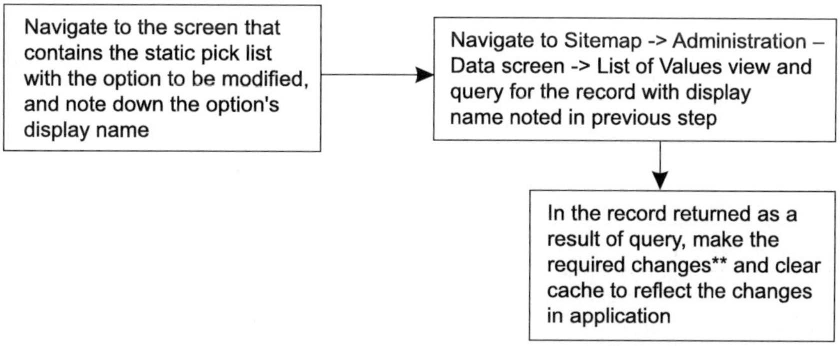

Fig. 18.5 *Steps to modify values in LOV*

** There are certain points to be kept in mind while making the changes in existing records in LOV:

- Never make any modification in the LOVs reserved for internal Siebel application's use.
- Never change the LIC of values, as it is used by internal Siebel application.
- Modifying the display value for some record does not update the historical data with new value.
- Along with display value of the record noted in first step in above flow diagram, the "Type" values is also required to make modifications. To find the "Type" value, refer to the previous section.

18.7 MULTILINGUAL LIST OF VALUES

MLOVs is a special kind of LOV that allows us to display values in active language of the user. We can enable MLOV only for bounded pick lists that are not hierarchical pick lists. (For bounded pick lists and hierarchical pick lists, refer to Chapter 15). MLOVs also allow users working in other languages to retrieve the values selected by a user working in any other language.

The basic difference between an LOV and MLOV is that LOV stores Display Value in columns, whereas MLOV stores LIC. As discussed earlier, display value and LIC together uniquely identify a particular record in LOV. For monolingual LOVs (referred as LOVs), the value of display value and LIC are same, whereas for MLOVs, display value contains the language specific value of the record, whereas LIC contains a common value for the record across all the languages.

18.8 SUMMARY

LOV plays a crucial role in managing values to be provided to static pick lists. They make it easy and systematic for administrator to add and modify the value displayed in pick lists without the additional effort to compile the changes or bouncing the server. Apart from providing values to static pick lists, LOVs also significantly enhance the quality of scripting by eliminating the need of hard coding the values. Due to this, any change requests for values can be handled systematically without modifying the code. With this, we are going to start the final chapter of this part, Chapter 19, after which we will move ahead toward a sample project to make the understanding of all these aspects of configuration handy for us.

Chapter 19

CONFIGURING APPLICATIONS

An application can be considered as a collection of related screens. Applications are designed to encapsulate all the functionalities required to suit a specific business functional area. Some examples of Siebel applications are Siebel Loyalty, Siebel Marketing, Siebel Sales and so on. In Part 2 of the book, we have discussed functional significance of various Siebel Enterprise and eBusiness Applications. In this chapter, we will concentrate on the steps to configure these applications.

Major topics covered in this chapter are:

- Introduction to Application object
- Child objects of Application object
- Configuring Application object

19.1 APPLICATIONS

An application is a collection of related screens, designed to suit specific business requirement. Examples of applications are Siebel loyalty, Siebel marketing, and so on. Applications are configured in Siebel tools with the help of "Application" object type, which has two child objects: "Page Tabs" and "Screen Menu Items." Together they define which screens are accessible in application through tabs and menus (site map), respectively.

Before moving ahead with discussing about configuring applications, let us have a quick discussion about the child objects of application object type.

19.2 CHILD OBJECTS OF APPLICATION OBJECT TYPE

Application object has the following two child objects:

1. **Page tabs:** Screens added in "Page Tabs" object definition appear in the tabs in user interface. These screens can be accessed directly by clicking the corresponding tab. Page tabs are shown in Fig. 19.1.

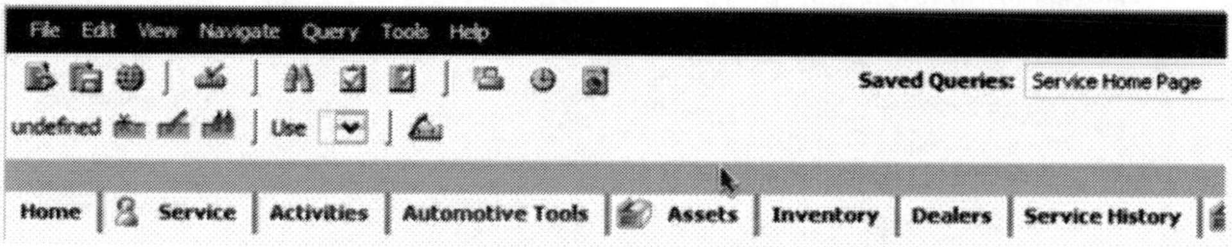

Fig. 19.1 *Page tabs*

2. **Screen menu items:** Screen added in "screen menu items" object definition appears in site map. For accessing these screens, we will have to click on site map button, which will open the list of available screens. From this list, we can select the screen that we want to access. The list of screens shown by clicking site map button is shown in Fig. 19.2.

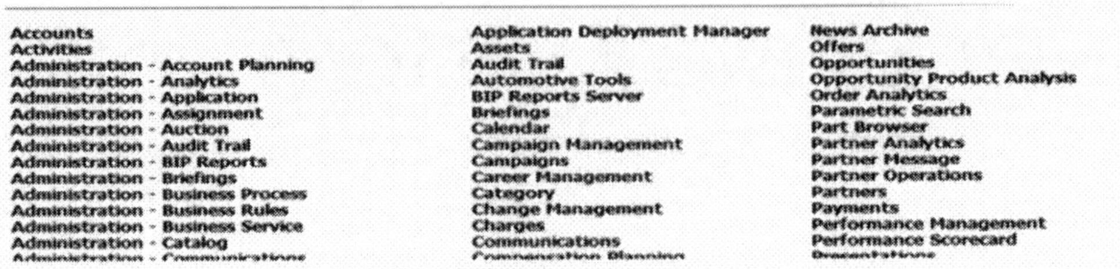

Fig. 19.2 *Site map*

19.3 CONFIGURING APPLICATIONS

Figure 19.3 shows the steps required to configure a new application.

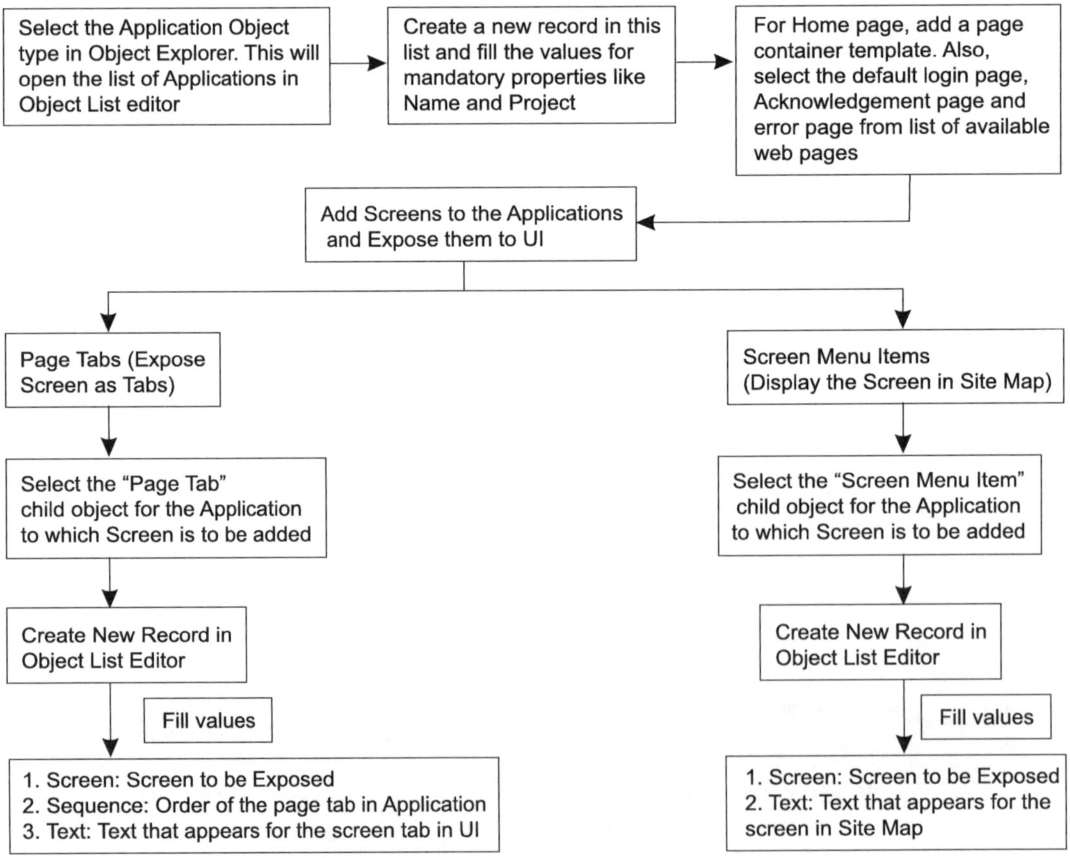

Fig. 19.3 *Steps to configure application*

19.4 SUMMARY

Applications are used to group together all the functionalities required by a particular business unit. These functionalities are provided by all the screens, views, and applets present in application. With this, we will wind up our discussion on Siebel configuration. In Part 4, we will together work on a sample project, where we will try to configure all the Siebel object types discussed throughout this section. While working on our sample project, we will try to use all the best practices that we discussed during this part of book.

PART IV
IMPLEMENTING SIEBEL BUSINESS APPLICATIONS

This part of book is dedicated to enterprise-level implementation of Siebel business applications. Till now, we discussed mainly about navigating and configuring Siebel applications at our local machine. Now, we will take up our discussion at enterprise-level implementation of Siebel projects. Just like other projects in organizations, Siebel projects also need a systematic planning and execution to ensure the expected success.
In this section, we will discuss various aspects of implementing Siebel projects. A systematic approach is very crucial for a successful implementation of project. Implementing Siebel projects is basically a four-step process. These steps are as follows:

- Planning and defining organizational structure
- Siebel server and environment setup and administration
- Developing and providing solutions
- Post-deployment support

At each step, there is a need of resources (persons) having step-specific expertise to carry on the tasks efficiently. Various teams participating at each step are as follows:

1. At first step, the major role is played by organization's executive and collaborative committees, which contain various higher management resources. These people are responsible to define an organizational structure to carry on the Siebel project.
2. At second step, the most crucial role is played by Siebel administrators. They are responsible to set up Siebel servers and environments, and administering them.
3. At third step, the major role is played by Siebel developers, technical architects, and testing teams. Developers are responsible to plan and develop the solutions based on the organization's requirements, while testing team is responsible for pre-deployment and post-deployment testing and reporting the bugs back to development team. At this stage, Siebel administrators also play an active role while repository migrations and solution deployment.
4. Tasks at fourth step are taken care by support professionals. Their responsibilities include supporting customers with the solution provided, reporting and fixing the bugs identified in solution, and routing requests raised by customers to appropriate team.

Throughout this section, we will have a detailed discussion about all the four steps discussed above, which will include various sub-steps of each step, tasks carried on at each step and role played by various members in the teams responsible to handle the step. This section is divided into four parts, one part specific to each step. We will start with planning, move ahead with setup and administration, followed by developing and deploying the solution and wind up with supporting the solution.

Chapter 20

IMPLEMENTING SIEBEL BUSINESS APPLICATIONS

In this chapter, we will discuss about organization-level implementation of Siebel applications. We will look on various steps of implementing a Siebel project, along with the important roles and responsibilities in each step. We will start our discussion with the first step of every Siebel project, that is, planning and defining organizational structure. Here, we will discuss various aspects of planning the Siebel project, along with the responsibilities in this phase.

Moving ahead, we will discuss about second stage of implementing Siebel projects, that is, setting up Siebel environments. Here, we will discuss about various types of Web clients and their significance. Also, we will look on various servers that take part in setting up Siebel environment. We will also discuss about the roles and significance of each server in an environment.

The third stage discusses about developing and providing solutions. This is based on the planning done during first stage, and uses Siebel environment developed during second stage. This is the stage where actual coding work starts. Here, we will also discuss about Siebel eRoadmap methodology and its significance in delivering an efficient solution.

The final stage will be post-deployment support. This stage basically comprises of a support team and clients. Clients raise requests against any defect found after solution is delivered, and persons working in a support team are responsible to address those issues. Along with defects, clients may also raise change requests, or enhancement requests for the solution delivered. Along with working on various requests raised by clients, support team is also responsible to collaborate with multiple teams and route requests to appropriate team, based on their expertise.

Major topics covered in this chapter are:

- Planning and defining organizational structure
- Setting up Siebel environment and servers
- Siebel Web Architecture
    - Siebel Web Client
    - Siebel Web Server
    - Siebel Enterprise Server
- Developing and Providing Solutions
    - Siebel eRoadmap Methodology
- Post – Deployment support

20.1 PLANNING AND DEFINING ORGANIZATIONAL STRUCTURE

This step comprises of deep analysis for defining organizational hierarchy, starting from executive committee till the team members. The analysis is typically done in top to bottom manner, where the top management and executive committees are planned first, and correspondingly each team and team members are planned. Following are the sub-steps of the "Planning" step:

1. Defining organizational executive committee
2. Defining collaborative executive committee
3. Defining the mission of project
4. Defining the scope of project
5. Defining project management structure
6. Defining risks and steps to manage them
7. Change management

1. **Defining organizational executive committee:** Organizational executive committee consists of top management from organization. It is indispensable to decide the executive committee before any other planning, as these are the persons who play a crucial role for the further planning of project. Organizational executive committee comprises of the following key roles:
   - **Chief Executive Officer (CEO)**
   - **Chief Operating Officer (COO)**
   - **Chief Information Officer (CIO)**
   - **An executive sponsor**
   - **Project General Manager**
   - **A technical architect**

The major activities done by organizational executive committee along with collaborative executive committee include defining the goals and scope of a project, providing direction to the project, analyzing and approving the implementation strategies and guidelines, deciding the important deadlines and staff configuration to achieve the goals in these deadlines, along with analyzing and approving various infrastructural resources and filling the loopholes achieving the desired goals.

2. **Collaborative executive committee:** This committee is made up of executives representing organization and Siebel. It works as a "Join" between the organization and Siebel, and is designed to collaboratively plan the road maps to achieve the requirements, along with conflict resolution and finalizing the plans made by organizational executive committee. The key roles in this committee include the following:
   - **An executive sponsor**
   - **A project manager** (Typically one manager both from organization and client)
   - **A technical lead**
   - **Business analysts and all key contacts from organization and its client**
   - **Siebel consultants and team leads**
   - **Senior management representatives from organization and client**

The major responsibility of this committee is to review and finalize the implementation road map made by organizational executive committee, resolve any kind of conflicts between the two participating parties, dividing the tasks into subtasks and deciding the corresponding deadlines along with implementation plan to achieve them. This committee basically provides a cooperative environment to plan and achieve the desired goals.

3. **Defining the mission of project:** After the organizational and collaborative executive committees are planned, the next step is to start the planning for a project. The planning starts with deciding the mission of project. An ideal mission of project aligns with the organization's mission, and is planned to achieve the goals set by them. It comprises of a deep analysis of organization's goals and targets for next 3¬--5 years and defining project's mission to achieve those goals in most efficient ways.
4. **Defining the scope of project:** In this step, organization's executive committee and collaborative executive committee sit together to analyze the scope of project. The main aim in this step is to utilize most of the Siebel standard modules, along with various Siebel industry applications to effectively utilize the information captured by the Siebel systems. At this step, a proper planning differentiates Siebel from normal store and reporting systems, as the information captured by Siebel systems is used as a resource, like manpower and materials. Along with this, the planning also comprises of integrating all the sites and offices at various locations of company on board the Siebel centralized platform.
5. **Defining project management structure:** Project management structure basically contains persons from collaborative executive committee. This structure is a hierarchy of roles that are responsible to manage the Siebel projects. At the top of this hierarchy lies the Chief Project Officer. He basically works as Business Analyst, and should be familiar with business environment and functionalities. He should also be technically proficient to handle a team of Siebel consultants and other key users. He is the person who supervises the entire project, which includes accepting deliverables, providing required sign-offs, deciding deadlines, and configuring staff based on requirements. Along with this, he also works as a single point of contact for Siebel consultants for addressing their administrative and infrastructural issues, along with guiding Siebel and its implementation partners about company's specific business requirements.

   The next role that comes under this hierarchy is **Project Manager**. Project managers are appointed to supervise individual sites, and are responsible to accept the deliverables (for their site) and delivering them on pre-decided deadlines, along with ensuring the quality. They also appoint the manpower based on the staffing plans, and manage their request locally at site. Their other responsibilities include arranging required training programs for technical and functional consultants and getting business users' attention for relevant issues whenever required.

   After the site management, the next role requires module management. This role is Module Leader. A **Module Leader** is responsible to efficiently implement specific Siebel modules to meet organizational goals. A module leader is basically a person having Siebel technical knowledge and experience, along with required Siebel functional knowledge.

The roles discussed till now in Siebel project management structure are vertical roles, which lie top to bottom in the hierarchy. Along with these vertical roles, we have two horizontal roles as well. These roles are **Resource Manager** and **Training Manager**. Resource managers are responsible to provide infrastructural resources, such as hardware and software, at each stage of the project. They are the key contacts for approving resource-related requests and budgets, along with ensuring proper on-time installations and quality. Training managers are responsible to conduct trainings when and where required. The trainings include technical as well as functional trainings for employees. For conducting these trainings, training managers have to ensure the availability of competent trainers at the site, and arranging training slots based on employees' availability.

6. **Analyzing risks and defining steps to manage them:** Risk management steps involve identifying the potential risks in implementing Siebel projects and take proper precautions and measures to address them effectively. The risks associated with Siebel projects are different from traditional software implementations as Siebel is a package of standard modules. Various risks associated with implementing Siebel project include a lack of clarity on project scope and mission, lack of competent resources, inefficient designs and developments, inefficient trainings to users and developers, inefficient integration with other systems to get an updated data and information, missing deadlines, switching to new systems, conflicts with users, and infrastructure failures.

   During the phase of risk management, organizations need a deep analysis of all these potential risks and plan a road map to avoid or manage these risks.

   Siebel eRoadmap implementation methodology: Siebel eRoadmap implementation methodology is a tool that ensures accelerated execution of all success factors of a Siebel project. This methodology focuses on reducing the business risk and maximizing customer's ROI. It consists of the following seven steps to ensure the effective execution of all success factors. These steps will be discussed in detail later in Part 3 "Developing and Providing Solutions." These steps are iterative in nature, so that organizations can revisit the previous steps to fine-tune them for improved results. The seven steps of Siebel eRoadmap methodology are shown in Fig. 20.1.

7. **Change management:** Although many tools are employed during developing Siebel projects, there are certain adjustments required in most of the cases. This is the situation where change management comes in picture. Change management involves managing the required changes. An efficient change management is required to decide "Go/No - Go" for the changes made in the projects during implementation cycles. Change management basically involves changes in one or more of the following:

   - **Business processes**
   - **Systems**
   - **Job roles**
   - **Organizational structures**

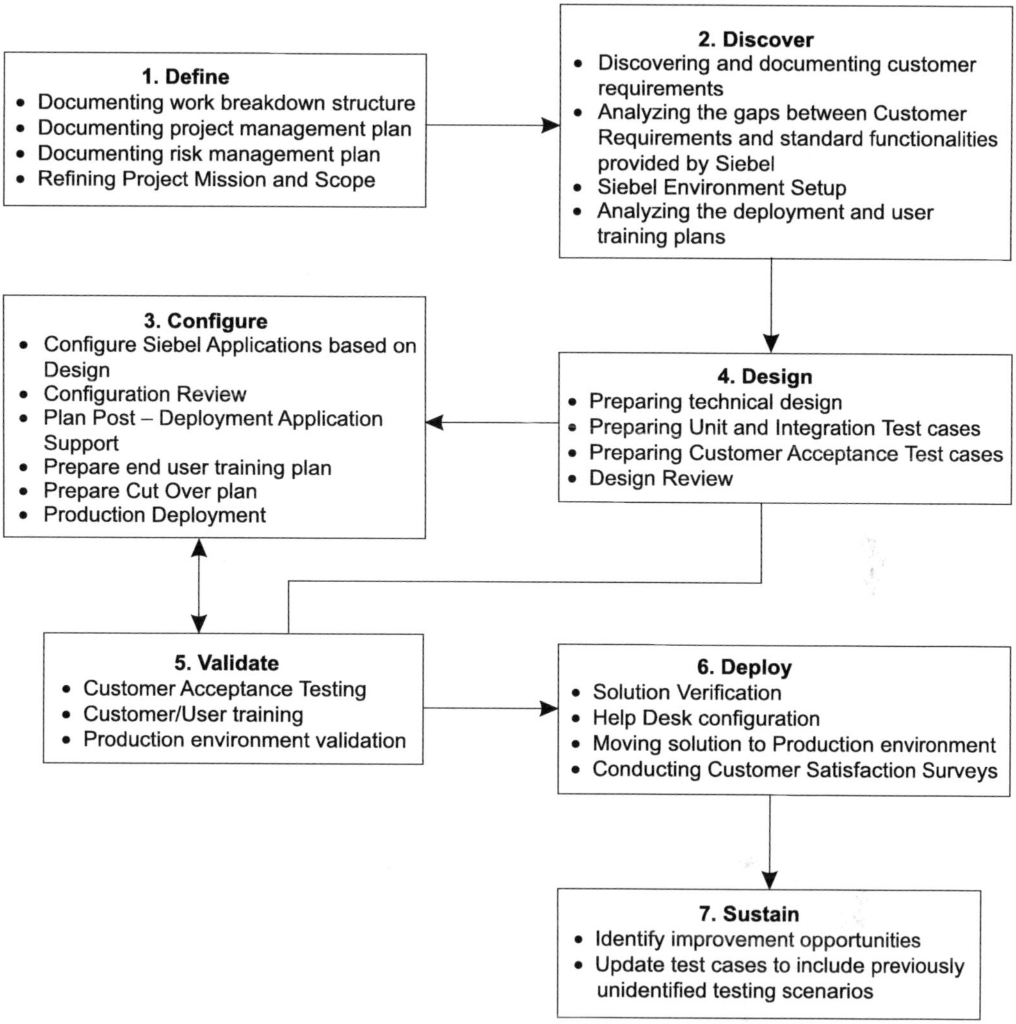

Fig. 20.1

The reason behind these adjustments is to adopt a better way to reach the desired goals. The main areas of focus may be cost reduction, streamlining the information flow, problems resolution, exploring more opportunities, and so on. Change management is a three-step process that involves the following:

- Planning for change
- Managing the change
- Support the change

20.2 SIEBEL SERVERS AND ENVIRONMENTS—SETUP AND ADMINISTRATION

In this part, we will discuss about setting up Siebel applications environments. Environment includes Siebel servers, clients, and database, along with other necessary software, hardware, and network resources. After planning the Siebel project, the next step is to set up various environments required for the project. These environments are as follows:

1. **Development Environment:** Required for developers to develop the solution based on the functional specifications and technical design documents. Unit testing is also performed on this environment.
2. **Test Environment:** Required by test team to carry on the testing for the solution developed by developers to ensure its alignment with the functional specification document provided by client. System integration testing takes place in this environment.
3. **UAT Environment:** After the solution passes the system integration testing, it is moved to user acceptance testing (UAT) environment, where client can test and validate the solution.
4. **Production Environment:** Production environment is the one that is used by client's business users and customers. The code accepted and approved by client during UAT is finally moved to production environment and made available for his business users and customers.

The setup process for all the environments discussed above is almost same. They typically differ in data, as production environment contains the live data relevant for organization, whereas all other contain dummy or test data required to validate the functionality of product.

Let us now direct our discussion toward Siebel Web architecture, where we will discuss how components are involved in setting up Siebel environment. Installation of each of these components is discussed in section "Installing Siebel Environments."

20.2.1 Siebel Web Architecture

Siebel Web architecture basically contains the following six components. These components are presented in Fig. 20.2.

1. Siebel Web Clients
2. Siebel Web Servers
3. Siebel Enterprise Servers
4. Database Servers
5. Siebel File System
6. Siebel Gateway Name Servers (optional)

20.2.1.1 Siebel web clients

Siebel Web clients enable users to access data present on server using web browser. This allows users to connect and access the data present on server without installing any software. There are five types of Siebel clients provided by Oracle. They are as follows:

- Siebel Web Client
- Siebel Developer Web Client
- Siebel Tools Client
- Siebel Mobile Web Client
- Siebel Wireless Client

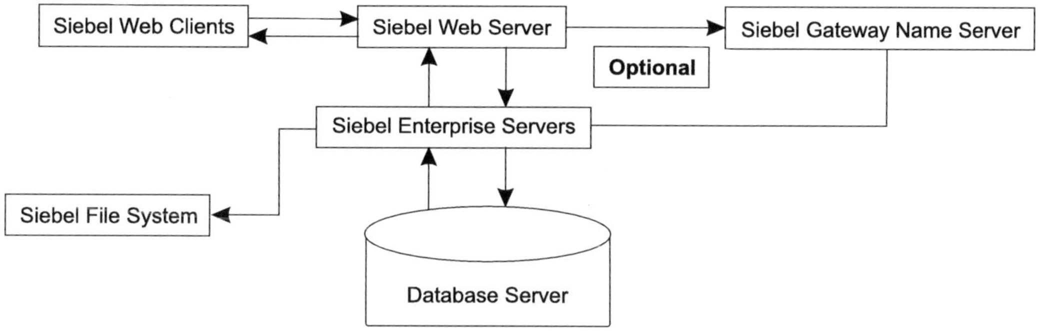

Fig. 20.2 *Siebel Web architecture*

1. **Siebel Web client:** Siebel Web clients are present on client's personal computer, and use standard browser to connect to Siebel server through Siebel Web server. This means that all the requests from a Web client go to Siebel server via Siebel Web server. At Siebel server, all the business logics and data access requests are handled. These clients run only on the supported Web browsers with required settings. For a list of supported Web browsers, please refer to Section "Installing Siebel Environment."
2. **Siebel Developer Web Client:** Siebel developer Web client is meant especially for Siebel developers and administrators. It connects directly to the database server, thereby enabling Siebel developers to perform quick development and testing and verification for the designs and coding done by them. It also facilitates Siebel administrators to perform administrative tasks directly with the database server. It is a highly interactive client delivered through Microsoft Internet Explorer.
3. **Siebel Tools Client:** Siebel tools client is a dedicated client for Microsoft Windows users, and it helps users to access Siebel tools. More about Siebel tools is discussed in Section "Siebel Tools."
4. **Siebel Mobile Web Client:** Siebel mobile Web client is meant for the field users who cannot stay connected to the server all the time. These clients also use Web browser to launch and access the data from database. The difference is that a copy of database is present locally in case of mobile Web clients. These clients connect to this locally present database, and need periodic access to Siebel server to update and synchronize it with server database.
5. **Siebel Wireless Client:** Siebel wireless client is designed for users accessing Siebel applications using PDAs, cell phones, or any other mobile device. They do not require any software installation at client side. They connect to Siebel server via Web server and can run on a variety of WML and HTML browsers.

The installation of Siebel Web client and Siebel tools client is discussed in Section "Installing Siebel Client, Tools and Sample Database."

20.2.1.2 *Siebel web server*

Siebel Web server work as an intermediary between Siebel Web clients and Siebel enterprise servers. It accepts and identifies the Siebel requests generated by Siebel Web clients and passes them to Siebel enterprise servers. In response, it accepts the response given by Siebel enterprise servers and passes it to Siebel Web clients. It consists of a third-party Web server with following three main components:

- Configuration File
- Siebel Web Server Extension (SWSE)
- Virtual Directories

Figure 20.3 represents Siebel Web server architecture:

Fig. 20.3 *Siebel Web Server Architecture*

Configuration file: This component contains the configuration information for all the Siebel applications. This information includes login details, security settings, and connectivity information, along with a connect string for all Siebel applications.

Siebel Web Server Extension: This component is responsible to accept and parse inbound HTTP requests from Siebel clients and passing them to appropriate Siebel enterprise server's component by establishing TCP connections. If the architecture requires a load balancing server, then SWSE establishes a TCP connection with it for information sharing.

Virtual Directories: This component is required for Siebel eBusiness applications. Accept and route the requests from Web clients for eBusiness applications to SWSE.

20.2.1.3 *Siebel enterprise servers*

Siebel Enterprise Server is basically a logical blanket covering the Siebel servers that access same database and file system. It facilitates a user with common administration of all Siebel servers via Siebel server manager.

20.2.1.3.1 Siebel servers These are the main servers where whole business data resides. They support various front-end and back-end processes that include interactive (Web clients running Siebel applications), background (e.g., workflows) and batch processing (e.g., EIM data transfer). Siebel server has the following important files and components.

20.2.1.3.1.1 Important files in Siebel server

Siebel server has the following important files:

- Siebel Repository files (.SRF)
- Configuration files (.CFG)
- Web Template files (.SWT)

Siebel Repository File: A binary file that contains data specific to one or more Siebel applications in complied form. All the changes configured by using Siebel tools are compiled into this file, and applications use it to launch and present the data, business rules, and processes.

Configuration File: An application-specific file that contains application-specific details including enterprise server name, database server name, repository file name, and other application parameters during application start.

Web Template File: An HTML file with embedded Siebel tags having content enclosed in them. It is used to specify the user interface's look and feel. Typically, we will have a collection of these files in "Web Template" folder, with each file specific to a particular view or an applet.

20.2.1.3.1.2 Important Siebel Server Components Siebel server components are basically programs that execute on server to perform specific tasks. These tasks may include processing of requests generated by clients, data import, and export, and so on. The three major components are as follows:

- **Application Object Manager**
- **Data Manager**
- **Siebel Web Engine**

Application Object Manager: Object manager is the most important component in Siebel server, as it is the central processing site for the objects at all the three levels of Siebel Object Architecture (User Interface Layer, Business Object Layer and Data object Layer. Siebel Object Architecture is discussed in detail in Chapter - 6 "Introduction to Siebel Objects"). The other two major components, data manager and Siebel Web engine, work as facilities inside the object manager.

Data Manager: Data manager works as an intermediary between object manager and database. It is a facility inside object manager that accepts the database requests generated by object manager and issues SQL queries to database. The data retrieved in response is given back to object manager.

Siebel Web Engine: Siebel Web engine is responsible to generate user interface for Siebel applications, allowing users to access and modify the data. It generates HTML pages on server and uses HTTP protocol to pass them to Web browser, where users can access them. It also tracks the modifications made by users in any applet and uses notification mechanism to notify the server to update the data instantly at other locations, so that all the other applets can show the updated data in their respective views.

So, how does Siebel Application operate?

Figure 20.4 shows the operation of Siebel applications. User uses a URL to navigate to application that is hosted on a Web server. This application gets the HTML pages generated by Siebel Web Engine, which works as a facility in Object Manager. Siebel Web

Server Extension (SWSE presents at Web Server and Siebel Web Engine Service present at Siebel Server are the components of Siebel Web Engine. They collaborate with each other to manage the HTTP requests. SWSE provides the HTTP requests with extension (.swe) to Siebel Web Engine Service, which in turn generates response and gives back to SWSE. Siebel Web Engine Service generates the user interface for Web server hosted application, which is displayed to user to access and modify the data. For displaying the applets at run-time, SWE obtains the relevant data related to applet, which includes various list columns or controls in the applet and its associated Web template and generates a Web page that is sent to Web browser to be displayed.

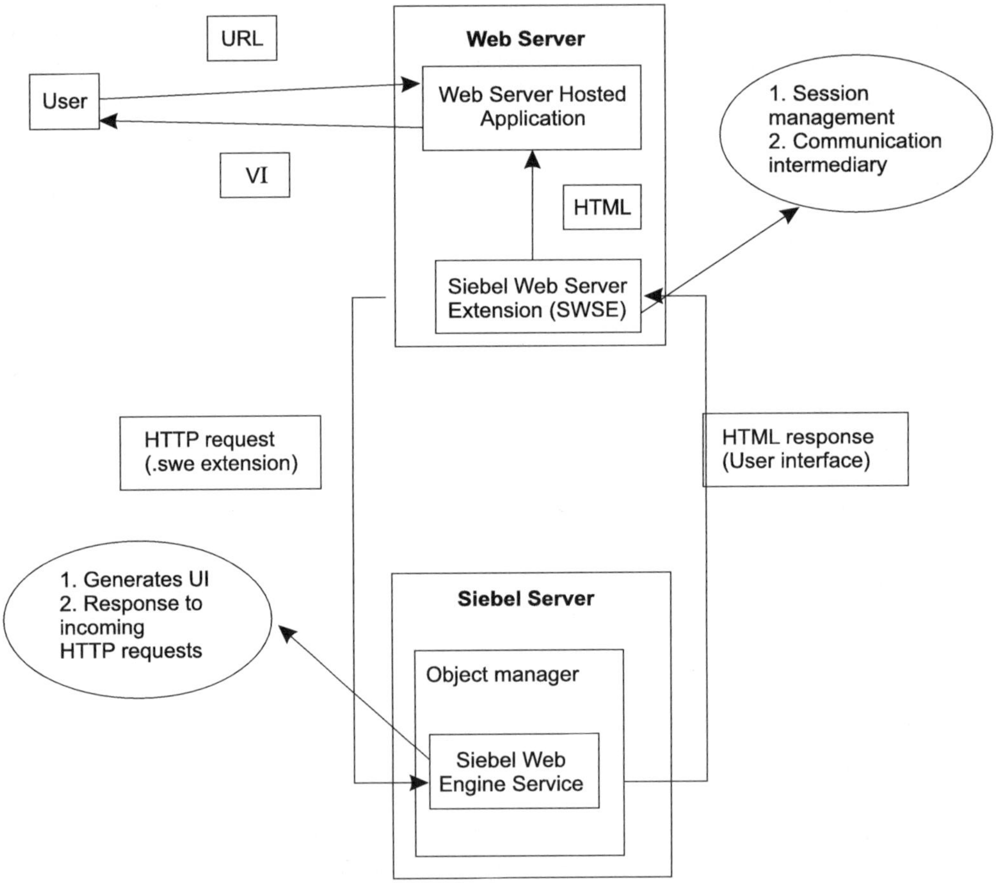

Fig. 20.4 *Siebel application operation*

1. **Database Server:** Database server contains the data used by Siebel applications. It supports a wide range of third-party RDBMS. The data is stored in predefined schema, and is accessed by Siebel server by using Data Manager, which works as a facility in object manager.
2. **Siebel File System:** Siebel clients and enterprise servers use various files. Siebel file system stores these files in compressed form. Siebel server has a component called

"File System Manager," which controls the read or write access to file server.

3. **Siebel Gateway Name Server:** Siebel Gateway Name Server works as a backup for Siebel servers. It contains a file called siebens.dat that stores information about Siebel server configuration, which is read by Siebel server at startup. This information includes connectivity details, components definitions and assignments, and other operational parameters. At startup, each Siebel server marks its attendance in Siebel gateway name server, which registers its availability information. This information is used by enterprise components to check the availability status of a Siebel server.

Installation and setup of all the components discussed in this section is covered in section "Installing Siebel Environment." With this discussion, the organization gets ready to use Siebel environment to provide solutions to clients. In next section, we will discuss about developing and providing solutions to clients.

20.3 DEVELOPING AND PROVIDING SOLUTIONS

Till this point, we have discussed about the pre-implementation tasks for Siebel project. Sections 20.3 and 20.4 cover implementation and post-implementation tasks. The implementation phase basically consists of steps for developing and delivering the solutions. This phase stands on a strong foundation of "Siebel eRoadmap Methodologies," which is a seven step suite of methodologies designed to accelerate the execution of all success factors of a Siebel project. As discussed earlier in Section 20.1 (refer to Fig. 20.1), the seven steps of Siebel eRoadmap methodologies are as follows:

1. **Definition:** This step basically comprises of defining project's mission and scope. It sets a foundation for all subsequent stages. Some of the major tasks done during this stage are defining the project structure, which includes identifying the roles and responsibilities of various teams and their members, creating project plan documents to be used as a reference in next stages, analyzing risks and necessary steps to avoid or mitigate them, planning for design and configuration reviews by expert resources, refining business mission and scope, and defining project management policies, standards and guidelines.
2. **Discover:** This is the stage where project team analyzes and finalizes the functional and technical specification documents. These documents contain organization's requirements, and should be modified after a deep analysis, so that they should align with the organization's goals. Along with refining these documents, project team also analyzes the gaps between the organization's requirements and standard features provided by them, so that an efficient gap analysis can be done to fill these gaps. This is the stage after which the development work starts. Hence, setting up development environment is also a major task in this stage. Development environment should resemble the actual production environment, so that developers and architects should be able to develop the solutions suitable for it. Development environment consists of clients, servers, and necessary software, hardware, and network resources. Along with these tasks, an end user training strategy is also analyzed and built during this

stage.

3. **Design:** This is the stage where development work starts. In this stage, a project team prepares a technical design document that contains the plan that works as a reference to develop the solution. This document typically contains business rules, screen definitions, data models, external systems (for integration) and steps to develop the solution. Along with preparing the technical design document, project team also prepares test cases for unit and system integration testing, and a plan for UAT. UAT plan contains the test cases that should be satisfied in order to get client's approval to move the changes to production environment.

4. Configure: In this stage, the solution is configured in development environment based on the technical design document prepared in previous step. An ideal solution should satisfy all the client's requirements mentioned in functional specifications document, prepared in Discover stage. After this stage, the testing phase starts. Hence, a testing environment, including all the required hardware, software, and network resources, is set up during this stage. Along with this, a deployment plan is prepared to move the changes from development to test, test to UAT, and finally UAT to production environment. An end-user training plan is also prepared to be transitioned to concerned members from testing team.
5. Validate: In this stage, the main role is played by the testing team. They use test environment to test the changes made by development team and validate if they satisfy the client's requirements mentioned in functional specifications document. After the changes pass the testing, they are moved to UAT environment. Hence, a UAT environment is also set up during this stage and changes are moved to it. Client checks and validates all the changes in this environment. Production environment setup also takes place in this stage. It should contain all the required software, hardware, and network resources.
6. **Deploy:** After client verifies the changes in UAT environment, they should be moved to production environment. This happens in this stage. All changes made during development phase and validated in testing phase are moved to production environment. Along with this, a helpdesk is also set up in this stage to handle all the issues raised by clients. After successful deployment of solution, customer satisfaction surveys are done to get their feedbacks and implement them for future.
7. **Sustain:** In this stage, analysis is done to find the improvement opportunities in the solution provided to the client. Along with this, ownership transfer also takes place, which includes helpdesk knowledge transition, end user trainings, and management training workshops.

Table 20.1 summarizes the roles of various teams taking part till the end of this phase.

Moving ahead, we'll discuss about the various post deployment activities.

Table 20.1 Various Teams and Their Roles

Serial number	*Team*	*Roles/responsibilities*
1	Steering Committee	Responsibilities discussed in Part 1
2	Project Management Team	• Comprises of client's project manager and Siebel project manager • Client project manager ensures that organization's goals are met, resolves escalations, manages the changes, and accepts and sign off the deliverables • Siebel project manager documents project plans, plans resources, budgets and deadlines, ensures better customer acceptance, manages the changes, addresses quality issues, and supervises the risk management
3	Technical Architects Team	• Manages infrastructure resources, which include hardware and software. Also manages the servers • Database administration • Maintains ongoing Siebel processes
4	Business Analysts Team	• Identifies business process flow • Identifies client's functional requirements • Analyzes organization's requirements and compares them with Siebel standard functionalities, along with documenting the changes (if required)
5	Siebel Configuration Team	• Analyze client's requirements and prepare technical design • Develops the solution and does unit testing • Knowledge transfer to support teams
6	Deployment Team	• Data migration between various environments, which include development environment to testing environment and testing environment to production environment migration • Supports end users and resolving system errors
7	Training Team	• Plans end user training • Create training material for end users

20.4 POST DEPLOYMENT SUPPORT

This section focuses on providing support to clients after the successful implementation of solution provided in previous stages. This stage revolves around the enhancements identified in the solution. Enhancements requests can be raised by client, or can be suggested by organization to clients. Along with enhancements, any kind of functional or technical issues raised by clients are also addressed in this stage. Some of the major tasks done in this stage are as follows:

1. Solution roll out
2. Addressing enhancement requests raised by clients
3. Supporting clients in using the solution
4. Performance monitoring and maintenance
5. Upgrading Siebel applications
6. Retaining Siebel consultants and providing continuous training to keep them updated

1. **Solution Rollout:** The success of Siebel projects can be maximized only when the solution provided to clients is present at all the client sites present at different locations. Typically, during the implementation phase, the solution is developed and deployed at client's base site. This step focuses on moving the solution to all the client sites. Before movement of solution, it is required to set up the solution environment, including requirement of software, hardware, and network resources, at all the sites. Along with this, end-user and support professionals' training is also done, so that they can become familiar with using the solution and handling any kind of possible issues in future. After moving the solution to various sites, an integration testing is done to make sure that it is integrated properly and works fine with other sites.
2. **Addressing Enhancement Requests raised by Clients:** This task focuses on enhancing the solution provided to client. Enhancements are typically required to optimize the solution to adopt a better way to reach the goals set by client. These enhancements may include optimizing the functional as well as technical aspects of solution. Addressing enhancement requests involves a deep "Impact Analysis," which involves analyzing the functional and technical impacts of enhancements to be made on existing solution, and plan the steps to mitigate any kind of negative impacts. As enhancements require changing existing solution, most of the steps of "eRoadmap Implementation Methodology" are executed here. These steps include preparing or updating functional specification, technical specification, and technical design documents. Also, test cases are prepared for Unit, System Integration and User Acceptance testing. As development, testing, and production environments are already set up during implementation period, we can use them to carry on the required tasks.

   After document preparation and approval, project team needs to do required enhancements in development environment and perform unit testing, after which the changes are moved to test instance to perform system integration testing. These testing steps focus mainly to make sure that the enhancements are developed properly and are not putting any negative impacts on existing solution. After system integration testing, the changes are moved to UAT instance to be approved by user, before moving it to production environment.
3. **Supporting clients in using the solution:** In this stage, the key role is played by customer support professionals. The main focus here is to address the issues and escalations raised by client while using the solution, and resolving them in defined service level agreement (SLA) time. Along with this, support professionals also assist clients with any kind of difficulties they face in using the solution, or any module of

it. Typically, a service desk is set up by organizations to support their clients. Service desk is basically a module-specific team of support professionals, who remain in direct contact with client via various communication channels including e-mails, direct phone calls, instant messaging and tickets, and assist them with the problems faced by them. Service desks are managed by incident manager, who is responsible to manage customer support professionals and ensure quality of solution given to client for the issues or escalations raised by them.

4. **Performance Monitoring and Maintenance:** In this stage, a continuous monitoring of performance of solution is done and appropriate recurring maintenance steps are taken to ensure its proper functioning. Performance monitoring is done to ensure the optimal efficiency of solution, both in case of time and resources consumed. Typically, the performance may degrade due to heavy data transfer, lot of concurrent scheduled jobs, EIM data loads from multiple environments, network outages, and so on. In order to keep business intact from any kind of performance degradation, a continuous monitoring is required. If any kind of performance impact is seen, appropriate maintenance activities should be taken immediately to resolve the issues, along with a proper analysis and changes (if required) to ensure that it does not happen in future.
5. **Upgrading Siebel Applications:** Siebel applications upgrade basically means installing new patches or versions of application that are beneficial to clients. Siebel applications come with a comprehensive suite of upgrade and customization tool, which make this task easy and quick. Siebel applications facilitate users with customizable installation programs that allow them to install only the components required to configure unique application software based on their needs. Along with this, Siebel provides easy data extensibility that helps developers to extend application's database schema without impacting consistency of application's upgrade path.
6. **Retaining Siebel Consultants and providing continuous training to keep them updated:** Once implemented, Siebel projects cannot be considered as complete. They require upgrading and development of new integration with various applications. Hence, retaining Siebel implementation team is a crucial task for organizations. If organizations are not able to retain the Siebel implementation team, they will need recurring trainings to new team members about the delivered solution in order to carry out future upgrades and new integration requests that will consume a lot of valuable time.

   Along with retaining Siebel implementation team, organizations should ensure proper timely trainings to them in order to keep them updated with latest Siebel version releases and new emerging applications that need to be integrated with existing solution. Also, "skill upgrading" is also a crucial factor for organizations. Skill upgrading means upgrading the skills of a team member to next level. For example, skills of a Siebel configuration resource can be upgraded with Siebel EAI or Siebel eScripting skills. This will benefit both organizations and employees. Organizations will get an advantage of having more skilled resources who can handle more tasks, whereas employees will get the benefit of continuous learning and upgrading their skills.

20.5 SUMMARY

Implementation of Siebel applications is basically an end-to-end approach for implementing projects. It covers all the aspects of a project, right from planning the organizational structure till post-deployment support. Various steps discussed in this chapter, if followed properly, ensure the success and expected outputs from a project. With this, we will wind up our discussion in this part. Moving ahead, we will look on a sample project, which will refresh all the concepts related to configuring Siebel objects.

Chapter 21

INSTALLING SIEBEL CLIENT, TOOLS AND SAMPLE DATABASE

This section is dedicated to installing Siebel Web Client, Tools and Sample database. Installing Siebel at our local system is very crucial before we can start learning it, as a side by side practice and reference will be very helpful throughout our learning. Most of the tasks discussed here are part of Siebel Administration process, and are done by Siebel Administrators. Typically, in most of the organizations, developers get the whole environment ready to start developing the solutions. But, it is important for everyone to be aware of the basics of installation. As we've planned to focus more towards developers' role, we'll focus on Siebel Web Client, Siebel Tools and Siebel sample database installation on Windows platform. For practicing and referring, this would be sufficient for readers. For further queries about installing Siebel Enterprise Server, Siebel Gateway Server and Siebel Web Server, please refer Siebel Installation Guide provided in Siebel 8 Bookshelf.

In this chapter, we'll discuss on following topics:

- Downloading Siebel and Creating installation image
- Installing Siebel Web Client
- Installing Siebel Tools Client
- Installing Siebel Sample Database

21.1 DOWNLOADING SIEBEL AND CREATING INSTALLATION IMAGE

Following are the steps to download Siebel from Oracle's website:

1. Go to address http://edelivery.oracle.com and provide support - web user name and password to login. The next page will ask you to select the language.
2. Select the desired language and continue.
3. Complete export validation and continue.
4. Select the required Siebel product pack. We have two choices here, Oracle Business Intelligence (Siebel Analytics) and Siebel CRM, from which we need to select Siebel CRM. Also, we have to select the operating system and then click Go.
5. We will see the software available to be installed. We have to download all the related files in single directory and extract them in some other directory, which is referred as Siebel Installation Image directory.

21.2 THE INSTALLATION PROCESS

We will start our installation process with installing Siebel Web Client, followed by Siebel Tools and Siebel Sample database.

21.3 INSTALLING SIEBEL WEB CLIENT

Siebel Web client is used to access Siebel application using Web browser. Before starting our discussion on installing Siebel Web Client, let us first discuss about certain Pre-installation tasks for installing Siebel Web Client.

21.3.1 Pre-installation tasks for installing Siebel Web Client

Before starting the installation, it should be made sure that the system fulfills all the pre-installation requirements. For a complete list of pre-installation tasks for installing Siebel Web Client, refer "Pre-installation Tasks for the Siebel Client" in Siebel Bookshelf V8.0 under section "Siebel Installation Guide For Microsoft Windows".

21.3.2 Installing Siebel Web Client

Following are the steps to install Siebel Web Client on local machine with sample database. This discussion will be sufficient for the learners who are installing Siebel Web Client for reference and practicing.

For those who are installing Siebel Web client for practice and reference purpose on local machine, it is recommended to install Siebel Mobile Web Client, as it would be easy for them to get familiar with Siebel Applications using Siebel Sample Database.

- Move to Siebel Installation Image folder, and then navigate to Windows\Client location. Here, we can see three folders; Siebel_Tools, Siebel_Web_Client and Siebel_Sample_Database.
- To install Siebel Web Client, move into Siebel_Web_Client folder and double click install.exe file to start the installer.
- The first screen will be "Choose Setup Language" screen, where we can select the language in which the installation is to be conducted, and click Next.
- In the "Welcome" screen, the installer allows us to see already installed products, and de-install the previous versions. If we select "Deinstall Products", the installer flow moves towards the steps to de-install the existing product. If it is not required, click on "Next" button.
- The next screen will be the "Setup Type" screen, where we can see the default path for Siebel Client installation directory as C:\Program Files\Siebel\8.0\Web Client. We can accept default, or can change this path.
- In the same screen, we need to select Installation type out of three available options; Typical, Compact and Custom. For practice and reference purpose, Typical installation would be sufficient. After selecting the type of installation, click Next.

- The next screen will ask you to select Language Pack. Here, we need to select at least one language out of available languages and click Next.
- The next screen will be for selecting the Client type to be installed. Here, we will see 2 options, Mobile Web Client and Developer Web Client. The next steps which are highlighted are specific to Developer Web Client installation. If we select Mobile Web Client, we will skip these steps.
- In the next screen, we will see 4 options for selecting the Server Database type; Oracle Database Server 10g (CBO), IBM DB2 UDB for Windows and UNIX, IBM DB2 UDB for z/OS and Microsoft SQL Server. We will move our discussion towards using Oracle Database Server 10g (CBO). Select this option and click Next.
- The next screen will ask for Database Alias and Table Owner. Specify these details and click next.
- In the next screen, we need to specify the path for Network - based (Shared) Siebel file system. We can also use the default path provided by installer. Click Next.

  (It is recommended to create a shared folder (with full permissions) to be used by Siebel as its File System before starting the installation. If it is not created yet, leave this installer window and create this folder under the Siebel Installation folder and specify its directory path in this step.)
- The next screen will be Remote Server Information Screen. Click Next in this screen to accept the default.
- In next screen, specify following details:
  - Gateway Name Server Address: Specify the Network Name or IP Address of Siebel Gateway Name Server.
  - Enterprise Server Name: Specify the name of Siebel Enterprise Server.
- In the next screen, specify the name of the Siebel server having Server Request Broker component.
- In next screen, specify the Hostname and Port Number for the Search Server (If you are using Search Server product) and click Next.
- This step is specific to Mobile Web Client Installation ONLY. On clicking Next after selecting the Client Type, the next screen will ask for Siebel Remote Server connectivity details. Enter these details and click Next.
- The next screen will ask for the default folder, where the Siebel Web Client specific folders will be placed. Some of the examples of these folders are "Local", "Sample", "Bin", "Objects" etc. We can select the default folder, or can browse and specify other folder. Click Next.
- On clicking Next, we see the installation process is started. Wait till this process finishes. On the completion of this process, we will see an Internet Explorer browser window gets opened, with the file predeploy.htm loaded. This file downloads all the required ActiveX controls for Siebel High Interactivity client. Once the download finishes, a message saying "The download is complete, you may close the window." will be displayed. Close the browser window and verify the details present in various

logs that will be displayed in next steps. The Siebel Mobile Web Client / Developer Web Client installation process finishes here.

After installing Siebel Web Client, the next task for us is to install Siebel Tools Client. Following section encapsulates the steps to install Siebel Tools Client.

21.4 INSTALLING SIEBEL TOOLS CLIENT

Following are the steps to install Siebel Tools Client base product:

- Move to Siebel Installation Image folder, and then navigate to Windows\Client location. Here, we can see three folders; Siebel_Tools, Siebel_Web_Client and Siebel_Sample_Database.
- To install Siebel Tools Client, move into Siebel_Tools folder and double click install.exe file to start the installer.
- The first screen will be Choose Setup Language screen, where we can select the language in which the installation is to be conducted, and click Next.
- The next screen will allow us to select whether we want to add Language packs in existing installation, or install a new instance of the product. If we have Siebel Tools client already installed in our machine and we select to add language packs in existing installation, the installer flow will move towards adding new language packs. If we want to install new instance, we need only to click Next in this screen.
- Just like Siebel Web Client Installation, we see a Setup Type screen in this step, which will allow us to select one out of three available setup types available; Typical, Compact and Custom. For practice and reference purpose, selecting Typical would be sufficient.
- The next screen will ask us to provide a destination directory to install Siebel Tools. We can go for the default directory provided here, or can browse and select other directory and click Next. DO NOT install Siebel Tools in the same directory as Siebel Client, as it may result Memory Conflicts.
- The next screen will allow us to select the language to be installed. Select the language here and click Next.
- The next screen will ask to select the database for Siebel Tools. As we have installed web client with Oracle 10g, select Oracle Database Server in this screen and click Next.
- In the Database Identification Screen, specify the Database Alias and Table Owner, and click Next.
- The next screen will be Siebel File System Server Information screen. Here, we need to specify the directory path of the shared file system folder, created during Web Client installation and click Next.
- In the next screen, which is Siebel Remote Server Information Screen, we need to specify the Remote Server Hostname. As we are installing Tools client for reference and practice purpose in our local machine, we can select the default value and click Next.

- In the Enterprise Server Information screen, specify the Gateway Name Server Address and Enterprise Server Name. As we are installing Tools client for reference and practice purpose in our local machine, we can select the default value and click Next.
- In the next screen, select the default destination folder to install Siebel Tools and click Install to complete the installation.

The final step for completing our task to install and run Siebel Demo applications is to install Siebel Sample Database. Sample Database is basically designed to help learners to get familiar with the working of Siebel Applications with Siebel Mobile Web Client. We can also get familiar with Siebel tools using Sample Database. All we need to do to use Siebel Mobile Web Client and Siebel Tools with Sample database is to specify the full path of Sample database file (.dbf) in the "ConnectString" parameter in the client specific Configuration File (.cfg) . We will discuss this later, after our discussion on the installation steps for Sample Database.

21.5 INSTALLING SIEBEL SAMPLE DATABASE

Siebel Sample Database is designed to help learners to get familiar with the working of Siebel Applications using demo versions of Siebel Mobile Web Client. Before starting the installation of Sample Database, we should make sure that our machine meets all the platform requirements for it. For the complete list of these requirements, please refer Siebel System Requirements and Supported Platforms on Oracle Technology Network.

Following are the steps to install Siebel Sample Database:

- Move to Siebel Installation Image folder, and then navigate to Windows\Client location. Here, we can see three folders; Siebel_Tools, Siebel_Web_Client and Siebel_Sample_Database.
- To install Siebel Sample Database, move into Siebel_Sample_Database folder and double click install.exe file to start the installer.
- The first screen will be Choose Setup Language screen, where we can select the language in which the installation is to be conducted, and click Next.
- The next screen will allow us to select whether we want to add Language packs in existing installation, or install the new instance of the product. If we have Siebel Sample Database already installed in our machine and we select to add language packs in existing installation, the installer flow will move towards adding new language packs. If we want to install new instance, we need only to click Next in this screen.
- The Setup type screen will allow us to select a destination directory for the Sample database installation. We can select the default one, or can browse and provide a different directory.

In the same screen, we need to select Installation type out of three available options; Typical, Compact and Custom. For practice and reference purpose, Typical installation would be sufficient. After selecting the type of installation, click Next.

- The next screen will allow us to select the language to be installed. Select the language here and click Next.
- The next screen will ask for the program folder, where the Siebel specific folders will be placed. We can select the default folder, or can browse and specify other folder and click Next.
- The next screen will display the Event Log. After verification of information present here, click Next.
- In the next screen, click Next to complete the Siebel Sample Installation. After the installation, we will find the shortcuts for demo applications (E.g. Siebel Services DEMO - ENU)

21.6 CONFIGURING SIEBEL WEB CLIENTS AND TOOLS WITH SAMPLE DATABASE

This section is specific to beginners and learners who want to get familiar with the working of Siebel Applications. Here, we will discuss configuring Siebel Mobile Web Clients and Tools Client to be used with Sample Database. After completing installations, we need to take certain steps before using Siebel Web clients and Tools with Sample database. These steps are mentioned below:

- Configure the ODBC connection to connect to underlying database (in our case, this is Oracle database).
- Make following changes in Tools' configuration file tools.cfg present at path <Siebel Installation Folder>\8.1\Tools\BIN\ENU:
  - In [Sample] section's ConnectString parameter, put the full path of sample dbf file. Typically, the name of this file is sse_data.dbf.
  - In RepositoryFile parameter, put the full path of srf file. Typically, the name of this file is siebel_sia.srf.
- Make the same changes in client's cfg file. Each client has a specific configuration file,e.g. Siebel Loyalty's cfg file is loyalty.cfg and Siebel Services' cfg file is sfs.cfg. You can find the collection of these files at location <Siebel Installation Folder>\Client\BIN|ENU.
- After making these changes, you are ready to work with Siebel Web Client and tools with sample database.

21.7 SUMMARY

The steps mentioned in this chapter for installing Siebel Client, tools and sample database are generic steps. Based on the type of installation, these steps may vary slightly. Readers are advised to be in touch with Siebel Administrators or refer Siebel bookshelf to get more details on these steps, if required.

Chapter 22

SAMPLE PROJECT

Let us start our first project in Siebel. This project is designed to work as a refresher for all the topics discussed throughout the book. While working on this project, we will discuss all the phases of Software development project. At this point, I assume that everyone has Siebel environment ready on their PC.

Before starting our project, let's first discuss various steps in a typical software project. Typically, Software Development Lifecycle can be divided into four phases:

1. Requirements Gathering.
2. Planning.
3. Development.
4. Support and Maintenance.

While developing our project, we will discuss about these phases and their significance in Software Development Lifecycle. During these phases, there are certain persons who play key roles. During the development of our project, we will keep on changing our roles based on the phase.

22.1 PROJECT TITLE: ADD A SCREEN IN SIEBEL LOYALTY APPLICATION

A new screen in Siebel Loyalty Application is required, which will show a list of all the members added in last one month. The Screen should contain two applets, one list applet on top, showing all the members added in last one month, and a form applet at bottom, which will show all the details of the member selected in list applet.

22.2 PHASE – 1: REQUIREMENTS GATHERING AND CLARIFICATION

Reader's Role: Business Analyst

In this phase, the major role is played by the Business Analyst. A Business Analyst is a person who has knowledge of Client's Business Functionalities, along with the software and tools used (here Siebel Loyalty and Siebel Tools) to build and deliver the solution. Throughout this phase, he stays in touch with clients to gather all the requirements and gets clarifications on the points which look confusing.

In this phase, we will play the role of a Business Analyst and try to get all the details about requirements. At the end of this phase, we will prepare a final list of requirements, and get them signed–off from clients. A clear picture of requirements is very important for the successful delivery of a Software project. It should be made sure that developers understand all the client's expectations, and build the solutions accordingly. Following section covers a typical conversation between a Business Analyst (BA) and Client.

22.2.1 Requirements Gathering Conversation

BA: Who can view the Views present in this new Screen?

Client: The views should be visible to all the employees of organization.

BA: Which fields should be displayed on User Interface?

Client: We want the following fields to be displayed on User Interface.

- Member Name
- Start Date
- Status
- Members
- Member Type
- Membership Scheme
- Last Updated By
- Last Updated

BA: Will the fields present in the List or Form Applets editable by Employees?

Client: We want some of the fields to be editable by employees. Rest of the fields should be read–only.

BA: Which fields will be editable?

Client: Only "Member Name", "Start Date" and "Status" fields should be editable.

BA: Will Employees be able to 'Query' the members in the list or form applet?

Client: No, Employees should be able to query members in the list applet only.

BA: Will Employees be able to create new members in the list or form applet?

Client: No. We want employees to only view and edit member's details. They should not be able to create new members in these applets.

BA: Which fields in the list applet should be sortable?

Client: Only "Member Name" field should be sortable in the list applet.

BA: Will Employees be able to delete any member from the list applet?

Client: Yes, they should be.

BA: Which fields should be visible in the list applet, and which should be in the form applet?

Client: We want only "Member Name", "Member Type", "Membership Scheme" fields to be visible in the list applet. The form applet should contain all the fields.

22.2.2 Requirements Document

Based on this discussion, the BA prepares a draft Requirements document. This document will contain following points:

1. A new screen to be created in Siebel Loyalty Application.
2. The screen should contain a list view and a form view.
3. The list view should be at the top and the form view should be at the bottom.
4. The list view should show all the members registered in last one month till today's date and the form applet should show the details about the member selected in the list applet.
5. The list applet should contain the following fields:
   - Member Name
   - Member Type
   - Membership Scheme
6. The form applet should contain the following fields:
   - Member Name
   - Start Date
   - Status
   - Member Type
   - Membership Scheme
   - Last Updated By
   - Last Updated
7. The views present on screen should be visible to all the employees across the organization.
8. Only "Member Name", "Start Date" and "Status" fields should be editable in the list as well as the form applet.
9. Employees should be able to query the members in the list applet.
10. Employees should not be able to add a new member using this view.
11. Employees should be able to delete the members from the list view.

After BA prepares this document, he will ask the client to review this document and provide their comments and / or approval. If client feels any kind of modification in requirements listed by BA, they intimate it to BA and get them modified. Once they feel that the requirements listed by BA satisfy their expectations, they provide their approval. After their approval, the requirements get frozen, and no modifications are allowed in them. This marks the end of requirements phase, after which BA provides the requirements document to a team of technical architects and developers and explain them the requirements. He also clears any doubts raised by teams related to requirements.

22.3 PHASE – 2: PLANNING AND DESIGN

Reader's Role: Technical Architect

In this phase, the major role is played by a team of technical architects. Technical Architects are the persons having a thorough technical knowledge of the software used to develop the solution (here it is Siebel Loyalty Application and Siebel tools) and business functionalities. Typically, technical architects have sound experience on all the phases of software lifecycle. They are the persons responsible to analyze the requirements and plan the steps to develop the solution. They also give their expert comments to developers during development phase.

The role of technical architect team starts with getting the requirements document from BA and ends with preparing a technical design document. Technical design document provides a step-by-step guidance to developers to build the solution. For building the technical design documents, technical architects have to do a deep analysis of requirements. Next section contains a sample technical design document which will cover the steps to develop our project.

Most of the objects required to fulfill a typical requirement are provided by Siebel. In most of the cases, we will not need to create new objects. All the objects required for developing our project (e.g., tables, columns, business components, etc.) are also provided by Siebel. We just need to customize them to fulfill our requirement. But for learning purpose, we will create most of the objects. It is always advisable NOT to create any new object until it is actually required. Always try to use the existing objects provided by Siebel for developing solutions.

22.3.1 Technical Design Document Preparation

In our requirement, we need to create a new screen. This screen will have two applets, a list applet and a form applet. These applets will show some fields. For creating applets, we would require to create a "Business Component" having all the required "Field" objects (An Applet is based on a Business Component. The Fields of Business Component are mapped to controls and list columns present in Applets). But before that, we would require a Table object and its Column Objects (A Business Component is based on a Table. The Columns of table are mapped to the fields of Business Component).

Before starting the planning for our project, let us first open Siebel Loyalty application and check the available fields. In Siebel Loyalty application, we can see a screen named "LOY Members" in screen tabs. This screen contains the entire details specific to all the loyalty members. On navigating to this screen, navigate to Application Level Menu -> Help menu -> About View option. On clicking on this option, we will see the details about the view. Here, we can see that the view showing the list of loyalty members is based on "LOY Member" business object. Also, the list and form applets present in this view are based on "LOY Member" business component. This shows that LOY Member business component contains all the required fields for storing details of loyalty members.

In Siebel tools - > Object Explorer, navigate to Business Component object type and query "LOY Member" business component in Object List Editor. Here, we will try to find out the base table and columns used to store the data displayed in required fields. On querying LOY Member business component, we will see that it is based on S_LOY_MEMBER table. Now, our task is to find out the columns on which our required fields are based. Next section shows the fields required in our project, along with the column details.

22.3.2 Fields and Columns Required for Project

As we already have table and columns which store the data to be displayed in our screen, we have to use those tables and columns for creating our Business Component (BC). We will just require creating a new business component based on S_LOY_MEMBER table and map the existing columns to its fields.

Ideally, we should use LOY Member business component for our applets. But, since this project is for our learning purpose, we will go for creating new business component.

Following are the fields required for our project, along with the column details:

1. **Member Name:** On querying the LOY Member fields for Member Name field in Siebel tools, we'll find that this field is based on "NAME" column. This shows that Member Name is stored in "Name" column. Also, the "Join" property of this field is blank; hence we can say that this field is getting data from "NAME" column of LOY Member business component's base table, i.e., S_LOY_MEMBER. Hence, the new field to display data in our new screen should be based on "NAME" column of S_LOY_MEMBER table.
2. **Start Date:** On querying LOY Member BC, we will find that this field gets its data from START_DT column of S_LOY_MEMBER table.
3. **Status:** Similar to above two fields, we can find that this field is getting its data from STATUS_CD column of S_LOY_MEMBER table.
4. **Member Type:** This field gets its data from MEM_TYPE_CD column of S_LOY_MEMBER table. Please check and verify the same it tools.
5. **Membership Scheme:** Analysis of this field requires a special attention. If we query "Membership Scheme" in LOY Member BC, we will not find any field with this name. Then from where this value is getting displayed in applet? Any guesses?

   Actually, this shows that the display name of this field in the applet is different from its actual name in LOY Member business component. For getting the actual name of the field, we need to go to that particular applet is Siebel tools, and get the actual name from there.

   After getting the exact name of the applet, navigate to Application Level Menu - > Help menu -> About View option. Here, we can easily find out the name of applet as "LOY Member List Applet". Now, in Siebel tools' Object Explorer, query for this applet, navigate to List - > List Column child object and query for "Membership Scheme" in Name property in Object List Editor. Here, we can see that the field corresponding to this list column is "Membership Scheme Name". This is the actual name of this field in LOY Member BC. If we search fields in LOY Member BC with this name (Membership Scheme Name), we'll find that the column corresponding to this field is "Name".

   But, there is one more twist in the story. If we see that "Join" property of this field, we can see that it contains a non-null value. The Join name is "Membership Scheme". This means that this field is getting value from "Name" column, which DOES NOT belong to S_LOY_MEMBER table. At this point, we know that this field is getting data from some other table using a join named "Membership Scheme". But we don't know that this join "Membership Scheme" fetches data from which table. To get this detail, select "Join" child object of Business Component object, and query for "Membership Scheme" in "Alias" property. On querying, we will find that this join fetches data from S_PROD_INT table. So now we know that our field "Membership Scheme Name" fetches data from S_PROD_INT table using join "Membership Scheme".

Now, here's a million dollar question. A Join requires a Primary key and a Foreign key (See chapter – "Joins' for more detail on Primary and Foreign keys). So how this join relationship is implemented? What are the columns from S_LOY_MEMBER and S_PROD_INT which take part in this relationship?

For getting answer to these questions, select "Membership Scheme" join object and navigate to its child object "Join Specification". Here, we'll see that "Destination Column" contains the value "ROW_ID" and "Source Field" contains value "Membership Scheme Id". Hence, we can say that the join is between ROW_ID column of S_PROD_INT table and the column corresponding to "Membership Scheme Id" field in S_LOY_MEMBER table. (It is an exercise to everyone, find out the column corresponding to Membership Scheme Id field in LOY Member BC).

So now, we have a clear picture of Membership Scheme. Membership Scheme control in the list applet gets its data from Membership Scheme Name field in LOY Member BC. This field in LOY Member BC takes its data from NAME column of S_PROD_INT table using a join named Membership Scheme. This join is between "ROW_ID" column of S_PROD_INT table and MEMSHIP_SCHEME_ID column of S_LOY_MEMBER table.

6. **Membership Scheme Id:** This field is required to create a join between S_LOY_MEMBER and S_PROD_INT tables. This field is getting its data from MEMSHIP_SCHEME_ID field of S_LOY_MEMBER table.
7. **Last Updated By:** For this field in our BC, we will use the system column LAST_UPD_BY (For reading about System Columns, please refer to chapter – Tables and Columns).
8. **Last Updated:** For this field in our BC, we will use system column LAST_UPD.

We can, and should use the existing fields for our requirements. We can use all the above mentioned existing fields to create our new applets. But for our learning, we will create new fields. These new fields will be the exact replica of existing fields.

After this discussion, let us first summarize the fields required in our new BC and corresponding columns to be mapped from S_LOY_MEMBER table. Table 22.1 provides the summary. The last column of table lists the names of new fields that we are going to create in our new BC. These fields will be exact replica of the fields mentioned in corresponding column – 1 of table. For example, Sample Project Member Name field in new BC will be exact replica of Member Name field in LOY Member BC.

Table 22.1 Field and Columns required in project

Sl. No.	*Field*	*Column*	*Base table*	*Join*	*New Field's Name in new BC*
1.	Member Name	NAME	S_LOY_ MEMBER	Column is coming directly from base table of BC. Hence no join is required here	Sample Project Member Name
2.	Start Date	START_DT	S_LOY_ MEMBER	Column is coming directly from base table of BC. Hence no join is required here	Sample Project Start Date
3.	Status	STATUS_CD	S_LOY_ MEMBER	Column is coming directly from base table of BC. Hence no join is required here	Sample Project Status
4.	Member Type	MEM_ TYPE_CD	S_LOY_ MEMBER	Column is coming directly from base table of BC. Hence no join is required here	Sample Project Member Type
5.	Membership Scheme	NAME	S_PROD_ INT	Membership Scheme join is used here. This column is coming from S_PROD_INT table.	Sample Project Membership Scheme
6.	Last Updated	LAST_UPD	S_LOY_ MEMBER	Column is coming directly from base table of BC. Hence no join is required here	Sample Project Last Updated
7.	Last Updated By	LAST_UPD_ BY	S_LOY_ MEMBER	Column is coming directly from base table of BC. Hence no join is required here	Sample Project Last Updated By
8.	Membership Scheme Id	MEMSHIP_ SCHEME_ ID	S_LOY_ MEMBER	Column is coming directly from base table of BC. Hence no join is required here	Sample Project Membership Scheme Id

Now, we have data for our new BC. We will now discuss about creating our new BC. This new BC should be based on S_LOY_MEMBER table, as we will use the columns from this table for most of our fields.

This should be kept in mind that we should create new objects only when it is really required. At this point, we can use existing LOY Member BC for our requirement, as it contains all the fields that we need for our requirement. But we are creating a new BC just for learning purpose.

22.3.3 Business Component required for project

For our project, we will require one business component to be created. This Business Component should be based on S_LOY_MEMBER table, and should contain all the fields mentioned in table 22.2. Corresponding columns are also listed in table.

Table 22.2 Fields required in Business Component

Sl. No.	*Field Name*	*Column*	*Table*
1.	Sample Project Member Name	NAME	S_LOY_MEMBER
2.	Sample Project Start Date	START_DT	S_LOY_MEMBER
3.	Sample Project Status	STATUS_CD	S_LOY_MEMBER
4.	Sample Project Member Type	MEM_TYPE_CD	S_LOY_MEMBER
5.	Sample Project Membership Scheme*	NAME	S_PROD_INT
6.	Sample Project Last Updated	LAST_UPD	S_LOY_MEMBER
7.	Sample Project Last Updated By	LAST_UPD_BY	S_LOY_MEMBER
8.	Sample Project Membership Scheme Id	MEMSHIP_SCHEME_ID	S_LOY_MEMBER

Please refer to the steps to create new BC in chapter – "Business Components". Also, you will find the steps to add new fields and mapping those fields to base table's columns. At this point, just create the fields and map corresponding columns to them. In next section, we will discuss about creating Joins.

22.3.4 Joins required for project

In our project, we will require one join between S_LOY_MEMBER and S_PROD_INT tables. While defining, we will define it as a join between our new Business Component and S_PROD_INT table. Following are some of the important points about this new join:

1. Join should be defined in the "Join" child object of our new BC.
2. Let us give our join name (Alias) as "Sample Project Membership Scheme".
3. Give table name as S_PROD_INT.
4. Navigate to Join Specification child object of this join.
5. Create a new record and do the following:
    - Give "Sample Project Membership Scheme Id" as Source Field. This field is mapped to MEMSHIP_SCHEME_ID column of S_LOY_MEMBER table.

- Give Destination Column as "ROW_ID". This is the ROW_ID column of S_PROD_INT table.
- Give Name as Sample Project Membership Scheme.

6. Now, navigate to "Field" child object and query for "Sample Project Membership Scheme" field.
7. Give "Sample Project Membership Scheme" in the "Join" property. This will ensure that this join will be used to fetch data from S_LOY_MEMBER table.

With this step, we are done with Business Component side configuration. Now, our next step is to create applets needed to fulfill our requirement. These applets will be based on our new BC. Next section discusses creating new applets.

22.3.5 Applets Required for Project

Based on our requirement, we will need 2 applets; One List applet to display the list of members enrolled in last one month and one Form applet to display the details of the member currently selected in the LIst applet. Refer to Chapter – 10 for steps to create a new applet and adding controls into it. Following are some important points about our applets:

1. Both the applets should be based on our new BC.
2. As users should be able to edit some of the fields through list applet, define the list applet in "Editlist" mode.
3. As users should be able to edit some fields through form applet, define the form applet in "Edit" mode.
4. Navigate to "List" child object of List Applet and create a new record. Name it as "List. Navigate to "List Columns" child object and create 3 new records with the values mentioned in Table 22.3. Also map them to the corresponding fields mentioned in next column in same table .

Table 22.3 List Column objects for applet

Sl. No.	*Name*	*Display Name*	*Field*
1.	Member Name	Member Name	Sample Project Member Name
2.	Member Type	Member Type	Sample Project Member Type
3.	Membership Scheme	Membership Scheme	Sample Project Membership Scheme

5. Also, refer to the Table 22.4 to provide values to some important properties:

Table 22.4 List Column properties

Sl. No.	*Property Name*	*Value*
1.	Available	Should be checked for all the list columns
2.	Field Retrieval Type	Provide the value "Field Data"

Sl. No.	Property Name	Value
3.	HTML List Edit	Check only for "Member Name" list column, as we want only this to be editable in list applet.
4.	HTML Row Sensitive	Check for all the list columns.
5.	HTML Type	Provide value "Field" for all.
6.	Read Only	Check for Member Type and Membership Scheme List Columns.
7.	Text Alignment	Should be Left.
8.	Type	Should be Textbox.
9.	Show in List	Should be checked for all.
10.	Width	Let us make it as 25.

6. In the form applet, navigate to Control child object and add new record for each of the controls mentioned in table 22.5. Also, map these controls to the respective fields listed in next column in same table.

Table 22.5 Applet Control properties

Sl. No.	Name	Caption	Field
1.	Member Name	Member Name	Sample Project Member Name
2.	Start Date	Start Date	Sample Project Start Date
3	Status	Status	Sample Project Status
4.	Member Type	Member Type	Sample Project Member Type
5.	Membership Scheme	Membership Scheme	Sample Project Membership Scheme
6.	Last Updated	Last Updated	Sample Project Last Updated
7.	Last Updated By	Last Updated By	Sample Project Last Updated By

7. As my designing sense is not very good, I am leaving it to you to design the web layout of applet.
8. Along with this, provide values mentioned in table 22.6 to some of the important properties of Controls:

Table 22.6 Important Control object properties

Sl. No.	*Property*	*Value*
1.	HTML Type	Should be "Field" for all.
2.	Automatic Horizontal Scroll	Check for all.
3.	Height	Lets' make it 25 for all.
4.	HTML Row Sensitive	Check for all.
5.	Read Only	Check for all the controls except Member Name, Member Type and Status.
6.	Text Alignment	Lets' make it "left" for all.
7.	Type	Textbox for all.
8.	Visible	Check for all.
9.	Width	Lets' make it 120 for all.
10.	Field Type	"BC Field" for all.

9. Before starting the editing of web layout, navigate to View Menu -> Toolbars and check "Configuration Context" there. Make sure that there should be proper target browser, along with "Siebel Loyalty" as Application and Interactivity should be "High".

Now we are ready with our applets. The next step is to dispose these applets to User Interface. For this, we will require a view to which these applets can be mapped. The next section discusses about creating a view and mapping applets to it.

At this point, we are done with creating new applets for our requirement. But, this does not fully satisfy our requirement. Our requirement says that applets should show only the members added in last 30 days. This requirement can be achieved using applet's search specification. Applet's search specification is discussed in chapter – "Applets". We just need to provide a search specification in the list applet that will check the created date of record should be SYSDATE – 30. With this search specification, applet will fetch only the records created within last 30 days. Here is a very good question to readers: Can you tell the reason of providing search specification at applet level, and not a BC level?

As both the applets (List and Form) are based on same BC, the record selected in list applet will be populated in Form applet. Hence, our requirement will be fulfilled with this implementation.

Finally, let us discuss the last three requirements:

- Employees should be able to query member records in List applet
- Employees should not be able to add a new member using this view.
- Employees should be able to delete the members from the list view.

For these requirements, we should keep in mind that since we are using Employee - Facing application (High Interactivity), we can fulfill these requirements with Editlist mode itself. But, in case on Standard Interactivity applications, Editlist mode can't be used.

22.3.6 Views Required for Project

As discussed in chapter - 13, a View is based on a Business Object. It can display only the applets which are based on Business Components that are mapped to the Business Object on which the view is based. Fig. 22.1 shows the diagrammatic representation of this confusing statement:

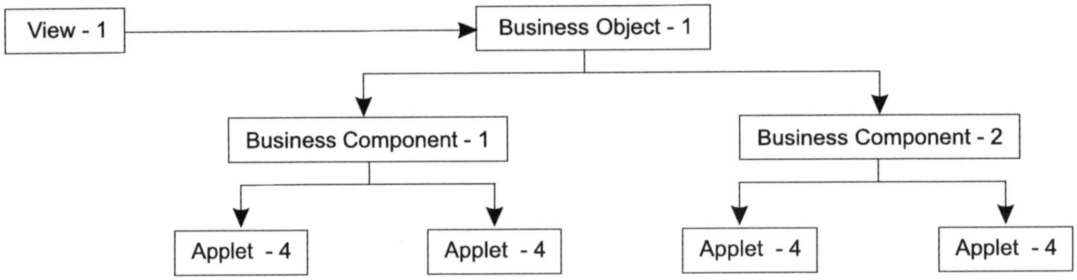

Fig. 22.1 *Relationship between View and Applets*

On analyzing Fig. 22.1 , we can say that View - 1 will be able to show only Applet - 1, Applet - 2, Applet - 3 and Applet - 4. There is no direct relationship between a view and applets that it shows. Till this point, we have created Business Component and Applets based on it. Now, for displaying these applets in a view, we will first require adding our Business Component in a Business Object, and then create a View based on that Business Object.

For our project, we will use the existing Business Object "LOY Member". It is an exercise to everyone to find out the Business Object corresponding to the view that displays the list of all Loyalty Members in Siebel Loyalty.

For adding our new BC to LOY Member Business Object, refer to Chapter - "Business Object". You can find the steps to add Business Components in existing Business Object.

After adding the Business Component in Business Object, let us have a discussion about creating our new view. Refer to chapter - 13 for the steps to create a new view and adding Applets in it. Following are some of the important points to be kept in mind while doing this:

1. The View should be based on "LOY Member" Business Object.
2. Use "Editlist" mode of List Applet and "Edit" mode of Form Applet.
3. Make sure that proper configuration context is used while editing the web layout.
4. Make sure that while designing the web layout, the list applet should be mapped at top and the form applet should be at bottom.

22.3.7 Adding View to the Screen

The next step after creating the view is to add it in screen. We will add this view in Loyalty Members' screen. It is an exercise to everyone to find out the name of "Loyalty Members" screen from application. Please refer to Chapter – 13 for adding view in this screen. Also, refer to chapter – 14 for adding a view tab corresponding to this view in screen.

The next step is to compile all the objects used in our project to the .srf file. As we have a lot of objects to be compiled, it is always suggested to go for full compile* instead of Incremental compile*. After full compile, we will get a new .srf file. Open the loyalty.cfg file and provide full path of this .srf file in "RepositoryFile" parameter. This will make your loyalty application to read data from new .srf file.

After full compiled .srf file starts pointing to application, the next step would be to add the view in application. For this, open application and navigate to Sitemap -> Administration Application -> Views view and register the view. For steps to register the view, refer to chapter – "Views". Also, while registering the view, add appropriate responsibilities to the view. Without this, the view will not be visible at application level.

* Full Compile refers to compiling all the projects in repository to a new .srf file. For doing full compile, select Tools -> Full Compile in Siebel tools. In object compiler window, select "All Projects" and click on compile. The .srf file will be created at the location mentioned in "Siebel Repository File" parameter of object compiler.

Incremental Compile refers to compiling objects in a existing .srf file. Incremental compile takes less time as compared to full compile. It is preferred only in the case where the number of objects to be compiled is less. Typically the size of incremental compiled .srf file is bigger than full compiled .srf file.

22.4 PHASE – 3: DEVELOPING THE SOLUTION

Reader's Role: Developer

The next phase deals with developing the solution. As a developer, our responsibility is to refer to the technical design document prepared in previous step and take required steps to develop the desired solution. During developing the solution, it should be kept in mind that steps in technical design document should be properly followed. If any kind of change is felt during development, it should be properly updated in design document as well. Also, we should ensure proper unit testing against all the requirements listed in Requirements Documents to make sure that all of them are met without solution.

22.5. SUPPORT AND MAINTENANCE

Reader's Role: Support Executive / Support Manager

After the solution is developed and deployed, support team comes into picture. This phase is required in order to ensure proper assistance to client in following situations:

- Client finds out some technical issue with solution
- Client has some problem in understanding the solution

- Performance related issues with solution
- Data correction
- Disaster recovery
- Any other unexpected problem with solution

22.6 SUMMARY

The objective of this project is to refresh reader's knowledge and to make them aware of the approach required for configuring Siebel applications. It DOES NOT present the entire lifecycle of software development project. While going through the project, I would request readers to work on tools in parallel to understand the concepts clearly. Those who are familiar with Siebel applications and reading this book just for reference can skip this project.

APPENDIX

This section is a challenge to everyone who is looking forward to test his / her Siebel skills. While going through this section, you are free to search content in this book or browse the web. These questions are the typical questions asked in an interview. If you can go through each question and find out its answer, you will be very well prepared to face most of the interviews for Siebel Configuration professionals. So, here we go!!!

1. How Multi value links are different from links?
2. Which Siebel Object types use Search Specification property?
3. Which Siebel Object types use Sort Specification property?
4. How Joins are different from Links?
5. How Customer Centricity is different from Sales Centricity?
6. What is a Command Object? Tell its significance.
7. At Siebel application's user interface, how will you differentiate between a Dynamic Pick list and an MVG? You have to find this only by seeing the user interface, and not by checking at tools level.
8. Which Siebel object type uses "Inter Table" property?
   - Join
   - Link
   - MVL
   - MVG
9. What is the meaning of "Inter Table" property?
10. What is a Pick Map? Why do we use a pick map?
11. What is the difference between Edit and Edit list mode of an applet?
12. What do you mean by Configuration Context?
13. Which Siebel Object type uses "Destination Link" property?
    - Join
    - Link
    - MVL
    - MVG
14. What does "Destination Link" property mean?
15. Suppose you have edited the web layout of a list applet in Edit List mode. In View - 1's View Web Template Item, you have created a new record corresponding to this applet. Here you have chosen mode as "Edit". In View - 2's View Web Template

Item, you have created a new record corresponding to this applet and given "Edit List" as mode. In which view this applet will be visible:
- View – 1
- View – 2
- Both the views, as the visibility of applet does not depend on the mode selected
- None of them.

16. Suppose you have made a field "Read Only" at Business Component level by checking "Read Only" property of that field. Where will this change get reflected?
    - All the Business Components which are using the column corresponding to that field
    - All the applets to which this field is mapped
    - At this Business Component and all the applets where this field is mapped
    - At all Business Components which are using the column corresponding to that field and all the applets associated to these business components.
17. How a view is related to Business Object?
18. What is the difference between Incremental Compile and Full Compile? In which case, the size of .srf file will be more?
19. Which file contains configuration details about Siebel clients and tools?
    - .srf file
    - .cfg file
    - .dat file
    - .mpeg file
20. In the RepositoryFile parameter of .cfg file, which file's location should be provided?
    - .srf file
    - .cfg file
    - .dat file
    - .mpeg file
21. What do you mean by srf file?
    - Siebel Repository File
    - Siebel Responsibility File
    - Siebel Restoration File
    - Siebel Restart File
22. Which of these is NOT an applet mode?
    - Base
    - Delete List
    - Query
    - Edit List
23. Suppose we have two Business Components, BC1 and BC2. Both of them have a field each which is mapped to "Created" column of S_LOY_MEMBER table. Now, if we inactivate the field mapped to this column BC1, is it possible to enter the value in this column using the field from BC2?
24. Can we have two different fields in same Business Component mapped to a single column of its base table?

25. Suppose we have a form applet FA1, which has a control CTR1. This control is mapped to a field in BC1. This field is actually a joined field, and it gets data from some table other than Business Component's base table. In which of the following scenarios this field can be modified at UI?
    - If the mode of applet is Edit, we can modify the field.
    - If the mode is Edit List, we can modify the field.
    - We cannot modify a Joined field.
    - We can modify this field only in base mode.
26. Describe MLOV.
27. Can we extend an Extension table?
28. Which two objects are involved in a link relationship?
    - A Master table and a Detail table
    - A Master Business Component and a Detail Business Component
    - A Master Applet and a Detail Applet
    - A Master Business Component and a Detail table
29. Differentiate between Roles and Responsibilities.
30. The Business Component property of a pick list is a non - zero value other than "Pick List Generic". What does this specify?
    - It is a dynamic pick list
    - It is a Static pick list
    - It is not possible to have a pick list with non - zero Business Component value other than Pick List generic
    - None of the above
31. Arrange below phases of developing a software solution in chronological order.
    - Technical Design
    - Requirements Gathering
    - Support and Maintenance
    - Developing the solution
32. Can we have two different views based on same Business Object?
33. Can we have a Business Object without Primary Business Component?
34. Can we have a link between a Business Component and a base table?
35. Which base table in Siebel stores data related to main organization?
    - S_ORG_EXT
    - S_ORG
    - S_ORGN_EXT
    - S_MAIN_ORG_EXT
36. Which one of the following is a 1:M extension table for S_LOY_MEMBER table?
    - S_LOY_MEMBER_X
    - S_LOY_MEMBER_XM
    - S_LOY_MEMBER_XX
    - S_LOY_EXT_M
37. Which base table stores data related to products?
    - S_PRODUCTS
    - S_PROD_INT

- S_PROD_FLOAT
- S_PROD_EXT

38. Suppose you get a requirement to add a new control in an existing form applet. Which of the following steps you will NOT take to achieve this?
    - Add the control to Form Applet
    - Compile the changes in .srf file
    - After making the change, register the updated view again in application
    - Launch the Edit Web Layout for the applet and add the control in it.
39. What is the purpose of Item Identifier property in Applet Web Template Item?
    - It specifies the ID assigned to the control that is mapped to the placeholder in the .swt file
    - It is a random unique identifier associated to the control
    - It assigns a default value to the control
    - It gives a sequence number to the control among all the controls present in repository
40. Which of the following Siebel Object type uses Destination Column and Source Field properties?
    - MVG
    - Applet
    - Business Component
    - Join
41. What does the Search Specification property of a pick list specify?
    - The Search Specification of originating Business Component
    - The condition based on which the records from Pick Business Component are filtered while fetching them
    - The condition based on which the records from originating Business Component are filtered
    - The search specification of Pick Applet
42. What does the Search Specification of an Applet specify?
    - The condition based on which records are displayed in Applet
    - The Search Specification of Applet's Business Component
    - The condition based on which records are supplied to the applet from its Business Component
    - None of the above
43. Can we have a Search Specification property for a Pick Applet?
44. What are the differences between a Pick Applet and an MVG Applet?
45. Which Siebel Object type uses "Immediate Post Change" property? What does it specify?
46. Which Siebel Object type uses "Outer Join" property? What does it specify?
47. Can we have two different MVLs with same Destination link?
48. Where can we find Siebens.dat file?
    - Web Server
    - Siebel Enterprise Server

- Siebel Gateway Name Server
- Siebel Database Server

49. Can we have a Siebel Web Client pointing to two different .srf files at the same time? If Yes, How?
50. Can we assign 2 different responsibilities to the same view at same time?
51. Is it possible to see a View in application if there is no responsibility assigned to it?
52. Describe Toggle Applets.
53. How data from extension tables is fetched in a Business Component based on their base table?
    - We will have to define a join between the business component and extension table
    - We do not need to do anything. There is always an implicit join defined between base table and extension tables
    - A join is not required here. Data from extension table will be fetched based on an implicit link.
    - We need to define a Link between the two tables.
54. Describe the importance of using unused columns in extension table rather than creating custom extension columns in base table itself.
55. If we have lot of joins in our implementation, will it affect the overall performance?
56. Why we should use multiple distributed enterprise servers?
57. Suppose you have a requirement to make some change in an applet. What would you do to get the copy of that applet to be edited in your local instance, which can be moved back to server after making the changes?
    - Do a "Get" of that applet
    - Do a "Check Out" of that applet
    - Do a "Full Get" for that applet
    - Do a "Check - In" for that applet
58. If I want to add an applet to a existing view, where I will create a new record corresponding to that applet?
    - View Web Template
    - View Web Template Items
    - Applet Web Template
    - Applet Web Template Items
59. Which of the following is NOT a property of Business Component object type?
    - Destination Table
    - Table
    - Name
    - Changed
60. Based on the requirement below, suggest the most suitable option from the options listed below:

    Requirement: We need to show a field in form applet. That field should display the address of all contacts selected in the Contact list applet. One contact can have multiple addresses associated to it. What would you use with the field?
    - A Static Pick list with LOV values corresponding to each address.
    - A Dynamic pick list based on a BC which stores all the addresses

- An MVG based on a BC which stores all the addresses
- None of the above

61. What is a command object? What will happen if we do not associate a command object with any toolbar item?
62. Suppose we have two Business Components; one for storing Account related data, and one for storing Service Request related data. Our requirement says that one account can have multiple service requests associated to it, whereas one service request can be associated to one account only. In such a scenario, how will you connect the two Business Components? Choose the most suitable option:
    - Using a Join between Account's Business Component and Service Request's base table
    - Using a link between two BCs
    - Using Multi value link
    - None of the above
63. In ConnectString parameter of configuration file, which file's path is specified?
    - .dbf file
    - .srf file
    - .mpeg file
    - .cfg file
64. Consider following requirement, and choose the most suitable option from the list:
    "There is an applet containing first name of members. This field should be a drill down field. The drill down on this field should be based on following conditions:
    1. If member is Active, it should navigate to View – 1.
    2. If member is Expired, it should navigate to View – 2.
    3. If member is Cancelled, it should navigate to View – 3.

    How can we fulfill this request?
    - By implementing Dynamic Drilldown object only
    - By implementing Static Drilldown objects for all the three views only
    - By implementing Static Drilldown objects for all the three views and associate them to the Dynamic Drilldown object using Dynamic Drilldown Destination object
    - By using link
65. What do "Source Field" and "Destination Field" properties of Drilldown object specify?
66. What do you mean by "Destination Drilldown Object" property of Dynamic Drilldown Destination object?
67. Consider the requirement below and choose the most suitable option
    "A new field is required in an applet. This field should display the names of all the schools available in City, and will allow user to select any one school out of them to be populated in the field. The list of schools changes frequently. All the changes made in school list should be reflected in the list of schools displayed in the field."
    Which object is required here along with "Field" object to fulfill this requirement?
    - A Static Pick list.
    - A Dynamic Pick list based on Schools BC

- An MVG based on Schools BC
- A Dynamic Drilldown.

68. Espider man needs to create an applet based on existing BC "BC - 1", and to display this applet in a new view "View – 1". He takes following steps to do this:
  1. Creates the applet based on the existing BC
  2. Creates the view "View – 1"
  3. Associates the new applet with the newly created view
  4. Adds "View – 1" to the desired Screen object and arranges it as required
  5. Compiles all the changes to .srf file and points it to the web client
  6. Adds the new View at application level from Administration -> Application – Views screen

  Now, when he tried to open the screen to see the view, he could not find it. What may be the issue? Investigate and explain.

INDEX

N

O

P

Q

R

S

AUTHOR'S PROFILE

Rishi Kumar Shrivastava is working as Systems Engineer with Tata Consultancy Services Ltd., Gurgaon. During his experience as Siebel professional, he has worked with Siebel Enterprise and eBusiness Applications and Siebel tools. His experience includes planning, designing and developing the solutions based on client's requirements, along with post-implementation maintenance and support. He has a Bachelor of Engineering degree with Computer Science and Engineering major from Samrat Ashok Technological Institute, Vidisha (M.P.) in 2008. He is from Bhopal (M.P.) where he lives with his parents and one elder sister.

Made in United States
Orlando, FL
04 November 2026

90200373R00149